Whose Wa

The battle for Welsh devolution and nationhood, 1880–2020

Whose Wales?

The battle for Welsh devolution and nationhood, 1880–2020

Gwynoro Jones
Alun Gibbard

This book is dedicated to the thousands of people in Wales who have battled for devolution over the last century and a half: the unknown campaigners who are not mentioned in this book, but who stood side by side with those who are.

Contents

Sir Deian Hopkin Preface

For many people in Wales, 1979 was a year to forget for many reasons, not least the deeply disappointing outcome of the Devolution Referendum vote on St David's Day. The defeat of the devolution project may have been clearly signalled some months beforehand and yet, even on the day of the vote itself, there was still some optimism that the Welsh electorate would grasp an historic opportunity and realise the dreams of devolutionists over the previous century. In the wake of that defeat, there were recriminations and much anguish, and yet, in less than twenty years, there was a very different, albeit narrow, outcome in a second referendum which led finally to the creation of the Welsh Assembly in 1997. It is just as important to understand why there was such an overwhelming rejection of devolution in 1979, by every part of Wales, as it is to examine its rapid revival, arguably the product of a profound reaction against the policies and conduct of the Thatcher administrations.

The authors of this book approach the subject matter from different perspectives. Gwynoro Jones has been one of the leading proponents of devolution for decades and was a key actor in the complex politics leading to 1979 and the fateful vote on 4 March. This narrative includes, but is not restricted to, his personal account. Alun Gibbard is an award-winning author and former BBC journalist, heavily influenced in his work by an interest in social history. His insightful documenting and analysis complements Gwynoro's experience and knowledge in a project that is unique in its scope and structure.

Together, the authors examine the longer history of devolution from the Cymru Fydd movement of the late nineteenth century, in order to provide a context for the intricate post-Kilbrandon campaigns of the 1970s. Gwynoro's experience as MP for Carmarthen from 1970 to 1974,

quite apart from his even longer engagement with Welsh and European politics, gives him unique insights into the twists and turns of those campaigns and, in particular, the fractious relationships between the key participants in the Welsh agenda, Labour and Plaid Cymru. He also seeks to explain how a promising campaign, clearly supported by Labour leaders and endorsed by successive party conferences, unravelled and foundered.

The rhetorical question in the book's title, *Whose Wales?* echoes the kind of questions which historians and political commentators have raised over the decades, from Gwyn Alf Williams' *When was Wales?* to Dai Smith's enigmatic question in the title of his book on Welsh politics, *Wales! Wales?* As the splendid television debate-documentary by Wynford Vaughan Thomas and Gwyn Alf expressed it so adroitly, the Dragon really does have two tongues. The fact that such questions have been asked, and continue to be asked, underlines the essential ambiguities which run through Welsh politics which, in turn, have hampered discussions of a clear Welsh political identity and, over many generations, undermined campaigns for devolution, let alone separation.

Yet, there were moments in the 1960s and 1970s when history might have been made. In the event, the devolution campaign became mired in the internal politics of the main actors and this is the central theme of this book. Given how deep the antipathies and animosities were in that period, it is all the more remarkable that less than twenty years after such a massive defeat in 1979, the Welsh Parliament in the Bay has risen from the ashes of failure and created a new Welsh politics. But that, as Gwynoro Jones and Alun Gibbard put it, is another story.

Professor Sir Deian Hopkin
Historian, former University Vice-Chancellor
and President of the National Library of Wales

Martin Shipton Preface

MYTHOLOGISING plays an important role in politics—much more than we give it credit for. Adherents to a particular party or cause like to believe they are following in the footsteps of heroes. The long struggle for Irish independence provides a textbook example of that. It's important to understand that certain kinds of myth are not made-up stories, but have their origins in real history. That's certainly true in the case of Ireland. But myths usually offer a partial and distorted view of reality.

In this book, Gwynoro Jones and Alun Gibbard disprove what they would see as a myth: the claim that Plaid Cymru was uniquely responsible for the circumstances that led to devolution in Wales.

Jones and Gibbard want it to be known that others had a hand in that part of history too. It's not surprising that Plaid Cymru seeks the lion's share of the credit for pushing the case for devolution (it's difficult to imagine that the party's foremost thinkers would really believe that no one else played any role at all in moving things forward). The party was formed in 1925 with the express remit of achieving home rule for Wales. For other parties, this may also have been an objective, albeit not an over-riding one: as Britain-wide entities, they necessarily had bigger priorities.

For Plaid Cymru, the purpose of maintaining the belief that it had the greatest influence over events has been two-fold: firstly, to validate its own members' understanding that they are part of an honourable tradition that serves the cause of Wales, and secondly to proselytise the cause to sympathetic outsiders in the hope that they will join the throng. Plaid cannot be blamed for this. But neither can pro-devolutionists from outside Plaid Cymru be blamed for wanting, as they would see it, to put the record straight.

Gwynoro Jones is not, of course, an impartial observer. But despite the titanic battles he fought against Gwynfor Evans in three successive General Elections, and the visceral bitterness between Labour and Plaid at the time, Jones has never flinched from a total commitment to the cause of Welsh devolution. It's a strong point in his favour. The book guides us through the history of those who argued for home rule from the late 19th century, citing the familiar names of Michael D. Jones, Tom Ellis, and David Lloyd George, as well as the short-lived movement Cymru Fydd.

They were, of course, relatively isolated figures, certainly in comparison with the mass Irish Home Rule movement that was gathering momentum at the time across the water. There's something quite farcical about the way Lloyd George apparently lost interest in the cause of a self-governing Wales after he was shouted down at an unruly public meeting in Newport. Arguably the wiliest political operator of the day, the future Prime Minister knew when to stop wasting energy on what would have appeared to him to be a lost cause. Looking back in retrospect on the unsuccessful attempts to drive devolution forward over many years, it is difficult not to be astonished that a National Assembly eventually came into being—and that it developed into a powerful Parliament whose ministers now hold very significant powers over people's lives, as the Covid-19 pandemic has shown. Throughout virtually the entire 20th century, devolution in Wales seemed a remote prospect.

The foundation of Plaid Cymru in 1925 was barely noticed, if at all, by the majority of Welsh people at the time, and it wasn't until more than 40 years later that the party saw its first MP elected.

Jones and Gibbard write about the way the Welsh home rule movement was hindered by the split between those who saw the campaign in purely political terms and those who viewed it more as a cultural battle— in other words, one associated with the preservation and nurturing of the Welsh language.

For a long time, the two elements did not coalesce, and then only fitfully and not across Wales as a whole.

It took until 1974 for Plaid Cymru to garner enough political support in the Welsh-speaking heartland of north west Wales to win two parliamentary seats there.

When, after his election as Plaid leader in 2018, Adam Price commissioned the former SNP Parliamentary leader Angus Robertson to conduct a "root and branch" review of the party, Robertson concluded that the Welsh language was both a blessing and a curse for Plaid. A high proportion of Welsh speakers saw Plaid Cymru as the natural party to vote for, but the perception of it as one that was predominantly interested in language issues at the expense of more bread-and-butter issues was shared by many non-Welsh speakers. That's part of the explanation for Plaid's failure to emulate the success of the SNP in Scotland, but also, plausibly, of the failure of a home rule movement to establish itself as a major force across Wales over many years.

During the 1979 referendum campaign, which resulted in a four-to-one defeat for the pro-devolutionists, those against the establishment of a Welsh Assembly shamelessly suggested that it would be run by Welsh speakers in the interests of Welsh speakers. The spurious allegation was believed by many.

As this book makes clear, those Labour MPs who supported the home rule cause repeatedly found it difficult to get a hearing at the highest level of the party. It wasn't seen as a priority at Westminster—and why would it be, with representation from Wales such a small proportion of the Commons' membership?

The flooding of the Tryweryn Valley in 1965 to create a reservoir to provide water to Liverpool quickly became part of Welsh nationalism's folklore, but although Labour MPs voted against the project, it didn't become a cause célèbre for the bulk of them in the same way.

Nor did the controversy result in much of a boost in support for Plaid Cymru, whose share of the vote across Wales varied over the years that the campaign was active, with 3.1% in 1955, 5.2% in 1959, 4.8% in 1964 and 4.3% in 1966.

In their detailed chronicle of the century from 1880 to 1980, Jones and Gibbard provide irrefutable evidence that people from all four political parties in Wales played a role in promoting the cause of home rule. All four of them, therefore, own a share of the devastating defeat that occurred in the 1979 referendum.

The two larger parties—Labour and Conservative—both had anti-devolutionists who campaigned for a No vote, encouraging belief in the different myth that Wales was incapable of managing its own affairs.

For anyone who doesn't know Wales' subsequent history, it would seem by the end of the book that the dream of political devolution was dead.

The seed of a future victory was, however, sown when Margaret Thatcher won power at the General Election in 1979.

What followed was 18 years of Conservative rule at Westminster that saw the end of the Welsh coal industry, mass unemployment and a growing understanding by many in Wales that they were ill-served under existing constitutional arrangements.

However, devolution only returned to the political agenda because of the support given to the case for a Scottish Parliament by Labour leader John Smith. As so often, Wales' involvement could almost be seen as an afterthought. After Smith's untimely death, the commitment to hold devolution referendums in Scotland and Wales was inherited by an unenthusiastic Tony Blair. Following Blair's landslide victory in the 1997 General Election, a devolution referendum was scheduled in Wales for September 18 of that year. It was narrowly won by the Yes campaign following a collaborative effort involving three of Wales' four main parties.

Nearly a quarter of a century later, the future of the UK is uncertain. Within a few years, both Scotland and Northern Ireland may have left the UK. At that point, the people of Wales would have to decide on their future. Would they be content to face permanent domination by their much bigger neighbour to the east? Or would they take the plunge and decide on independence?

Minority voices, of the kind described in this book, that argued for home rule in the late 19th century and most of the 20th century, would not be enough to create the momentum for the courageous latter choice. That would require a superhuman effort from a broad progressive coalition that had the confidence to argue the case for genuine home rule at last.

Martin Shipton,
Author and Political Editor-at-large, *Western Mail.*

Introduction

So whose Wales is it? Which political party can lay claim to having done more than any other to fight for a distinctive Welsh identity? Can one party claim to have done more to make Wales a separate political concept both from Westminster and within Wales itself? These are the questions that led to the writing of this book. It came from a Welsh language book that is the story of the rivalry between Gwynoro Jones and Plaid Cymru's first MP, Gwynfor Evans, in the late Sixties and early Seventies in the constituency of Carmarthen. That book, *Gwynoro a Gwynfor*, as the title suggests, concentrated more on the two personalities involved and their fierce rivalry in a period described as the most bitter in Welsh politics.

But in turning to write this book, the remit has broadened considerably. It isn't only about those two personalities and it isn't only about that one period in the story of Wales, in one constituency. This book goes back to the 1880s and traces the story of a political identity for Wales across the decades that followed right until the present day and the increasing clamour for Welsh independence.

That story is told in two ways. Its four parts are a combination of two different approaches. The over-arching narrative is looked at from a more detached historical perspective, but there are two sections that look at the topic as it was experienced directly by Gwynoro Jones as candidate, MP and after leaving Westminster. Then the thread continues chronologically, but breaks in style to be told in a different way on two occasions.

The first section looks at the period from 1880 until 1966 when four political parties enter the arena at various stages; the Liberals, Labour, Plaid Cymru and the Conservatives. Each party's contribution is looked at as and when they enter or leave the argument, and we do this in a more detached historical way.

The second section returns to the period dealt with in the Welsh language book, Gwynoro's fight with Gwynfor. It covers the aftermath of victory in Carmarthen in 1966, the run-up to the General Election in 1970, when Gwynoro beat Gwynfor Evans, Gwynoro's years as MP with specific reference to the devolution debate, and then the year of two General Elections, 1974. Gwynoro won the first but was defeated in the second. This story is told in Gwynoro's voice, based on his extensive collection of newspaper cuttings from the period.

The third section looks at the period 1974-1979, the years of a Labour government which had prepared the way for a referendum on devolution in 1979. This section is dealt with in the same way as the first, in the more detached historical style. It ends with the resounding defeat for the Yes campaign in Wales, and all the energy being drained from the Devolution for Wales movement.

The fourth section returns to the personal political and historical analysis of Gwynoro. Having been defeated in the 1974 October General Election, then being a founder member of the new SDP party, he left politics at the beginning of the Nineties and stayed away from it for nearly two decades. In the last few years, however, he has renewed his political interest and enthusiasm in a Wales that by then had an Assembly. The last section of the book gives us his analysis on the current climate in Wales, the Welsh Government, Yes Cymru and the call for Welsh independence.

The Appendix of the book brings the argument up to the present day. In it, there is a summary of what has happened in Wales between 1880 and 2020, culminating in Plaid Cymru publishing their Commission on Independence in September 2020. The argument for confederalism, one option included in Plaid Cymru's Commission publication, is outlined here by the person credited in that commission report for developing and advocating that idea, Glyndwr Jones. The argument for federalism is outlined in the appendix by Member of the Senedd, and leading Conservative thinker, David Melding.

This book aims to take a broad look at how many arguments over a century and a half and under the banners of more than one political party have contributed to the forming of a political identity for Wales. It contains elements not brought together before in one volume. The archive collected by Gwynoro Jones gives an additional distinctiveness to the telling of the story.

We are both indebted to Sir Deian Hopkin for reading Section 1 and Section 3 and for his invaluable comments and amendments on historical facts and interpretations. Needless to say, any errors remaining are our own. Thanks are also due to author and Political Editor at Large for the *Western Mail*, Martin Shipton, for reading the book prior to publication and for writing the foreword.

Gwynoro Jones,
Alun Gibbard.
April 2021

Timeline of key events in the devolution debate

Legislative and administrative milestones

The General Election of 1868, following the extension of the franchise in 1867, marked the beginning of 50 years of Welsh political nationalism.

1881   Sunday Closing (Wales) Act—first act to apply to Wales a legislative principle that did not apply to England

         First administrative admission of Wales as a separate entity was—
1889   Welsh Intermediate Education Act

1893   University of Wales

1896   Inspectorate and Examining Board to administer the Act

1907   Liberal Government proposed a Council for Wales composed of representatives from Welsh local authorities to regulate education policy in Wales. Passed in the Commons but defeated in the Lords. There came instead—

1907   Welsh Department of the Board of Education, National Library of Wales and National Museum

1913   Welsh Health Insurance Commission

1919   Welsh Board of Health and Welsh Department Ministry of Agriculture

1920   Welsh Church Disestablishment Act 1914 came into force

1940   Welsh Board of Health acquired a range of local government services

1942   Welsh Reconstruction Advisory Council—new decentralised administrative system to solve post-war problems in Wales

1945   Heads of Government Departments in Wales (15 of them)—annual report on government economic policies started

1946   Welsh Regional Hospital Board

1947   Wales Gas Board, South Wales Electricity Board and Merseyside and North Wales Electricity Board

1948   Welsh Joint Education Committee and the nominated body, the Advisory Council for Wales and Monmouthshire, meet in private, exchanging views and information, inform the government of the impact of policies on general life of the country)

1951   Minister for Welsh Affairs. Part of Home Office

1957   Minister for Welsh Affairs in Housing and Local Government department

1957   Welsh Department of Education permanent secretary given an office in Cardiff and officer in charge of Welsh Department of Ministry of Agriculture upgraded

1957   Council of Wales produced a memorandum setting out case for the office of Secretary of State and a Welsh Office

1964   Office of the Secretary of State established with Jim Griffiths MP as the first charter Secretary

1965   Welsh Office set up and by 1970, the department acquired a range of government executive powers such as housing, local government, roads, economic planning, health, education, tourism and part control of agriculture

1968   Mid Wales Rural Development Board, later became Development Board for Rural Wales

1967   Welsh Language Act, based on Hughes-Parry Report

1969   Development of Tourism Act—Wales Tourist Board established

1971   Bowen Commission Report on bilingualism

1976   Land Authority for Wales

1976   Welsh Development Agency established

1978   Wales Act setting up a Welsh Assembly subject to a referendum held March 1 1979

1992   Tourism (Wales) Act, responsibility for overseas promotion

1993   Welsh Language Act, placed the Welsh language on equal footing with English language in Wales

1998   Government of Wales Act

1999   First National Assembly of Wales established

2005   Government White Paper 'Better Governance of Wales' in response to the Lord Ivor Richard Commission

2006   Government of Wales Act—enacted formal separation between legislature (National Assembly) and the executive (Welsh Government). Assembly able to pass 'Assembly Measures' over 20 areas but requiring consent of Westminster and the secretary of State for Wales.

2009   All Wales Convention recommended a referendum on full law-making powers

2011   Referendum granting Assembly full law-making powers. Yes vote was 63.5% on a turnout of 35.6%

2011   Silk Commission on Devolution of financial powers set up by The Con-Lib Coalition government

2014   Wales Act. Devolution of powers over stamp duty, business rates and landfill tax. Able to hold a referendum on the devolution of income tax.

2014   Part two of the Silk Commission report published

2015   'St David's Day Agreement' between the four main Assembly political parties and the Secretary of State. It incorporated most of the Silk Commission proposal, but not on policing and criminal justice.

2017   Wales Act 2017 which introduced a 'reserved powers model' similar to Scotland

2017   Commission on Justice in Wales chaired by Lord Thomas of Cwmgiedd. Reporting in October 2019, recommended the devolution of policing and justice to the national assembly.

2020 Senedd and Elections (Wales) Act. Changed the name of the National Assembly to Senedd Cymru/Welsh parliament and lowered the voting age for elections to 16.

Political milestones

1886 Cymru Fydd

1891 National Institutions (Wales) Bill—proposing a Welsh Education Department, National Council for Wales and Secretary of State—overwhelmingly rejected

1914 E. T. John's Government of Wales Bill envisaging a 95-member assembly with legislative and financial powers. Heavily defeated. Period when Home Rule for Wales was viewed in context of Ireland

1918 The Llandrindod Resolutions—conference of Welsh notables—calling for a Welsh Parliament. Endorsed by 11-17 Welsh counties

Labour Conference in Cardiff approved a policy of Federal Home Rule for Wales.

**End of the period of debates on nationalism and home rule. Turned now to devolution and decentralisation of government **

1920 Speakers Conference reported deeply divided between those who wanted limited but separate legislatures for Scotland, Wales and England and others who proposed Grand Councils for Scotland, Wales and England.

1922   Dissatisfied Scottish and Welsh MPs introduced Government of Scotland and Wales Bill. The Welsh component envisaged a bicameral legislature (Senate and Commons) with substantial taxation powers.
Break up of Lloyd George coalition and deepening economic crisis removed devolution from the agenda for 30 years.

1925   Plaid Cymru established, calling for Dominion Status

1938   Chamberlain rejected the Welsh parliamentary party request for a Welsh Office and a voice in the Cabinet, something Scotland had since 1860s

1943   Churchill similar—grounds of cost, administrative disruption and, unlike Scotland, did not have a separate legal and administrative system and was too closely entwined with England

1947   Formation of Welsh Regional Council of Labour, merger of the party's South Wales and North Wales organisations

Post-war Labour government—vehement opposition to devolution from notably Morrison and Bevan—'would divorce' Welsh political activity from rest of UK

1955   S. O. Davies's Parliament for Wales Bill following petition signed by 250k—14% of the Welsh electorate

1966   Welsh Liberal Party formed after amalgamation of its South Wales and North Wales federations enjoying widespread autonomy from the UK party

1967   Royal Commission on the Constitution established under Lord Crowther who died some months later. The new chair was Lord Kilbrandon.

1972 Conservative party renamed as the Conservative Party in Wales

1972 Local Government Wales Bill. Welsh Labour group of MPs amendment for an Elected Council for Wales—Rejected

1973 The Kilbrandon Commission on the Constitution reported

1979 First Welsh Assembly Referendum

1982 SDP Council of Wales formed

1988 The above merges with the Welsh Liberals

1997 Second Welsh Assembly Referendum

PART ONE:

The Devolution Crucible
1880–1966

1.

The Devolution Baby

As the Welsh Government celebrates only the first twenty years of its existence, it would be easy to think that devolution is a new concept. Some recent publications seem to more than suggest that 'Welsh politics' itself was only born in the last two decades. That's one thing that this book sets out to show isn't the case.

Welsh politics has come of age in the devolution period. For example, when the Welsh Government legislated to allow the vote for 16- and 17-year-olds in the next Assembly elections, it was not only a historic vote but also the first time that Wales has changed its own system of governance. That's quite a moment. Therefore, in one sense, of course, it's possible to argue that devolution is in its infancy. The UK Nations of Wales, Scotland and Northern Ireland have only known law-making devolved governments of their own since the turn of this Millennium, a mere fraction of time in terms of the parliamentary democracy calendar of the British Isles. But talk of devolution, or Home Rule, or self-governance, or independence, whichever label has been in currency, goes back over twenty years and then a hundred more.

Such a lengthy period has, of course, seen governments of various political hues and sensibilities come and go. The times in which these governments have served have varied considerably, from the last twenty years of Queen Victoria's reign, through two World Wars and so much more, to the first twenty years of the twenty-first century.

It would be rather simplistic to assert that any one party has had a total monopoly on driving the devolution agenda. Plaid Cymru usually gets the popular credit for this, such was the perceived reality in recent decades at least. We could go further; Plaid Cymru seem to demand that

31

we give them such credit and move on to claim sole ownership of the future governance of Wales. As foolish as claiming that Welsh politics is less than a quarter of a century old, is the thinking that it's only recent political activity and protest that has given us a Senedd in Cardiff Bay. Again, such activity is usually attributed to that carried out under Plaid Cymru's banner and/or organisations affiliated to them through ideology or otherwise. Others within the Labour Party claim that no one has done more to advance devolution in Wales than they have, and there then follows a long list of 'achievements' that have led to such a claim. Establishing the first Secretary of State for Wales is close to the top of the list. A third party, the Liberals, enter the debate when they claim that they were the ones who were there in the very early days of devolution debates, before the Labour Party and Plaid Cymru were formed. There's no shortage then of those who want to jump on the bandwagon of crediting their party for devolution advancement. Often, however, more often than should be the case, they do this without bothering to find out who was involved in building the bandwagon.

In fact, four political parties have played their part in the unfolding devolution drama from the days of Victoria through to Elizabeth, and every George and Edward in between. The Liberals, the Conservatives, Labour and Plaid Cymru, in that general chronological order, gave the first contributions to the debate. Since those primary contributions were made, the order has chopped and changed, of course. We shall look at all four in this argument. But there are two key players that stand out in the Welsh devolution arena, above the others; two parties who have dominated the devolution debate in Wales for over half a century, and two who shared power in the devolved Welsh Government once it was established. They are two protagonists who aren't brought together in any other context but who are linked in the war of devolved power. This is where they come head to head. There's not a lot of love lost between Plaid Cymru and the Labour Party. Historically, there has been a strong hatred between the two, often a bitter, acrimonious one, as both argued in the name of their particular perception of Welsh identity. The acrimony came to a head during the period from the early Sixties to the late Seventies, described as the most bitter period in Welsh politics. The second part of this book looks at that bitter period through the eyes of a Labour MP who stood eye-ball to eye-ball with Plaid Cymru's first MP during that time, and their arena was the quiet market town of Carmarthen.

One prominent debate during this period has come to prominence again as these words are being written. Socialism and nationalism were constantly pitted against each other, not only between the parties, but within the two parties too. This is an argument that the First Minister of Wales, Mark Drakeford, has again raised in recent times. The united plight of workers in the Rhondda and in Stoke and in Glasgow is of more importance than any accident of birth, he claims, citing why he joined the Labour Party and not Plaid Cymru as a young man growing up in Carmarthen.

Devolution, the actual realisation of the political ideal, has to a large extent, brought the two foes, Plaid Cymru and the Labour Party, to sit at the same table. They even shared power in a coalition government in the Cardiff Senedd for some years. But the path to get there was a rocky one, and it can't be said that all is well even now. But let's look at the relationship between these two parties in a little more detail, beginning with where their relationship began. Plaid Cymru and the Labour Party first became aware of each other during a very colourful and dramatic decade, a hundred years ago.

A roaring ten years

They called the 1920s Roaring because it was a time of sudden and immediate change in the political and cultural worlds of the USA and Western Europe. It was also, however, a decade that saw severe economic hardship. In the UK, we suffered a recession and a General Strike in 1926. When the decade started, the coal industry the Valleys are famous for had already reached the peak of production. The black diamond itself became a symbol of a battle of opposing political ideologies—was it to be publicly or privately owned?

Once the General Strike and the Depression hit, unemployment soared in South Wales in particular. Amongst the coal miners specifically,

UNDER WHICH FLAG?
JOHN BULL: "ONE OF THESE TWO FLAGS HAS GOT TO COME DOWN—AND IT WON'T BE MINE"

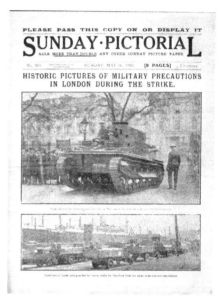

unemployment rose from 2% in April 1924 to 12.5% in January 1925, then to 28.5% in August of that year. This period saw the first halt of the industrial growth that had been experienced in Wales for the previous 150 years. That is a sobering statistic. It had major political repercussions.

The Americans well remember the ten years of the Twenties as the decade when more of them lived in cities than farms for the first time. The rest of Britain might remember it for the living realities created by the statistics mentioned and also for the rise of the dominance of the Labour Party in Parliament, which is the most relevant to our narrative here.

As the sound of the guns of World War One gave way to the roar of a new decade, there were six by-elections in Wales in the first two years of the Twenties. The Labour Party won all of them, and each one of those constituencies was in a mining area. Such results were a clear indication of what the 1922 General Election would give. And that's what happened. In that General Election, Labour won 142 seats in the UK and, in doing so, became the second-largest political party in Westminster. They became the official opposition under the leadership of Ramsey MacDonald. The following year, they consolidated their newfound position. The Conservatives lost their overall power even though they won most seats, and the resultant negotiations led to Ramsay MacDonald becoming the first-ever

Labour Prime Minister in January 1924, even though he only had a third of the House of Commons MPs. In four years, Labour had gone from being a minority party to being the official opposition and then to govern.

Such a Labour victory, however, had no immediate benefits for Wales in terms of its separate political identity. John Davies, in *A History of Wales*, says that in the elections of 1922, 1923 and 1924,

... Wales as a political issue was increasingly eliminated from the agenda.[1]

But such a fact is not of necessity a reflection of any anti-Welsh feeling or political philosophy. These were unprecedented economic times, which shifted priorities and perceptions. Jobs and day to day living became the pragmatic political focus. Pressing needs took over from any political ideals.

The election campaigns themselves were noted as being almost devoid of any Welsh issues. That was to come. But Labour's newfound power had been established, specifically in the thriving mining communities of Wales. Significantly, they had succeeded in knocking the Liberals off their perch in Wales and established a dominance that has continued to this day.

A year later, in Wales, a brand new political party was formed. There was an increasing urge amongst many in Wales to make Welsh identity the focus of political activity. In the year of the 1924 General Election, two specific Welsh groups existed to argue for a distinctive Welsh national identity. A man from the slate-quarrying culture of North Wales established Byddin Ymreolwyr Cymru (The Army of Welsh Home Rulers). Y Mudiad Cymreig was the other, The Welsh Movement. Their most significant member was Saunders Lewis, a lecturer in Welsh and a man from the greater Liverpool area. Three members of Yr Ymreolwyr and three from Y Mudiad came together during the Pwllheli National Eisteddfod of August 1925 and formed a new political power, Plaid Genedlaethol Cymru, The National Party of Wales.

This new party argued that it should sever all ties with the London-centric seat of government and cut ties with other more Britain-centric parties. This was Saunders Lewis's distinctive contribution. He insisted that

---

1. John Davies: *A History of Wales*. London: Penguin Books, 2007, p. 531.

Lieut. J. Saunders Lewis, B. A., mab y Parch. Lodwig Lewis, Lerpwl, ac wyr i'r diweddar Dr. Owen Thomas. Enillodd ei B. A. yn Athrofa Lerpwl. Tra yn y coleg enillodd wobr a gynygid gan y "Review of Reviews."

Army Officer Saunders Lewis 1916.

any previous manifestation of Welsh nationalism had pandered too much to Westminster. It had also, he argued, pandered too much to co-operation with other political parties. Such parties, he argued, had interests over and above Wales' specific ones and as a result, they could not give full fair play and attention to Wales. Only a Welsh party could do so.

It might well have had great trouble in establishing a credible, authoritative power base, but it was a party that was now existing at least. Although its membership was very small, as John Davies says, '… its members believed that the establishment of the party was an achievement in itself; merely by existing, the party was a declaration of the distinctiveness of Wales.'

Two years after establishing Plaid Cymru, its membership was only 400, predominantly made up of 65 quarrymen, 50 farmers, 25 ministers of religion and 70 students. As Gwynfor Evans says, in his book *The Fight for Welsh Freedom*:

Such was the movement that challenged British imperial might in Wales.[2]

Four years after their formation, they fought Caernarfon in the 1929 General Election. They secured 609 votes, 1.6% of the total votes cast. They had moved on steadily.

---

2. Gwynfor Evans: *The Fight for Welsh Freedom,* Tal-y-bont, Ceredigion: Y Lolfa, 2006, p. 131.

The years since the 1924 General Election and the formation of Plaid Cymru in 1925 were turbulent times, dominated by disputes, depression and the General Strike of 1926. As Labour grandee Jim Griffiths says of those years, in the book *James Griffiths and His Times*, and referring to Wales:

> *Politics became secondary to industrial problems... The valleys were filled with men without work and were stricken by economic paralysis. This was the stormy background of the mid-twenties dominating politics in Wales...*[3]

The General Election of 1929 was significant for two reasons. It was the platform for a fresh bid for power on behalf of David Lloyd George. The Liberals sought to take advantage of the economic conditions. They succeeded in increasing their vote and their number of MPs, but not as much as the Labour Party did. The Liberals secured 58 MPs; the Labour Party, 288. With the Conservatives only winning 260 seats, Labour was the dominant party in Westminster for the first time.

The Liberal attack, under Lloyd George, had failed in the UK, and the same was true in Wales as well. They won 9 seats in Wales, one less than in 1924 and a far cry from the 22 seats they had won in 1906, which was the pinnacle of success for the Liberal Party, akin to Attlee's landslide in 1945 and Blair's in 1997. The Liberals secured their landslide because of an electoral pact with the emerging Labour Party.

The Tories sank to their lowest ever number of seats—just the one. Labour won 25 seats. Jim Griffiths again:

> *... this was the last big effort of the Liberals to oust the Labour party— and it failed... The failure in Wales must have been a blow to Lloyd George's pride. Once the idol of Wales, he was now rejected.*[4]

---

3. J. Beverley Smith; James Griffiths: *James Griffiths and his Times*. Labour Party Wales, Llanelli Constituency Party, 1977, p. 30.
4. Ibid., p. 31.

David Lloyd George, the Welsh Wizard.

That's how the Twenties came to a political end in Wales. It was a decade of change. The Labour party were in the ascendancy and dominant. Plaid Genedlaethol Cymru were new and establishing an ascendancy, even though theirs wasn't an overtly political presence. This is the decade of the three leading devolution parties existing at the same time, for the first time. It's when the dynamic of that argument changed significantly, with one leading player, the Liberals, dropping out of the picture and moving back into the wings. Labour moved to centre stage, Plaid Cymru stepped onto the stage, while the Conservatives stayed up-stage.

2.

Home Rule and Dry Pubs

But let's step back for a while. It will help set the bigger picture. We have seen how the 1920s were the beginning of an awareness that Plaid and Labour existed in Wales, but it's true to say that, as far as the parties themselves were concerned, Plaid were more aware of Labour than vice versa. But what of the development of the devolution argument before that decade, before the Liberals left the picture? That's what we turn to next, before turning back again to Labour and Plaid themselves.

As the 1920s was a significant decade for Plaid and Labour, the 1880s was a significant decade for the wider Home Rule debate in Ireland and Wales. There were advances under a Liberal banner. One government Act in that decade led to a monumental change in the Welsh political landscape; a significant step in Wales' political growth. It's an Act that has been described as heralding a '… new kind of politics in Wales.'

The Reform Act of 1884 sounds potentially dry and boring, like its many predecessors, but for Wales, it was a huge step forward. It increased the number of people who could vote. As Kenneth O. Morgan says in *Rebirth of a Nation: Wales 1880-1980*,

The enfranchisement of the householder in the counties made Wales something resembling a political democracy for the first time.[5]

This was in the last few years of the Nineteenth Century, less than a century and a half ago. The emphasis, then, is not so much on devolution

---

5. Kenneth O. Morgan: *Rebirth of a Nation: Wales 1880-1980*. Oxford: Clarendon Press, 1981, p. 27.

being in its infancy, but on Welsh political democracy being young in terms of the nation's existence. In the same work, Kenneth O. Morgan says that in this decade,

> *... a sense of Welsh nationality and of national distinctiveness within the wider framework of the United Kingdom was present as never before.*[6]

It was also a decade of significant firsts.

Dry Sundays

This was what Wales could claim was the first recognition of its existence as a separate entity within the United Kingdom. Where did that happen? In the world of pubs! Or more accurately, where the world of pubs met the world of chapels. That would happen on a Sunday, of course, when worshippers and imbibers would flock to both establishments; more often than not, from one to the other. Welsh towns and villages were full of chapels and pubs. They were the definitive bricks and mortar. Could both be open and busy on the same day? No, was the firm Welsh reply!

Again, it was Gladstone who was in Number 10 when the issue arose. The momentum behind the call to close pubs on a Sunday in Wales came, maybe surprisingly, from those of the working class. They knew of their need to slake their thirst at the end of a hard shift in the two foot six. But they also knew about God. Sunday was his day. The chapels and the Temperance Movement were as strong a lobby in this argument as any brewer or landlord. In 1881, the Act was passed and pubs could not open on a Sunday in Wales. Its significance, however, stretched far beyond the end of the bar. It was the first time since the Act of Union between England and Wales, almost four hundred years before, that Wales was recognised as a separate entity to England and they passed an Act that applied to Wales but didn't apply to England. That was followed in the same decade by the Welsh Intermediate Education Act, 1889, introduced by a Conservative Government, supported by Liberal Unionists.

---

6.   Ibid., p. 90.

A young Welshman and Cymru Fydd

In the General Election of 1886, one Welsh candidate was the first to include the argument in favour of self-government for Wales in his manifesto. Thomas Edward Ellis was a tenant farmer's son from Bala in Merionethshire, North Wales. He loved the stories he heard at home of some political evictions in his area during two General Elections in 1859 and 1868. But more significantly, he was heavily influenced, to the point of discipleship even, by Michael D. Jones, best known for being the man who led a group of people to create a new Welsh colony in Patagonia, Argentina. Michael D. Jones was a dominant figure in Welsh politics and consciousness in the century before last, perhaps rarely considered in the wider devolution debate. Gwynfor Evans has no doubt about the significance of his contribution, as he wrote in his book, *Land of My Fathers*,

> *Michael D. Jones was the greatest Welshman of the 19th century and the greatest nationalist after Owain Glyndwr.*[7]

Michael D. Jones

He was Principal of the Theological College in Bala and from the same square mile as Tom Ellis himself. But ironically, even though he was a man whose convictions led to Welsh people leaving their motherland and settling thousands of miles away, they also regard him as one of the fathers of Welsh nationalism. He had a rather strong dislike of anything that suggested influence from across Offa's Dyke. He was one of the first, if not

---

7. Gwynfor Evans: *Land of my Fathers: 2000 Years of Welsh History* (transl. from Welsh). Swansea: John Penry Pr., 1974, p. 405.

the first, to formulate a political basis for a separate Welsh identity. Little wonder that one who fell so heavily under his influence was the first to put home rule for Wales in his election manifesto. Ellis had been immersed in the Welsh folk-lore and culture of his homeland. His view of a Welsh identity and the need to affirm the separate-ness of that identity, comprised two clear, strong strands; culture and politics.

In 1886, Ellis was one of 27 Gladstonian Liberals sent to the House of Commons from Wales in that Election. This new batch included many who heralded a departure from the old liberalism of the previous generation and the birth of a liberalism which focused far more on Wales and Welsh issues. They regarded Ellis, in particular, as a man who breathed some fresh air into the Liberal Party. The Liberal Party dominated Welsh politics from this point right up to the 1920s.

When Tom Ellis got to Westminster, he joined a small group of MPs that would argue causes relevant only to Wales, besides their usual duties. This happened in two different forums.

The year in which Tom Ellis took his seat in Westminster saw the formation of an organisation established to further the cause of Welsh self-governance, Cymru Fydd (The Wales that is to be). They argued for federal self-rule for Wales, reflecting the significant interest in Home Rule in Ireland by the Liberals, of course.

This proved to be an influential organisation, but one that also would show a distinct feature of the nationalist cause in Wales from then up to the present day—the tension between a political and a cultural nationalism.

Before Cymru Fydd, and during its early years, there was a strong resurgence in Welsh culture in terms of poetry, prose and

T. E. Ellis

the printed press. Daniel Owen's novels, the poetry of John Morris Jones and Elfed, for example, established a renaissance in Welsh culture.

But there wasn't a political expression to champion a Welsh identity attached to this renaissance. Llewellyn Williams, who promoted his Welsh cause in the journalistic field, decried a 'nationalism that was divorced from everything except politics'. Other advocates came from the academic, literary and educational fields of Wales. All fell short of seeing the need for affirming their newfound confidence in their Welshness in political terms. Sir John Morris Jones and Owen M. Edwards were two leading figures. The former resisted any suggestion that Welsh literature and politics should ever be brought together. The latter sought to work through the channels of education to further an awareness of all things Welsh.

Political figures who argued for Home Rule in Wales were few—which increases the significance of Tom Ellis. With his arrival in Westminster, a cultural Welsh identity and a more political one drew ever closer together. Ellis couldn't see how any real advancement in Wales as a nation could happen unless it had a political framework of its own. The resurgence that had swept through Wales in the more cultural fields needed a structure to sustain and advance it. He saw no separation. Each aspect expressed a core identity. His views, however, were beyond the grasp of advocates of each of the two camps he sought to bring together. They were too woolly for the politically minded, and too political for the others. He drifted away from Cymru Fydd as his political career prospered, but lost none of his convictions for the need for a Welsh government until his untimely death at forty.

Cymru Fydd argued its case along cultural lines. The duality between cultural and political nationalism reared its head as long ago as this. A new monthly journal took the name of *Cymru Fydd* too. It first came out in 1888 and continued until 1891. It began its days arguing, along strong political lines, for a Welsh government. But this was too much for some leading Welsh nationalists who wanted it to be a more cultural publication. Again, as in so many other cases, this publication's significance was because they had started it at all. Another magazine called *Young Wales* was launched in 1895.

But as the decade went by, they developed a more political identity and grew ever closer to the Liberal Party. One very influential factor in this process was a certain young Liberal called David Lloyd George, who was a prominent spokesperson for Cymru Fydd in North Wales. As aware as he was of a distinct cultural Welsh identity, he also wanted Home Rule for Wales to be a Liberal Party policy. When he was elected as an MP for the first time in 1890, this strengthened the political foundation for Home Rule in Wales. It also meant that Cymru Fydd and the Liberal Party drew ever closer. They joined formally in 1894, in the name of the Cymru Fydd League. Cymru Fydd and the North Wales Liberal Federation amalgamated to form this League. Mid Wales was also on board.

The next step would be for the South Wales Liberal Federation to do the same, thus creating a unified, Wales-wide organisation. But that didn't happen. There was far more suspicion and outright opposition to anything that looked like separating from England in this industrialised part of Wales. This resistance was concentrated in the dock towns of Swansea, Barry, and Cardiff. In Newport, there was a particularly volatile meeting, described by the *Western Mail* as a 'bear garden'. Lloyd George himself said that he had been 'howled down' at the meeting. In the name of redressing the balance, historian Chris Williams points out that Lloyd George supporters were also guilty of making a lot of noise:

> *The howl that went up when Mr. Robert Bird [an opponent of Cymru Fydd] said there was a large community in South Wales which would not submit to domination and dictation [by the Welsh-speaking population] was as bad as the pandemonium on a football ground when the referee decided against the home team. Some delegates were like raving lunatics for a time...*[8]

The South Wales Liberal Federation rejected what the others had accepted, and in that rejection, turned considerable vitriol towards Lloyd George.

---

8. Robert A. Stradling; Harry Hearder: *Conflict and Coexistence: Nationalism and Democracy in Modern Europe: Essays in Honour of Harry Hearder.* Cardiff: University of Wales Press, 1997, p. 124.

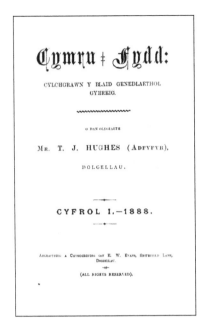

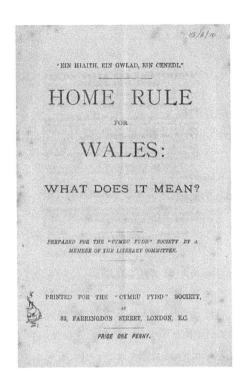

'The Magazine of the National Party of Wales', first edition.

He expressed his anger at both the outcome and the tone of this meeting in the Welsh language weekly, *Baner ac Amserau Cymru*,

> *Is the mass of the Welsh nation willing to be dominated by a coalition of English capitalists who have come to Wales, not to benefit the people but to make their fortune?*[9]

This was, in effect, the end of Cymru Fydd. The efforts of Michael D. Jones, Lloyd George and Tom Ellis to form a new political movement in Wales, if not a new political party, ground to a halt. In another of his books, *The Fight for Welsh Freedom*, Gwynfor Evans says,

> *The main political weakness of these able men was their failure to create an independent nationalist party as the Irish had done.*[10]

9.   John Davies: *A History of Wales*. London: Penguin Books, 2007, p. 466.
10. Gwynfor Evans: *The Fight for Welsh Freedom*, Tal-y-bont, Ceredigion: Y Lolfa, 2006, p. 126.

The Newport meeting shows a clear tension, a duality in the nationalist cause which is still with us. As a political idea and a cultural idea of Wales battle with each other, so do the industrial valleys and the rest of the nation.

This failure to be unified saw the demise of Cymru Fydd, and it ended the self-government emphasis in Lloyd George's politics. The exact role Lloyd George played in the development of the devolution story in Wales is still open to debate. Emyr Price, in his biography of Lloyd George, called him

> ... the first architect of Welsh devolution and its most famous advocate... the pioneering advocate of a powerful parliament for the Welsh people.[11]

Kenneth O. Morgan agrees that Lloyd George was a champion of the Welsh cause, saying that he did more than any of his contemporaries to make Wales a political and social reality.

But it wasn't the death knell of the surge in awareness of Welsh nationhood or in the call for self-government. That continued to gather momentum both in Wales and Westminster. In summing-up the legacy of Liberal domination in Wales from 1868 until this point, T. Graham Jones, in *Cof Cenedl VII*, refers to another crucial influence:

> *Yr oedd gwleidyddion Rhyddfrydol ifainc wedi sicrhau i Gymru le cadarn ar y llwyfan seneddol ac wedi ennill parch yn Nhŷ'r Cyffredin. Soniwyd am eu gweithgareddau'n rheolaidd yng ngholofnau'r wasg Gymreig, ac o ganlyniad dechreuodd llawer o Gymru ymddiddori o ddifri mewn gwleidyddiaeth am y tro cyntaf.[12]*

> *Young Liberal politicians had secured a place for Wales on the parliamentary platform and gained respect in the House of Commons. Their activities were mentioned regularly in the columns of the Welsh press, and as a result, many Welsh people started to show an interest in politics for the first time.*

---

11. Emyr Price: *Megan Lloyd George*. Caernarfon: Gwasanaeth Archifau Gwynedd, 1983, p. 208.
12. Geraint H. Jenkins: *Cof Cenedl VII: Ysgrifau ar Hanes Cymru*. Llandysul: Gomer, 1992, p. 170.

Mabon

Another dominant figure was a man who embodied the struggle to identify political and cultural Wales. Mabon was a character who stood tall in the politics of Wales at the end of Victoria's reign. He was a collier from Cwm Afan, a lay-preacher, the conductor of his chapel's choir, a Sunday School teacher, a member of the National Eisteddfod's Gorsedd of the Bards. In his coal-mining context, he was a leader of his fellow workers. He fought for the formation of a union and his biggest work was to build up a strong trade union

WILLIAM ABRAHAM. M. P.
COPYRIGHT Photo Russell

Mabon

organisation amongst the miners, which led to the formation of The South Wales Miners' Federation in 1898. He also secured a miners' holiday, called Mabon's Day, and was the first Welsh miner to be elected to parliament. Because of his many characteristics and activities, they hold him as an influential Welshman, who epitomised the culture and politics of Wales. He rose to prominence at the exact time the new Labour Party was beginning to emerge, under the leadership of Keir Hardie.

The Welsh MPs also formed a Welsh Parliamentary Party towards the end of the 1880s, which derived from a similar Welsh Parliamentary group that had existed for some years prior to that. They were effective in that they concentrated the attention of Westminster on Welsh matters in a way that had not happened previously. The Welsh Parliamentary Party ensured that Welsh Members could ballot jointly on private MPs' motions and lobby party leaders on Welsh issues. It didn't really have any teeth, but it expressed the political feelings amongst Welsh MPs for the first time.

During the 1890s, bills to create a Secretary of State for Wales were introduced. Seventy years before it actually happened, the debate was up and running, led by the major political figures of the period.

So the 1880s was a cauldron of a decade for the issues of Welsh identity and self-government. A collection of 'firsts' in culture, literature and politics amalgamated to have an impact far greater than their total parts. But there's one other crucial area in this decade where Welshness established a new, influential presence.

Welsh Not?

Developments in the schools of Wales also came from a newfound confidence in being Welsh and in the Welsh language itself. Before the 1880s, there was hardly any Welsh taught in schools, even though the overwhelming majority of pupils in their classrooms knew nothing but Welsh. This was the period of *Y Llyfrau Gleision, The Blue Books*—or as they are now referred to, *Brad y Llyfrau Gleision, The Betrayal of the Blue Books*. Well-known poet Matthew Arnold, who was at the time a schools inspector, was charged with writing a report on the state of education in Wales. His final report, referred to as *The Blue Books*, was a damning indictment not of Welsh education—although it was that too—but of Wales as a people:

> *It must always be the desire of government to render its dominions, as far as possible, homogenous... sooner or later the difference of language between Wales and England will probably be effaced... an event which is socially and politically desirable.*

Thus began the period that fostered the perception that English was the language of progress, and its converse, Welsh, the language of detriment. Organisations started in Wales to address this situation. They formed the Society for the Utilisation of the Welsh Language at the Aberdare

National Eisteddfod in 1895. It also had a Welsh title, Cymdeithas yr Iaith Gymraeg, The Welsh Language Society—but not the one we might be more familiar with today! The difference in titles is telling. Firstly, that there was a Welsh name and an English name, a necessity in the bilingual, but English dominated the formal word of Wales. But also the emphasis of the society's aims is different in both languages. The English is far more nebulous than the Welsh, which is more definite in its statement. It exists for the Welsh language, end of. The English is, therefore, its utilisation.

Whatever the nominal emphasis, the society's aim stated that their emphasis on the furthering of the Welsh Language was part of a wider brief 'for the better teaching of English'. Historian John Davies argues a reason for this:

> It is likely that the emphasis on English arose partly from the desire to put forward an argument which would be acceptable to the authorities.[13]

Its Welsh language propaganda was more favourable to Welsh only. Dan Isaac Davies, an inspector of schools in the Merthyr Tydfil area, formed the Society. He believed passionately in bilingualism and also believed that it was unacceptable not to educate children to speak the language of the country in which they were born.

If we think that the Welsh Government's 2017 initiative to create a million Welsh speakers by 2050 is new or ambitious, then we would do well to consider one of Dan Isaac Davies' publications, *Tair Miliwn o Gymry Dwy-ieithog ymhen Can Mlynedd*, Three Million Bilingual Welsh People in a Hundred Years. It would be interesting to know what his perception of the population growth of Wales was at the time of his writing! But there's no doubting his vision. The actual population of Wales, as shown in the 1911 Census, was 2.5 million, of which 43.5% spoke Welsh—8% of those spoke only Welsh and no English.

In 1890, the Education Committee of the Privy Council agreed to pay schools that were seen to teach Welsh successfully. This ground-breaking decision came because of a report submitted to a Royal Commission,

---

13. John Davies: *A History of Wales*. London: Penguin Books, 2007, p. 443.

set up by the Privy Council, by Cymdeithas yr Iaith Gymraeg. Dan Isaac was its author. It did not change the face of Welsh schools and it's been described as a grudging concession, but it was a crucial step. As John Davies says:

> ... it is only necessary to compare the fate of Welsh in the twentieth century with that of Breton—a language which did not succeed in winning a foothold in the education system—to appreciate the scale of their achievements.[14]

This Act also brings in another political party to the broader devolution debate. A Conservative government passed it, with Liberal Party backing.

Wales and the Conservatives

During this period, the Conservative party had not developed as clearly defined a policy on Wales as the Liberals had. For the twenty-two years between 1892 and the outbreak of World War One in 1914, the party's election campaign guides included the same statement on Wales:

> The laws, institutions and customs of Wales are the laws, institutions and customs of England. The Crown of England is the Crown of Wales, the flag of Wales is the flag of England. To deal with a corner of the country separately in relation to large constitutional questions, such as that of church and state, would be to introduce a system of particularism and parochialism into national affairs which would soon lead to most remarkable anomalies and undermine the whole fabric of uniform and orderly government throughout the country.

The mention of church and state is apposite. These were the years of debate regarding the disestablishment of the Church in Wales. The Conservative party were vehemently opposed to such a move. In 1914, the party's cam-

---

14. Ibid., p. 444.

paign guide includes a massive 61-page section on their stance on dises-tablishment—by far the largest single issue covered in that document. One of the party's previous publications on the issue, in 1895, argued on much the same principles, but the tone was more condescending in answering the question in its title, *Why We Oppose Welsh Disestablishment*:

> *Because the Church in Wales is absolutely the same as in England, and it is cowardly for those who dare not attack the whole body to try to ruin a small and poor part of it.*

Small and poor Wales! Electorally, this standpoint was reflected in Wales and showed a trend that has continued over the years. Wales traditionally return a minority of Tory MPs. One of the party's members in the Welsh parliament today, David Melding, says in his book, *Will Britain Survive beyond 2020?*

> *… despite the local services of a dedicated band of professional agents, the ability of the Party to organise on an all-Wales basis remained very weak until the 1950s.*[15]

The Irish Question

This impetus for forging a distinct Welsh identity was part of a wider debate on home rule for nations within the United Kingdom. The push for Home Rule across the water from Wales, in Ireland, was by far more advanced than any such stirring in Wales when the nineteenth century drew to a close. First surfacing, as far as Westminster was concerned at least, in the General Election of 1886, Irish Home Rule dominated Ire-land's dealings with Westminster for the last decades of the century before last, right up to the end of the First World War. It came from a clear awareness of what it meant to be Irish and the wrongs that the Irish felt

---

15. David Melding: *Will Britain survive beyond 2020?* Cardiff: Institute of Welsh Affairs, 2009, p. 140.

they had suffered under the hands of English dominance. The English, they felt, had taken over their land and their people but interestingly, not necessarily their language, as the influence of the Latin of the Catholic church had been great on the indigenous population of Ireland before. One should not underestimate the extent to which the translation of the Bible into Welsh by William Morgan in 1588 promoted continued usage of the language into the times under consideration.

Following the Act of Union in 1800, Ireland became a part of the United Kingdom of Great Britain and Ireland in 1801. However, opposition to this union remained vociferous throughout the nineteenth century. By the end of that century, Irish attempts to establish Home Rule were being carried out in the Westminster arena. The Irish campaign was a robust one. They secured the reading of the First Irish Home Rule Bill during Gladstone's time as Prime Minister in 1886. That failed, but there were three more Home Rule Bills after that. The Second Irish Home Rule Bill was Gladstone's second attempt to push such legislation through Parliament, in 1893, during his second period as Prime Minister. No such acts were introduced while the Conservatives, under Lord Salisbury, were in power between 1886 and 1892. The Liberals introduced a third Irish Home Rule Bill. The debate for this happened between 1912 and 1914. Unlike the previous two, this one was passed, leading to the Government of Ireland Act 1914. This was the first time in history that the British Parliament had made any concession toward devolution for a member nation.

However, its implementation was delayed by the onset of World War One. This delay, and the violent and volatile Easter Rising of 1916, led to more than one postponement and the Act was never implemented. The situation was, of course, far more complex than this paragraph suggests, but in the narrative of this book, establishing such facts is sufficient. Their significance for this book is the efforts to which the Liberal Government went to forge Irish Home Rule, having introduced three Bills, in two separate Governments, over twenty-eight years.

The Fourth Irish Home Rule Act was passed and implemented as the Government of Ireland Act 1920. The initial plans were for Ireland to be divided into Northern and Southern, with Home Rule in each. This happened in the North. In the South, discussions in the name of the

Anglo-Irish Treaty led initially to an Irish Free State in the South, which then eventually led to the Irish Republic we know today. The Prime Minister at the time of the Government of Ireland Act was Welshman David Lloyd George.

The impetus behind the Irish drive for recognition spilled over into the national awareness of the other Celtic countries, Wales and Scotland. It's fair to say that such a consciousness was far stronger in the other two countries than it was in Wales. Scotland secured a Scottish Office and a Scottish Secretaryship in 1886, But Wales felt the benefit of the nationalistic expressions of the other two countries in terms of morale and inspiration. Many MPs believed that the Liberal party's backing of Home Rule for Ireland was of benefit to Wales as well. There were more in Wales who favoured the Irish Home Rule movement than opposed it. They considered Ireland an example for Wales. As one MP said;

The Irish Question is helping Wales by helping to make a Welsh Question.

Some in Wales fell under the influence of the writings of Thomas Davies, of the Young Ireland Movement, which, in turn, was part of a broader, European nationalistic expression, as seen in the writings of people such as Young Italy's Mazzini. Wales saw *Young Wales* emerge, which was an accurate description of what was happening, even if there was no common perception of it.

Labours' roots take hold

The Liberal political dominance was waning as the 1880s drew to a close. The man who would lead the new political party that would challenge Liberal domination was someone who initially supported the Liberal cause. In fact, Keir Hardie was initially an ardent follower of Gladstone. When Hardie entered parliament as an Independent MP in 1888, the Liberals did not field a candidate to stand against him. In that same year, Hardie established the Scottish Labour Party. In 1893, he took part in the formation of the Independent Labour Party. For all his previous support for the Liberals, he believed that the working class needed a party of its own. They elected him to West Ham in 1892, but he lost his seat in 1895. He was back in Parliament again in 1900 as the MP for Merthyr Tydfil.

Swansea University

Keir Hardie speaking in Dowlais, 1900

In that year, he was again instrumental in the formation of a Labour movement, this time, the Labour Representation Committee. Deian Hopkin describes the LRC thus:

The LRC was not a union-based organisation, although trade unions were a key element—it was an alliance of groups, including the Cooperative movement and the ILP, and others. In 1906, the term Labour Party was adopted but largely for Members of Parliament. In fact, until 1918, there was no individual membership of the LRC—you could only affiliate either through a trade union or the ILP or other organisations. And the term "labour movement" refers to the whole history of labour and socialism from the 1860s onwards, arguable even from the Tolpuddle Martyrs of the 1830s.

After the 1906 General Election, with Hardie's place in Parliament secured once more, they chose him as the chair of the Parliamentary Labour Party. He led a party which had won 29 seats in that landslide election for the Liberal Party.

When Hardie resigned in 1908, in favour of Arthur Henderson, he passed on the baton to a person who was as fervent a Home Ruler as he was himself, and indeed, this was the new party's policy until 1926. Kenneth O. Morgan called Keir Hardie, Labour's greatest pioneer and its greatest hero.

It's interesting to note a particular meeting that took place in Carmarthen in 1911. The meeting itself is significant, but it takes on a greater significance in this book because of where it took place. They held the National Eisteddfod of Wales in the town that year, with the Ivy Bush Hotel a focal point. Down the road, in the vestry of a Baptist Chapel, a group of young Welsh people met to discuss the establishment of a Welsh Labour Party. The meeting resulted from a growing interest in devolution within the Independent Labour Party. There were twelve chapel ministers, trade union leaders and prominent poets in their midst. Ironically, Keir Hardie opposed the proposal to form a Welsh ILP and nothing came of it.

Mabon speaking in Tonypandy, 1911.

Sir Deian Hopkin, in *Cof Cenedl VI*, says that the year they held the meeting was significant because of unrest that was stirring and boiling over in South Wales. The Tonypandy Riots had just taken place and the Llanelli Railway Riots were only a few days away. The electoral success mentioned above had buoyed the Labour Movement generally. But Hopkin gives more reasons why this meeting was a significant one.

Dyma'r elfennau a gynrychiolid ganddynt: cysylltiad mewn addysg a diwylliant fel allweddi i gynnydd cymdeithasol, a chred yr un mor gadarn mewn esblygiadaeth yn yr ystyr o ddiwygiadau graddol. Yr oedd tueddiadau cryf yn eu plith tuag at Ffabianaeth a chysylltiadau eang â'r ILP (Y Blaid Lafur Annibynnol) yng ngogledd a de Cymru, ac yr oedd llawer ohonynt yn weithgar mewn mudiadau llenyddol cyfoes... Yn fwriadol y trefnwyd i'r cyfarfod gyd-ddigwydd â'r Eisteddfod Genedlaethol, a hynny er mwyn dangos gallu sosialaeth i fod yn rhan annatod o fywyd diwylliannol y Gymru Gymraeg.[16]

These are the emphases they represented: a link between education and culture as keys to social progression, and a strong belief in evolutionism in the sense of gradual reforms. There were strong tendencies in their midst towards Fabianism and wide connection with the ILP (The Independent Labour Party) in north and south Wales, and many of them were active members of contemporary literary movements... The decision to hold the meeting during the Eisteddfod week was deliberate, in order to show socialisms' ability to be an integral part of the life of Welsh-speaking people.

The creation of the ILP worried the Liberals, making them afraid that the ILP would win the working-class votes—which is exactly what happened. One has to wonder about the political judgment of the Liberal Party for not forming their own alliance with the Trade Union movement and therefore aligning themselves with the working class.

---

16. Geraint H. Jenkins: *Cof Cenedl VI: Ysgrifau ar Hanes Cymru.* Llandysul: Gomer, 1992, p. 165.

Church and State

In more political terms, the role of the Liberal Party in the drive to recognize self-government for Wales was abundantly clear. Besides what's been already noted, it was the Liberals who granted a Charter to the University of Wales in 1893. Later on, in 1907, they were to grant a Charter to The National Museum of Wales and the National Library of Wales. In that same year, the Welsh Department of the Board of Education was founded. These three were signs of an increasing constitutional recognition of Wales. In addition, they established a Welsh Department in the Board of Education in 1907, followed by the Welsh Cemeteries Act in 1908. In the following decade, the Welsh Insurance Commission was set up in 1911 and the Welsh Board of Health in 1919. In that year also, a Welsh Department in the Ministry of Agriculture was established.

That same year, there was a Speaker's Conference, called by the Speaker, James Lowther, who had been a Conservative MP before he was Speaker. His proposal for a conference was to establish Grand Councils for Scotland, Wales and England, with MPs from those countries serving on their respective councils. The proposal was discussed, but not passed. One Scottish MP, Murray MacDonald, wanted separate legislatures for the three countries. The Conference was divided on this, and they implemented nothing.

A big step however was passed as the guns of World War One started rumbling. It has the rather long title of An Act to Terminate the Establishment of the Church of England in Wales and Monmouthshire, and to Make Provision in Respect of the Temporalities thereof, and for Other Purposes in Connection with the Matters Aforesaid. In other words, The Welsh Church Act of 1914! There had been calls for a very long time, for many generations before then, for the Welsh Anglican Church to be separated from its English mother church. There was a growing resentment among Welsh Anglicans that they had to pay their dues to an English Church and had no say on decisions that involved them. Cymru Fydd played an active role in this campaign, as did the Liberal Party. There was also a strong resentment that the Anglican Church enjoyed a power and dominance out of proportion to the actual nature of church and chapel attendance in Wales. The Nonconformist chapels, predominantly Welsh-speaking, dominated Welsh worship and social life.

THE MORE FAVOURED NATION.

Nations compared in *Punch* magazine.

The Act was passed but not implemented, because of the First World War. It became law in 1920. On the first of April in that year, Anglicanism ceased to be the official religion in Wales. Welsh bishops would no longer be in the House of Lords. But more significantly, all other manifestations of the Christian faith, Baptist, Methodist, etc., were seen as equal with the Church in Wales. To this day, Wales is the only country in Britain that has no official religion.

Such ecclesiastical changes had their wider significance, of course. In a global context, what happened in Wales was happening in other countries around the world. As former Empire nations gained their independence, so too did their Anglican churches. Within the Welsh context that has been outlined in this book, it wasn't quite the same way round, but there was a similar correlation. The disestablishment of the Anglican Church in Wales was another sign of a broader need for Wales to have its own structures. The centenary of that particular separation was much celebrated in Wales last year.

Central elements of Welsh national ambitions had been cast in this decade then: the tension between cultural and political nationalism, between industrial South Wales and the rest of the nation, and between the two languages spoken there. But also, throughout all this, there was a strong sense of internationalism.

3.

War and the Shape of Wales

Moving on to the decades after the 1929 General Election, Wales was ever-changing. It had lost 40,000 men in the First World War. Between 1925 and 1939, its population decreased by 390,000. Unemployment hit over 15%. And ahead lay the Second World War. The cauldron of the second global war had an enormous impact on Wales and every aspect of its life. It played a big part in defining the relationship between Plaid Cymru and Labour, in a specific, defined Welsh context.

If we look back at the First World War, specifically the years in which it was looming ever closer, the Labour Party was hesitant to support the impending conflict, believing war itself to be a capitalist offensive. That attitude might well have changed after the guns started firing, however. Grass-root members became more positive in their support of the reasons for Britain to enter the conflict. Ramsay MacDonald continued to oppose it but resigned his leadership to make room for the more pro-war Arthur Henderson. When he took over, he made an uncompromising statement in 1918:

The Labour party is pledged to the widest and most generous measure of Home Rule that can be devised... we regard the claim of Wales to self-government on these lines as strictly analogous to those of Ireland... Nationalism means the vigorous development of the material and moral of the whole people. It is hardly possible to conceive an area in which a scheme of parliamentary self-government could be established with better chances of success than in Wales... given self-government, Wales might establish itself as a modern utopia, and develop its own institutions, its own arts, its own culture, its own ideal of democracy in politics, industry and social life, as an example and an inspiration to the rest of the world.[17]

This statement is worth contemplating and pausing for a moment or two to ponder! That's what Gwynfor Evans did in *The Fight for Welsh Freedom*:

The weight behind the words is hard to exaggerate... This was the language that Plaid Cymru would speak. At no time has it been attached to the 19th-century concept of an absolutely sovereign nation state which independence entails.[18]

That was World War One. There was far less hesitancy on their reaction to the war itself, on Labour's part, when the Second World War started. There was a more cross-party united front in 1939, claiming the second global conflict as a clear-cut just war, opposing as it did the powers that threatened democratic systems and human values. No doubt that conviction was boosted by the 'workers fight' in the Spanish Civil war only a few years previously, and sending men to battle in that conflict. It was also a war that did much to sharpen Welsh political consciousness on an international level.

Not so much for Plaid Cymru, however. In his book, *The Fascist Party of Wales?* director of the Wales Governance Centre in Cardiff University, Professor Richard Wyn Jones, says of Plaid's stance during this conflict:

17. Gwynfor Evans: *Fighting for Wales*. Tal-y-bont, Ceredigion: Y Lolfa, 1991, p. 26.
18. Gwynfor Evans: *The Fight for Welsh Freedom*, Tal-y-bont, Ceredigion: Y Lolfa, 2006, p. 129.

Labour delegates in their conference, Llandudno 1930.

... international relations were not high on the agenda of the Welsh Nationalist Party of the mid-1930s. The Party leadership's priority was rather to discover or invent a symbolic cause around which it might evangelise; a cause that could form the focus of a campaign of national redemption capable of shaking Wales from its torpor in the run-up to the four hundredth anniversary of The Act of Union.[19]

Penyberth

That symbolic cause came in the response to the UK Government's 1935 decision to establish a Bombing School on an old farm on the Llŷn Peninsula. The campaign led to including the word Penyberth in Plaid Cymru's vocabulary of nationalist battles: the first real entry. Penyberth, an old farmhouse that had been both a centre for poets and writers and a stopping place for pilgrims on their way to

Lewis Valentine

Bardsey Island, was taken over by the Government as a camp for the RAF. It was referred to as the Bombing School. The then Plaid Cymru President, playwright Saunders Lewis, spoke of this move as turning one of the 'essential homes of Welsh culture, idiom and literature into a place for promoting a barbaric method of warfare.' Saunders Lewis and two others set fire to the building and then turned themselves over to the police. They were tried in Caernarfon and then tried again at the Old Bailey before being sentenced to imprisonment. They also sacked Saun-

---

19. Richard Wyn Jones: *The Fascist Party in Wales? Plaid Cymru, Welsh nationalism and the accusation of Fascism.* Cardiff: University of Wales Press, 2014, p. 50.

ders Lewis from his job as a lecturer in Swansea University. From that point on, for many years to come, Penyberth defined the Plaid Cymru cause. Because it was a Bombing School, with the obvious implication that whatever was learned there wouldn't be applied on British soil, there was an international element to the opposition to it. But as Richard Wyn Jones sums up,

> There can be no doubt, however, that their primary concern centres on Wales, Welsh identity, and the future of the Welsh language.[20]

The global conflict

The opposition to war from the Left of the political spectrum in the second global conflict came from a brand new direction. Plaid Genedlaethol Cymru, the Plaid Cymru we know today, was into its second decade. When it arrived, they did not back the Second World War, choosing instead a position of neutrality based on a definite political view of national identity and pacifist values. Plaid Cymru's position was that Wales, as a nation, had the right to decide that it didn't have to take part in the war. Quoted in John Davies's seminal volume, *A History of Wales*, A. O. H. Jarman, editor of Plaid Cymru's journal, *Y Ddraig Goch*, says this about the party's stance:

> Neutrality was a state of mind... the maintenance of the right of the Welsh nation to decide its own attitude to the war.[21]

Of course, many Plaid members would have objected to war based on the traditional values on which they had been brought up, which centred on Christian pacifism. They had a constitutional right to object to going to war on such grounds, and many did. Welshmen from different political backgrounds objected to the war based on these Christian principles.

---

20. Ibid., p. 50.
21. John Davies: *A History of Wales*. London: Penguin Books, 2007, p. 581.

What Plaid leader Saunders Lewis was calling for, however, was for party members to object on political principles: the political position that Wales was a distinct nation which didn't have to take its orders from England, even in a time of World War. About two dozen stood up to the authorities in such a way, and twelve were sent to prison for their stance.

Such a stance, almost inevitably, led to Plaid Cymru being on the receiving end of many direct and negative accusations, not least of which was that they were pro-Nazi and Fascist. It was an early test of identity for this fledgling political party.

As with most political accusations, many of those aimed at Plaid Cymru were opportunistic and not of necessity based on any coherent argument. That does not negate their impact on the political scene of the time or on the popular perception of Plaid Cymru. It was vehemently claimed by many that the party, in refusing to back the Allies, were endorsing more power to the Nazis. Further, in taking such a stance, they demonstrated that their dislike, if not hatred, of England and its political and cultural dominance over Wales, was stronger than their opposition to what Hitler stood and killed for.

The roots of such perceptions take us back to the Spanish Civil War of the mid-1930s and a personal decision of faith made by Saunders Lewis at around this time. Saunders Lewis made a public declaration of his conversion to the Catholic faith. In so doing, the leader of the Welsh Nationalist party was advocating the cause of a Welsh identity based on a liberal, non-conformist faith, but who was now a Catholic himself. For many, that was too much to swallow. Richard Wyn Jones adds:

> It was the Spanish Civil War that created in Wales the tendency to con-
> flate Catholicism and Fascism, a conflation that featured so prominently
> in the subsequent attacks on Plaid Cymru.[22]

Most Welsh primary school children, going back many generations, would have taken part in the annual "Neges Ewyllys Da" tradition, the

---

22. Richard Wyn Jones: *The Fascist Party in Wales? Plaid Cymru, Welsh nationalism and the accusation of Fascism.* Cardiff: University of Wales Press, 2014, p. 51.

Good Will Message. This involved children from Wales broadcasting a message of peace and good will to children in many other countries. The instigator of this tradition was the Reverend Gwilym Davies. He was the main accuser of Saunders Lewis. Richard Wyn Jones argues that Davies's argument on Saunders Lewis's Fascism comprised two parts:

1. *Implicit: that Charles Maurras, the 'father of Fascism', was the dominant influence on Plaid Cymru's political thought.*
2. *Explicit: that Fascist ideas were central to the Nationalists programme for the future of Wales. Specifically, (i) the party intended to found a one-party state in Wales, and (ii) the nature of the political institutions that the Party proposed for an 'Independent' Wales was Fascist. Plaid Cymru would also adopt Fascist methods after the war by creating a paramilitary wing.*[23]

Plaid Cymru's actual stance on the Second World War has been very much in keeping with the majority attitude of the people of Wales; not the political leaders, but most of the country's people.

But such is the political game. Their opponents, of more than one political colour, made enough of this to make the accusations of their alleged Fascist tendencies stick—and for long enough to cause them considerable political difficulties which did not disappear when the War ended.

The effect of war

The Second World War, then, played a definite part in defining some issues of political identity in Wales. International events had forced Plaid Cymru to make a stand on issues far broader than those on which they were founded. But they also attacked those very same core principles. Their members believed that the war would endanger the future of the language and of Wales itself. In his *History of Wales*, John Davies says:

---

23. Ibid., p. 9.

The Second World War, like the First, did much to strengthen Britishness. At the same time, it seemed to be a death blow to Welshness.[24]

They deemed such a death blow to have come from more than one direction, in many aspects of day-to-day life, most of them far removed from the actual trumpet and drum of war. In broadcasting terms, for example, the BBC brought all their programming under the umbrella of the Home Service. Regional broadcasting was ended, including in Wales. They took away any existing Welsh identity on the airwaves. The War Office had acres and acres of Welsh land in its sight, needed for different aspects of preparation for combat. This not only 'took away' large chunks of Wales, but offended the deeply held sensibilities of many Welsh people, now facing military activity on their doorstep. The sending of evacuees to Wales was another grave cause for concern. The prospect of thousands of people moving into Welsh towns and villages caused worries and uncertainties for the future of those very communities and the language.

Wales and wartime Westminster

Jim Griffiths addressing a miners demo in 1936.

24. John Davies: *A History of Wales*. London: Penguin Books, 2007, p. 585.

When Plaid Cymru were arguing the principles of why Welsh people should not go to war, the Labour Party was also debating the same issue. Recently elected MP for Llanelli, Jim Griffiths, asked the Government of the day, in 1939, what provision was there for those from Wales who wished to conscientiously object to going to war, and who wanted to do so in their mother tongue. Would they be allowed, he asked, to make their case in a Tribunal in Welsh? He himself did not endorse pacifism, but he argued the right of those who did to be allowed to defend their position in their first language. On 26 October 1939, he received an answer from the Labour and National Service Minister, Ernest Brown. They would allow Welsh people to argue their objection to going to war in the Welsh language.

But Jim Griffiths' wartime contribution was far greater than that significant victory. Before the War started, they chose him as the Secretary of the Welsh Parliamentary Party in 1938. It was a responsibility he greatly cherished. This was the platform given to Welsh MPs of all political parties to work together. On 30 June 1938, in the middle of a volatile international situation, he was a member of a deputation from the Welsh Parliamentary Party to see Prime Minister Neville Chamberlain. Their request was clear. They argued that Wales needed a Welsh Office and a Secretary of State. On 29 July, they received a written reply from Chamberlain. He did not believe that Wales needed such provision. It would be far too costly. Wales, he argued, already received special treatment. Any comparison with Scotland, he maintained, was irrelevant, because that country already had its own legal and administrative structures. He continued:

Wales, since Henry VIII Act of 1535, has been closely incorporated with England and there has not been, and is not now, any distinct law or administrative system calling for the attention of a separate Minister.[25]

Leading Labour light and Welshman Aneurin Bevan in effect agreed with Chamberlain. His argument to his fellow Labour Party members was that

---

25. D. Ben Rees: *Cofiant Jim Griffiths: Arwr Glew y Werin*. Tal-y-bont, Ceredigion: Y Lolfa, 2014, p. 140.

Wales did not have any unique issues. The circumstances which faced the workers of any community in Wales were the same as those of any community in Britain.

Jim Griffiths was undeterred, however. This was the period when he was also arguing for official status for the Welsh language in the courts of law and in public life. The cultural institution that is the National Eisteddfod of Wales, in Cardiff in 1938, served as an unlikely occasion for Jim Griffiths to share a platform with Saunders Lewis. And to add to the political intrigue, William George, the brother of David Lloyd George, chaired that meeting. The rallying call of that meeting was to promote official status for the Welsh language. They set a petition up to nurture support for just that. World War II halted the completion of the petition. But when it was brought to an abrupt stop, it had a quarter of a million signatories. That was a significant step that could have led to some actual changes had not the war interrupted the debate.

However, Jim Griffiths's campaigning for more political recognition for Wales continued unabated.

In the first full year of the Second World War, 1940, there were developments at Westminster that affected Wales. The Welsh Board of Health, established twenty-one years previously, was given increased responsibilities. Housing, water services, local sanctions and other local government services were added to its portfolio. This trend continued throughout the war years, so by the War's end in 1945, fifteen government departments had offices in Wales.

In 1942, Jim Griffiths was asked to be a member of the Wales Consultative Committee. They met for the first time on 17 July of that year. One of the Committee members was Clough Williams-Ellis, the architect and creator of Portmeirion's Italianate village in North Wales. The Committee was to concentrate on issues of industry and agriculture, education and youth, transport and public services, as they affected Wales. Jim Griffiths failed in his attempt to add a Planning Authority for Wales to the Committee's remit.

He secured a notable victory, however, in that same year, when guided the Welsh Courts Act through Parliament. This gave a Welsh person the right to give evidence in court in Welsh if it was a disadvantage for him or her to give the evidence in English.

He steadfastly stuck to his belief that Wales needed a Secretary of State and the resultant political recognition that would give the nation. Deputy Prime Minister Clement Attlee refused such a request once more in 1943. This led to a robust campaign in Wales, led by the Welsh language weekly paper, *Y Cymro, The Welshman*. On 26 July 1943, it published a letter on its front page, in English only so that government leaders would understand it, asking,

> *How can Mr Attlee be so blind as to try to damp the desire of the Welsh members for a Welsh Secretary of State?*

That same year, five years after the deputation to Prime Minister Neville Chamberlain, Jim Griffiths sent a letter to Prime Minister Winston Churchill re-iterating the call for a Welsh Office and a Secretary of State for Wales. The response was equally negative, but far more dismissive. It took eighteen months and more for Churchill to respond. When he did so, in January 1945, this was said:

> *The difficulty is that a proposal of this nature has such far-reaching implications in the administrative sphere that detailed consideration has to be given by the many authorities concerned. These authorities are of course heavily burdened with war tasks.*

Jim Griffiths' biographer D. Ben Rees, says:

> *Roedd y rhyfel yn ddigon o reswm i Winston Churchill gladdu'r argymhellion yn gyfangwbl. Er cydnabod ei fawredd fel gwladweinydd adeg y rhyfel nid oedd ganddo lawer o gydymdeimlad â dyheadau gwlatgar y Cymru. Yn wir, trwy gydol yr Ail Ryfel Byd ychydig iawn o gydnabyddiaeth o roddwyd i genedligrwydd Cymreig gan Churchill nac Attlee. Y ddau eithriad oedd Deddf y Llysoedd yn 1942 a'r Diwrnod Cymreig ar 17 Hydref 1944, y cyntaf erioed yn hanes Senedd San Steffan.*[26]

---

26. Ibid., p. 143.

The war was reason enough for Winston Churchill to bury the proposals once and for all. Despite recognising his greatness as a wartime states-man, he had very little sympathy with the nationalistic aspirations of the Welsh. Throughout the Second World War, they paid very little attention to Welsh nationalistic arguments by either Churchill or Attlee. The two exceptions were the Welsh Courts Act 1942 and the Welsh Day on 17 October 1944, the first ever in the history of Westminster.

Jim Griffiths, Chair of the Labour Party 1949

It's difficult to argue with the overall conclusion made by Rees. It is possible to add to the examples he gives in that quote the White Paper on Welsh Affairs that was published from 1946 onwards. But in the broader context of this narrative, even in a time of world war, the arguments for greater political recognition for Wales were being championed, and in Jim Griffiths's case, vociferously and passionately so. There's no doubting that there were advancements made in arguing the Welsh cause.

However, the Labour Party made their moves when the War was over. In 1947, they formed the Welsh Regional Council of Labour. It was still controlled centrally, but it recognised Wales' separate identity. A year later, Clement Attlee's Labour Government established the Council for Wales and Monmouthshire, which was an advisory body to guide the government on matters relating to Wales. Its aim was to ensure that the government was 'adequately informed of the impact of government activities on the general life of the people of Wales'.

Still, Attlee dismissed the calls for a Secretary of State for Wales, believing that the formation of such a role took Wales too close to nationalism. Many prominent Labour MPs were staunch opponents of any form of devolution, Aneurin Bevan being the most vociferous. Historians such as Peter Stead argue that Bevan, from the 1940s onwards, was the main obstacle to any further recognition of Welsh separateness. But because there were many within the party who did back devolution for Wales, for example, Grenfell, Mainwaring and in particular, Jim Griffiths, the formation of the Council was seen as a compromise in their direction.

There were twenty-seven appointed members on the Council, made up of people from the Joint Education Committee, the University of Wales, the National Eisteddfod Council, The Welsh Tourist and Holidays Board, 12 from Welsh Local Authorities and representatives from industry and agriculture, on both the management and unions side. A Trade Unionist, Huw T. Edwards of The Transport and General Workers Union, was the Council's first chair. We'll talk more of him later.

The Council established many panels to look at various aspects of Welsh matters, including one for the Welsh Language.

In conclusion then, a new political picture was forming in Wales in the war years and immediately after. Labour backed the global conflict; Plaid Cymru didn't. So, by the time the guns were silent, they had fought out issues of being British and being Welsh at home in the context of an international war. In addition, the Liberal Party and the Labour Party were both strong in their support for the creation of a Secretary of State for Wales.

4.

Some Big Players

When the guns of war were silenced, the political seeds sown in the 1880s and the 1920s had long since taken root. 1945 was a year that saw more than one significant development in the devolution narrative, in terms of how events were to influence the course of Welsh devolution in the future. The Twenties' changes centred more on political parties. 1945 gave us significant cross-party individuals who would prove to be big players.

Far away from the newspaper and radio headlines leading thoughts on the possible shape of a peace-time Britain, another significant political milestone was happening in quiet Llangollen. On 6 August, they elected Gwynfor Evans as the new President of Plaid Genedlaethol Cymru, The National Party of Wales. He was an Oxford graduate, the owner of a market garden business in Carmarthenshire, and the son of a department store owner in Barry, Glamorganshire.

J. SAUNDERS LEWIS
Founder-member of Plaid Cymru, President 1926 - 1938

Plaid's first President, Saunders Lewis was by then disillusioned within and distanced without. During the Second World War, Lewis had stood for the University of Wales in the 1943 by-election. His opponent was Dr William John Gruffydd, who had been the deputy Vice-President of Plaid Genedlaethol Cymru, when Lewis was President. They had parted company, however, and Gruffydd joined the Liberal Party. He was very popular with the Welsh-speaking academics and the literary crowd. Subsequently, he secured a substantial majority in that by-election—53.2% compared to Lewis's 22%. Perceptions of Lewis's Fascism and Catholicism made him increasingly unpopular. This loss made Lewis a somewhat bitter man. He withdrew from active politics soon after. But for Plaid Cymru, however, ironically, it had been a very successful by-election. It had shown them to be a political party that could begin to challenge. Party membership rose significantly after it.

But Plaid's stance of wartime neutrality didn't go down well with the public. On becoming President, it was not an easy time for Gwynfor Evans within the party, or indeed, within his own family. The family department store in Barry, which took his father's name, Dan Evans, was vandalised. Some of their vans were daubed with paint. Amongst the slogans used were 'Spy', 'Traitor' and 'Fifth Columnist'. Family members felt the need to have words with Gwynfor about this. His brother urged him to remember that he was not just an individual but a member of a family too.

On 2 July 1943, Gwynfor received a letter from his father.

These are very trying for everyone, and the trials and worries caused by the war are beginning to have their effect on people's nerves and tempers. I need not remind you that we have never by word or deed attempted to interfere in your position of secretary to Welsh Pacifists... you are entitled to your opinion and you have never flinched in your attitude... you know also that neither Mam nor I are able to agree with their position... (not that I worry) but I lost the honour of JP through having a son as a CO (Conscientious Objector). You see therefore that your attitude and work for these societies is having a very unfair reaction upon us.

This letter made Gwynfor stop and think. It certainly made him think twice about becoming President of Plaid Cymru, as some party members were urging him to do. Saunders Lewis had stepped down. Abi Williams took over but Gwynfor was still being asked to be President. As a compromise, he accepted the Vice-Presidency, before becoming the Party President not long after.

This was the beginning of a new era for the party, which had existed for twenty years at that point. Many, including its own leaders, thought that it would not survive the World War, but it did, and it entered the post-war era with a new President. It would be another twenty years, plus one more, before Gwynfor Evans would be elected as his Party's first MP.

Labour's voice

In the General Election of that same year, a young solicitor stood for the Labour Party in the Anglesey Constituency. Cledwyn Hughes was born in Holyhead into an active Liberal family. The island's MP was Megan Lloyd George, the youngest child of her famous father and the first woman to be elected an MP in Wales. Cledwyn Hughes was taken to some of her public meetings by his father. But Cledwyn turned away from the Liberal party. He was convinced that the only hope for Anglesey was in what the Labour Party offered. In that 1945 Election, he lost to Megan Lloyd George. She appears more than once at key places in this story!

A central element of Cledwyn Hughes's politics was his Welshness. Many within his party were alarmed that he was being considered for the Anglesey constituency because of this. In *Yr Arglwydd Cledwyn o Benrhos*, a biography of Hughes based on a four-part series made by HTV in 1990 called Cledwyn, author Emyr Price describes these concerns:

Yn ystod etholiad 1945, er mawr ofid i drefnydd Cymreig y Blaid Lafur, Cliff Prothero, roedd ymgeiswyr Llafur yng Ngwynedd fel Elwyn Jones (Bwrdeisdrefu Caernarfon), Goronwy Roberts (Caernarfon), Huw Morris-Jones (Meirion), a Cledwyn Hughes, yn gefnogol i bolisi Llais Llafur—

polisi Cymreig answyddogol, a fynnai Fwrdd Dŵr i Gymru, gwasanaeth radio cyflawn, Ysgrifennydd Gwladol Cymreig yn y Cabinet, ac ymhen amser Senedd Federal i Gymru... Wele bwysleisio ar gychwyn ei yrfa boliticaidd fod cyplysu Cymreictod a Llafuryddiaeth yn rhan anhepgor o'i gredo politicaidd.[27]

It was of great concern to the Organiser of the Labour Party in Wales, Cliff Prothero, that in the 1945 election campaign, Labour candidates in Gwynedd such as Elwyn Jones (Caernarfon Boroughs), Goronwy Roberts (Caernarfon), Huw Morris-Jones (Meirion), and Cledwyn Hughes were supportive of the Llais Llafur (Labour Voice) policy—this was an unofficial policy calling for A Board for Water in Wales, a comprehensive radio service, a Welsh Secretary of State in the Cabinet and in time, A Federal Parliament in Wales... Here was emphasising right at the start of his political career that combining Welshness and Labourism was a central part of his political credo.

This point is further emphasised later on in the same book:

Er 1945 pan gefnogai bolisi Llais Llafur, credai Cledwyn Hughes, er mai plaid ganolog oedd y Blaid Lafur oddi ar y 30au, yn dra gwahanol i'r Blaid Lafur a'r ILP yng nghyfnod Keir Hardie, fod modd cyplysu Cymreictod, achosion Cymreig a Chymraeg, â Llafuryddiaeth. Credai hefyd mai llywodraeth Lafur oedd yr unig gyfrwng ymarferol i sicrhau, o fewn y cyd destun Prydeinig, gyfrifoldebau helaethach i Gymru a deddfwriaeth Gymreig o San Steffan.[28]

Since 1945 when he supported the policy of Llais Llafur, Cledwyn Hughes believed, even though the Labour Party since the 1930s was a centralist party, in stark contrast to the Labour Party and the ILP in Keir Hardie's period, that there was a way of linking Welshness, issues of Welshness and language with Labourism. He believed also that a Labour

---

27. Emyr Price: *Yr Arglwydd Cledwyn o Benrhos.* Caernarfon: Cyhoeddiadau Mei, 1990, p. 14.
28. Ibid., p. 24.

government was the only practical means to secure, in a British context, broader responsibilities to Wales and Welsh legislation from Westminster.

Both Gwynfor and Cledwyn, and the parties they represented, were a part of the changing political climate in post-war Wales. Both parties used the phrase New Age to describe what they perceived to be happening in Wales. If they were two completely different parties, with opposing ideologies, there was a theme that could unite some Labour MPs and Plaid Cymru members in a common cause—albeit a unity hidden under the surface and never acknowledged by one or the other. In a generic phrase, it could be called love for your country. Politically, it's nationalism, of course. It's defining your national identity and shaping the means for it to be realised. Members of both parties claimed their political vision was one that sought the best for Wales, and they thought in terms of a Welsh identity in distinction to a British one. In Plaid Cymru's case, the majority would herald a Welsh identity instead of a British one.

And two more

Two big players also first stepped onto the parliamentary stage in 1945 who would go on to play a direct role in the devolution debate that would unfold over the next three decades. Both won seats in the soon-to-be capital city of Wales, Cardiff. Both were Labour party candidates but they had their differences. Cardiff Central was captured by George Thomas and Cardiff South by James Callaghan. The former was to become the Speaker in the House of Commons, the latter, the Prime Minister in the decade that gave Wales a referendum on devolution.

Another future big player in the devolution debate made his mark in 1945 as well. It wasn't his first victory, but Llanelli MP Jim Griffiths secured a majority of 34,000 in 1945, the largest in the British Isles. We shall come back to these individuals.

The arena was set. The players were taking their place on the field, and Wales was an issue.

Towards defining devolution

The British Government sought to define Britishness through their British Nationality Act of 1948, whereby they sought to describe what a Citizen of the United Kingdom and the Colonies was. That process of definition was happening within three of the four nations that made up the British state. Scotland, Wales and, to a lesser extent Northern Ireland, sought to explain what citizenship meant to them.

Through the very soil that made Wales what it was, Labour and Plaid Cymru faced their new futures as parties in Wales and for Wales. The result was the development of an embryonic devolution agenda with a focus and drive that wasn't in existence before World War II.

There was one difference between the two parties, however. Most Plaid members would have sung from the same hymn sheet in regard to the issue. There was no such harmony amongst the Labour ranks. Certainly, there was not anything like the same view on Wales and all things Welsh amongst Labour members and MPs outside Wales. But neither was there such agreement within Labour in Wales itself. For many of its MPs, any talk of separating Welsh issues from broader matters relating to everyone in Britain was nothing more than nationalism in the negative sense. For those who held such belief, socialism, the living conditions of the working people, was more of a central value than nationalism. How the people of Stoke or Newcastle or Cardiff or Glasgow lived their day-to-day lives was of more importance than any accident of geography that would focus efforts on people who lived in a patch of land defined by an artificial boundary.

So, if there was a movement within Plaid and Labour for a more devolved Wales, even if the nature of such a new Wales would be defined differently by both parties, it would seem natural enough for there to be an element of co-operation at least between the two, in the name of a common goal. Maybe not. Plaid Cymru's new President had a clear view on his Labour opponents and how he could attract people to his party, as outlined in Rhys Evans's authoritative biography of *Gwynfor Evans, Portrait of a Patriot*:

*For one, following Labour's sweeping victory, he judged that it would
be a mistake to 'make too obvious any hostility' towards it. Rather, he
concluded that Plaid Cymru would do well to act as a pressure group
and urge the new government to carry out 'a substantial programme for
Wales'. The programme, he hoped, would include a Development Council
for Wales and a Wales Radio Corporation within the next few years. He
was aware that it would be a long time before the Welsh people would
begin to regard Labour with anything approaching objectivity, but was
confident that the day would come when the enthusiasm waned and the
electorate considered Labour 'more coolly and with a new poise'. It was
then when disillusionment with Labour had begun that Plaid Cymru
would seize the day.*[29]

Considering the bitter battles between Plaid and Labour in the Carmarthenshire constituency in the late sixties to the mid-seventies, this
does sound rather strange. Even in the 1940s and before that, Plaid were
only too ready to proclaim that Labour had done nothing for Wales.
Gwynfor Evans repeatedly said this throughout the subsequent Carmarthen battles. But even as early as the rebuilding process of the late
1940s, Gwynfor and his party would have been seriously struggling to
back up such a claim. Whatever Attlee's views on devolution, he didn't
ignore Wales in that post-war renewal. South Wales was declared a
development area which brought in industries and jobs. The NHS was
founded. The National Coal Board was as well. This was a challenge not
only to Gwynfor's claim that Labour had done nothing for Wales, but
also to his stated aim of not being negative towards Labour.

Many leading Labour politicians had some sympathy, at least with
Plaid's views on devolution. Many had come to a crossroads in their own
political awakening which had left them facing the choice of turning to
the Plaid highway or the Labour one. One leading Labour politician, who
we shall hear much more of later, Gwilym Prys Davies was just such a
person. He made analytical comments about late-1940's Wales as a Plaid

---

29. Rhys Evans: *Gwynfor Evans: Portrait of a Patriot.* Tal-y-bont, Ceredigion: Y Lolfa,
    2008, p. 103.

Cymru supporter. But he left that party and joined Labour soon after. He was not convinced that Plaid Cymru had the organisational ability to be a major force in Wales. He was greatly encouraged and inspired by the fact that there were at least five Welsh Labour MPs who supported devolution—the five who caused concern for the party's Welsh organiser in 1945 during Cledwyn Hughes's election campaign.

During his student days at Aberystwyth, Cledwyn Hughes had many nationalist friends and he was influenced by the events at the Bombing School on the Llŷn Peninsula. In the 1930s, mentioned earlier. Cledwyn Hughes was aggrieved by the taking of the farm by the RAF and all that it symbolised. It drew him to Plaid Cymru for a couple of years, although he was never a full member. In choosing to give his allegiance to the Labour Party in 1945, he took his views on Welsh identity and nationhood with him.

This common appeal of Plaid and Labour has been a recurring theme from the 1940s onwards. Leading Plaid thinker during the fifties and early sixties, Elystan Morgan, subsequently joined the Labour Party, was elected as an MP, was appointed a Minister in the Wilson Government of 1966-70 and is now a Labour peer Baron Elystan-Morgan. And in more recent times, former Welsh First Minister Carwyn Jones, following his political awakening during the Miner's Strike of 1984/85, faced a choice of joining Plaid or Labour. He considered Plaid for a short space of time, but the obvious choice for him was to turn to Labour. He considered that they were the party that could best serve the Wales he loved.

Therein lies the story of many a leading Labour politician in Westminster and Cardiff Bay over those post-war years. While there have been many Labour MPs and leaders who have been vehemently against any definition of a distinct Welsh identity, there have been notable examples of Labour MPs, over many decades and across a broad geographical electoral base, who have championed Welsh devolution—and despite overwhelming opposition from the rank-and-file members of the party and the party's leadership too. For anyone, including Plaid Cymru, to deny that flies in the face of history.

5.

From the Rubble of War

By 1945, when the noise of war had only just started to fade, the grief and mourning of loss were still to continue for a long time in so many countries. The wounds would need a lot more time to heal. The actual number of casualties in Wales and the UK, in general, were less in the Second World War than they were in the first, but the social and economic impact was greater. Rebuilding had to begin as soon as possible. The United Kingdom was no exception, and neither, of course, was Wales.

But politically, the question was, who would re-build postwar Britain? The politics of the country would change from 1945 onwards. That year heralded a landslide election victory for Labour who secured 393 MPs compared to 197 for the Conservatives. In Wales, Labour sent 25 MPs to Westminster, the Liberals 6 and the Conservatives 4. In Wales, Labour made seven gains and ended with 25 of the then 36 seats in the country, winning on the back of a manifesto that included the following priorities:

> *The nation wants food, work and homes. It wants more than that— it wants good food in plenty, useful work for all, and comfortable, labour-saving homes that take full advantage of the resources of modern science and productive industry. It wants a high and rising standard of living, security for all against a rainy day, an educational system that will give every boy and girl a chance to develop the best that is in them.*

Priorities were different on the back of a cataclysmic global conflict.

This was the beginning of a significant and long period for Labour in Wales, as Professor Roger Awan Scully noted in 2013:

... across the UK as a whole, the 1945 election constituted an exceptional electoral triumph for Labour, the scale of which was not to be repeated until 1997... Labour's new dominance of Welsh politics was to prove highly enduring. At every single one of the seventeen subsequent UK general elections, Labour has been the leading party in terms of vote share and has won a majority of Welsh seats.

Labour then, under Clement Attlee, would have the responsibility of shaping peacetime Britain.

As he chronicles in *The Rebirth of a Nation*, Kenneth O. Morgan summarises the effect of the 1945 election on Wales:

The general election of 1945 provides a suitable final comment on the ordeal of Wales during the twenties and thirties. The campaign was charged with folk memories and communal bitterness, which Churchill's talk of a Labour 'Gestapo' reinforced. It confirmed the arrival of a powerful, socially cohesive Labour elite, still Welsh in many of its instincts and aspirations, but far less committed to the native language and to political separatism than the old Liberal ascendancy had been. It emerged out of struggle and protest in the thirties to full authority, a symbol of revenge on a cruel past of depression and unemployment, and a beacon of hope for a more bearable and fulfilling world.[30]

This is what Plaid Genedlaethol Cymru faced. There's no doubt that they were an increasingly active new force and vociferous in some parts of Wales, even if they weren't yet a real political threat. Plaid had little electoral success in 1945. They chose seven candidates to stand in the 1945 election with only one keeping their deposit. However, the party had established their presence, and the performance was a big step up from that of 1935, when only Saunders Lewis stood for election.

Plaid were facing far more than euphoric Labour electoral success in

---

30. Kenneth O. Morgan: *Rebirth of a Nation: Wales 1880-1980*. Oxford: Clarendon Press, 1981, p. 303.

that first peacetime election after the war. Labour's political triumph, like others in the preceding years, were, as Kenneth O. Morgan says:

> ... *but the political or parliamentary facade for a growing radicalisation of south Wales during the depression years. Every major development in the industrial and economic history of the region from 1921 onwards underlined the fierce loyalty of most working people in the coalfield to their class and to its formal union representatives.*[31]

So, in the second half of the forties, both parties faced issues that had been defined by World War II, over which they would fight each other for decades to come. They faced these issues from positions of differing strength but the battle for Wales was on. It was union. It was nation. Two collectives. One championed by Labour, the other championed by Plaid. Both dealt with Welsh identity—in some ways similar, but with fundamentally different elements.

This land is our land

After 1945, one issue provided members of both parties with an opportunity to thrash out exactly what that Welsh identity meant and it was directly related to the Second World War. The Ministry of Defence set their eyes on both the land and some of the young men of Wales. They sought to commandeer large sections of land in Wales so it could train soldiers, many of whom would be from Wales. The Second World War might well have been over, but there was a Cold War to prepare for.

Even with the need for a strong military very much still in the minds of the people, following the victory of World War II, there was strong opposition to the taking of Welsh land for military use. The government targeted areas in Brecon, Pembrokeshire and Meirionydd for this purpose, totalling thousands of acres and involving many living communities. No doubt, the very thought of young Welsh men going through

---

31. Ibid., p. 283.

military training again, and so close to home, might well have been too much for the psyche of Wales at the time.

Gwilym Prys Davies, half out of shot, at the head of a War Office land protest, 1947

Baron Gwilym Prys-Davies, in his autobiography, sums up this threat:

Wrth edrych ar Gymru ar derfyn yr Ail Ryfel Byd yr oedd cyfrifoldeb gwladgarwyr Cymreig yn un dwys. Gwelem beryglon dybryd i rai o'r ardaloedd Cymreiciaf yng nghynlluniau amddiffyn Prydain a oedd yn hawlio rhagor o diroedd er mwyn hyfforddi milwyr.[32]

As we look at Wales at the end of the Second World War, the burden of responsibility on Welsh patriots was intense. The plans that the defence

---

32. Gwilym Prys Davies: *Llafur y Blynyddoeedd*. Dinbych: Gwasg Gee, 1991, p. 35.

*of Britain had to claim more land in order to train soldiers we saw as a
serious threat to the most Welsh of areas in Wales.*

Rhys Evans summarises the way Plaid Cymru saw the same situation. He
says that rather unexpectedly, militarism came to define the first five years
of Gwynfor's presidency. The War Office's grip on Wales was more likely
to strengthen than loosen.

*Gwynfor had not given much attention to the effects of this conditional
peace, but as soon as J E Jones received 'highly confidential' information
in November 1945 of a plan to occupy 7000 acres in Merioneth for
military purposes, the army's land use became one of the party's main
campaigns. In time, this would become the campaign that demanded the
lion's share of Plaid Cymru's attention.*[33]

The original Welsh language version of the same biography adds to the
last sentence of this quote. Having stated the campaign focused Plaid's
attention it goes on to say that it also increased the party's supporters.

In his analysis of the spirit of the time, Gwilym Prys Davies adds that
there was also a real perceived threat of a Third World War, and if that
was to be the case, then the fear was that Westminster would insist on a
uniformity of culture throughout Britain during the preparation for such
a conflict. The Welsh culture, as a result, would disappear.

The view from overseas

Both parties were also aware of political changes in other countries outside the UK. They could see the gradual disintegration of the former
British Empire. Gwilym Prys Davies:

---

33. Rhys Evans: *Gwynfor Evans: Portrait of a Patriot.* Tal-y-bont, Ceredigion: Y Lolfa,
    2008, p. 104.

Gwelem fod y wladwriaeth hithau mewn cryn berygl yn economaidd ac yn strategol. Roedd ei phwysigrwydd ymhlith y Galluoedd Mawr yn lleihau, nid yn unig oherwydd ei gwendid economaidd, ond hefyd oherwydd datblygiad y gwledydd newydd a fu gynt yn drefedigaethau o fewn yr Ymerodraeth Brydeinig.[34]

We could see that the state was in considerable danger economically and strategically. Her importance amongst the Super Powers was diminishing, not only because of her economic weakness but also because of the development of new countries who had been in the British Empire.

Gwynfor Evans saw things in the same way. Again, this is how Rhys Evans chronicles this point:

… roedd yna hyder ar draws Plaid Cymru bod dyddiau Prydain fel grym imperialaidd yn darfod fel mwg.

… there was a confidence across Plaid Cymru that Britain's days as an imperial force were disappearing like smoke.

The other country that served as a very real example of this was the one next door to Wales, in a westerly direction; Ireland. Both parties were more than aware of the journey the Irish cousins had taken from the violence of 1916 to the freedom of 1949. The two parties in Wales might not have wanted the same end, nor the same outcome as Ireland. But the path that country had taken did indeed speak to the Plaid and Labour narratives of the late-1940s in terms of their perceptions of the Wales they wanted to see.

They were two parties mindful of creating a new distinctive Wales, albeit from two different political ideological starting points. Would the Wales of either have it as good as everyone else in the UK? The Labour party without doubt, as the party with Westminster power, pushed ahead with plans to increase the accountability of the Welsh people for things

---

34. Gwilym Prys Davies: *Llafur y Blynyddoeedd*. Dinbych: Gwasg Gee, 1991, p. 35.

that happened in Wales, despite many of their own Welsh MPs aggressively disagreeing with the same need.

In the 1940s, Plaid Cymru was a growing force, in terms of public profile if not political impact. They improved organisationally, there's no doubt. But their presence and influence were predominantly in the Welsh-speaking communities. Their President, Gwynfor Evans, contributed to a published collection of essays in 1950 called *Seiliau Hanesyddol Cenedlaetholdeb Cymru* (*The Historical Foundations of Nationalism in Wales*). He describes Plaid Cymru's position during this period:

Ond yn lle cael ei ddinistrio yr oedd ar derfyn y rhyfel... yn gryfach nag y bu erioed; yn ddigon cryf yn 1945 i ymladd am ddeg sedd yn yr etholiad, ac yn 1946 i ennill pedwar ugain o seddau ar y cynghorau lleol; yn ddigon cryf i dreblu nifer ei swyddogion ac agor swyddfa newydd yng Nghaerdydd.[35]

But instead of getting destroyed, it was at the end of war... stronger than it had ever been before; strong enough in 1945 to fight for ten seats in the election and in 1946 to win eighty seats on local councils; strong enough to triple its officer numbers and to open a new office in Cardiff.

For Gwynfor, in his ever over-optimistic manner, this was the start of a new dawn for not only his Party but for the entire nation of Wales. Plaid Cymru shaped its campaign outside Westminster, in hearth and home, on the protest front, in the chapels and in local government.

Such post-war fervour for Welsh devolution wasn't restricted to Labour and Plaid Cymru either. In 1950, a young barrister called Emlyn Hooson stood as a Liberal Party parliamentary candidate for the first time in the then-new constituency of Conwy. It included a large section of Lloyd George's old Caernarfon Borough constituency. In that campaign, Hooson argued for devolution. He did not get elected in 1950, but would later serve Montgomeryshire as an MP for many years. In

35. Arthur W. Wade-Evans; T. Jones Pierce; et. al.: *Seiliau Hanesyddol Cenedlaetholdeb Cymru.* Caerdydd/Cardiff: Plaid Cymru, 1950, p 143.

1967, he introduced a Bill in the Commons '… to provide a scheme for the domestic self-government of Wales and for connected purposes.' This is part of his speech in the Commons when he introduced his Bill. It serves as a good summing up of the broader thoughts on devolution in immediate post-war Wales.

> *In seeking to introduce a Bill for a domestic Parliament for Wales, I do not come to the House of Commons looking to the past, although I am conscious of it. I do not come here nursing grievances or imagining injustices. I do not subscribe to the myth that the English are bent malevolently on the destruction of Wales. (There are exceptions, of course.) If that were so, we could easily deal with them and far more effectively. What I fear far more is their sympathetic but inactive benevolence. There is, in this House, a great measure of sympathy and kindly feeling towards Wales, but there is not here the time, the committed interest, the single-mindedness, the overwhelming concern to ensure that the economic, social and cultural life of the Welsh nation is properly safeguarded.[36]*

Thus ends the decade of World War II and thus begins the brand new hopeful decade of the 1950s. Within Wales, as the first pre-war years unfolded, there were fears and insecurities. Fears of an economic depression were real. Wales' narrow industrial base was a genuine cause for concern, as indeed was the nature of its very restricting and constricting geography. But they proved to be largely unfounded; prosperity and growth out-muscled fears and insecurities. For a while, at least. This is how historian Kenneth O. Morgan summed it up in *The Rebirth of a Nation, Wales 1880-1980:*

> *As the fifties broadened into more continued affluence, with domestic industry rejuvenated and able to participate in a more sustained upturn of world trade, it seemed that at last most of Wales, outside the more remote rural areas such as Anglesey and the Llŷn peninsula, was climbing*

---

36. Derec Llwyd Morgan (ed.): *Emlyn Hooson: Essays and Reminiscences.* Llandysul: Gomer, 2014, p. 136.

confidently out of the trough of economic depression into which it had been thrust for so long. At last, the Welsh people were putting the bad times firmly behind them.[37]

How this would play out politically is where we go next.

37. Kenneth O. Morgan: *Rebirth of a Nation: Wales 1880-1980*. Oxford: Clarendon Press, 1981, p. 310.

6.

Labour the Party of Wales

Politically, turning its back on the bad times, meant for Wales that the Labour Party were in the ascendency. They further developed and consolidated a dominance of the political situation in the country that continues to this day, even if they have had to form coalition administrations with the Welsh Liberal Democrats and Plaid Cymru over the last 20 years to keep going! According to Kenneth O. Morgan, 'a new society was blossoming in Wales from the rubble of war'. But, as he also says, it was the old Labour ascendancy of the twenties and thirties that presided over this new Wales. It was a domination that grew to be far greater than any it had before the Second World War. The new decade saw a General Election in its first year and another a year later. The 1950 election was the first to be held after a full term of Labour government. It was the first democratic election, following the abolition of plural voting, which had existed up to the Representation of the People Act of 1948. This meant for example that the University of Wales seat was abolished. This Election was also the first to televise the results—to the 350,000 who had TV licences. But how did the parties fare at the dawn of a new decade?

Liberal decline

That meant one thing specifically. Liberal dominance had gone. Maybe not completely, but it could only show weak traces of its former glory in Wales. That party had dominated public life in Wales since before the First World War. It gave Wales one of its most famous and influential politicians ever, David Lloyd George. But the times were changing. The once-dominant Liberals were becoming increasingly associated with a rural Wales, a Nonconformist Wales, as its industrial base declined. The General Election of the first year of the new decade reduced Labour's Westminster majority significantly. But the Liberals fared worse. They took only five seats in Wales, and all five were predominantly rural. They lost Pembrokeshire to Labour in that year, however. In 1951, the Liberals' plight could be further increased through their loss of Anglesey and Meirionydd. The afore-mentioned Cledwyn Hughes took Anglesey for Labour, and away from Liberal Megan Lloyd George, who had held the seat since 1929.

The 1950 General Election gave the Welsh political scene, and the devolution debate specifically, one Liberal who would become an influential champion of governance for Wales. As already mentioned, Emlyn Hooson stood as a candidate for the first time in 1950, for the Conway constituency. He was unsuccessful on that occasion, but as others from other parties had done before then as well, he stood on a strongly devolutionary platform. He failed again in the 1951 General Election. He succeeded in 1962, becoming MP for Montgomery, where he won again in 1964, 1966, 1970 and 1974. Labour Peer Elystan Morgan says of Hooson's view of devolution:

He was a devolutionist to the backbone, but two things must be said about his attitude to devolution. The first is that his commitment lay not with the geometric niceties of balancing government between the centre and the periphery by outward transfer of legislative and executive authority, but in securing for an ancient nation-community a meaningful and authoritative voice in its own affairs...... The second and equally pertinent comment I wish to make is that as much as anyone else in public life over the last half-century,

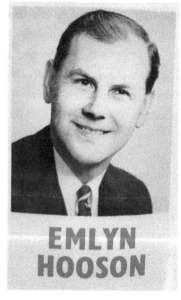

A 1962 election poster.

94

he had the classically correct concept of what devolution essentially was and is. It is the deliberate transfer of authority and responsibility from central government outwards to the periphery.[38]

With such a clear appreciation of Hooson's contribution to the devolution debate, it would mislead not to draw attention to him in a section that deals with the demise of the Liberal Party's influence in Wales. We shall hear more of him later.

Labour ascendancy

But as Hooson was cutting his political teeth, his party was losing its grip on Wales. Labour benefited. Following their landslide victory in the 1945 General Election, the Labour Party consolidated its position of power throughout many regions of the UK. In Wales, they spread their influence outside the traditional coalfield stronghold areas, spreading into more rural areas and to North Wales. In doing so, they established an increasingly firm grip on Wales itself. This grip grew ever firmer as the fifties rolled out and then turned into the sixties. This is how Andrew Walling sums it up in his chapter in *The Labour Party in Wales 1900-2000*:

Particularly in Urban Wales, voting Labour was a way of life, passed on from one generation to the next. Safe seats really were safe seats and thrashing Conservative opponents was the norm, not an exception. Whilst the party spent long periods in decline nationally between 1951 and 1964, in Wales quite the reverse was true, as Wales became an even more pronounced bastion of Labour strength. Labour made gains, returning twenty-seven MPs from thirty-six constituencies in 1951 and reaching a high water-mark of thirty-two in 1966.[39]

38. Elystan Morgan; Huw L. Williams: *Elystan: Atgofion Oes*. Tal-y-bont, Ceredigion: Y Lolfa, 2012, p. 134.
39. Deian Hopkin; Duncan Tanner; Chris Williams (eds.): *The Labour Party in Wales 1900-2000*. Cardiff: University of Wales Press, 2000, p. 193.

The devolution debate in Wales, from 1950 on, took place within such a political atmosphere. Labour was in a strong position of dominance. As this process gathered strength, Labour enhanced their claim to be the party that represented the nation. As John Davies says:

> *The more of the constituencies of Wales it won, the more Welsh interests it was expected to represent.*[40]

This had a direct influence on the British Labour Party. Wales grew in its importance to the wider Labour picture and its influence on the Party too. Welsh MPs gained dominant positions in the Labour Party. Jim Griffiths and Aneurin Bevan were figures of influence throughout Britain, not just in Wales.

Jim Griffiths was deputy leader to Gaitskell in the second half of the 1950s and Bevan, from 1945 to his death, was regarded as the acknowledged leader of the left within the party. It's interesting to note that Jim Griffiths beat Nye Bevan to become deputy leader. Griffiths was more of a Social Democrat than someone from the political left. Maybe that's why he hasn't had the full recognition within Labour circles that he should have had, considering his success and influence. In later years, he was to become a close colleague of Roy Jenkins.

Plaid Cymru and the Conservatives

Plaid Cymru and the Tories were very much of lesser influence in Wales as the fifties began. The Conservative Party has never enjoyed a particularly strong relationship with Wales. Conservative AM David Melding says that Wales is perceived as 'irreducibly radical and intractably anti-Conservative'. Regarding how the Tories entered the fifties, he says:

> *Little strategy and less policy emanated from the Party in Wales. They produced almost no Party literature for specific use in Wales, and leaflets*

---

40. John Davies: *A History of Wales*. London: Penguin Books, 2007, p. 638.

in Welsh were rare. The Party's archive contains three Welsh language leaflets published in 1909 and another published in 1927… the Campaign Guides of 1922, 1929, 1931, 1935 and 1945 contained no reference to Wales (and few to Scotland).[41]

If Liberal influence in Wales was well on the decline by now, the Tory Party were in no position to take advantage of that, as Melding says:

… the collapse of the Liberal Party created few opportunities for the Conservative Party in Wales. Rather, it was the Labour Party—which had as many difficulties on cultural and Welsh national issues as the Conservatives—that became the party of Wales.[42]

Plaid Cymru were obviously still a fledgling party in Wales, and the only one with a Wales-only political base. In the 1950 General Election, it fielded only seven candidates who polled 17,000 votes. They fielded only four in 1951, and they all did badly. Kenneth O. Morgan says that Plaid began this period, and remained so for some years to come, presenting no dangerous challenge to the existing parties:

… the party remained a small, largely rural-orientated movement, based on a declining constituency of Welsh speakers. Its social base was particularly limited, if intellectually distinguished.[43]

Such was the state of the parties and the nature of their influence in Wales. From such a base, how did the devolution debate itself develop? That's the next question.

---

41. David Melding: *Will Britain survive beyond 2020?* Cardiff: Institute of Welsh Affairs, 2009, p. 140.
42. Ibid., p. 141.
43. Kenneth O. Morgan: *Rebirth of a Nation: Wales 1880-1980*. Oxford: Clarendon Press, 1981, p. 381.

All parties together

Within the field of devolution, the dominant factor at the beginning of this period was not the campaign of any one party, but the emergence of a cross-party campaign that called for a modified home rule for Wales in a Welsh Parliament. Called Parliament for Wales, it gained considerable momentum after its founding in 1949. It based its campaign principles on those of Undeb Cymru Fydd. Lady Megan Lloyd George was its President. Kenneth O. Morgan says that Plaid Cymru *took a decision to back the campaign and take part in its propaganda—a decision which reflected the political awareness of Gwynfor Evans in contrast to the last-ditch intransigence of the almost apolitical Saunders Lewis.*[44]

One of Gwynfor Evans's biographers, however, takes a slightly different standpoint. In *Gwynfor Evans,* biographer Pennar Davies acknowledges the Parliament for Wales Campaign as the most important to unite like-minded people in their desire to secure some measure of political responsibility for the nation of Wales. He then credits the beginnings of this campaign:

Gellir olrhain cychwyn y mudiad i lythyr a ddanfonodd Gwynfor Evans i'r Western Mail yn haf 1949.[45]

The beginnings of this organisation can be traced back to a letter written by Gwynfor Evans to the Western Mail in the Summer of 1949.

So, the campaign existed thanks to Gwynfor! He further argues that they based the letter on a decision by Plaid Cymru's Summer School that year to call for a Parliament for Wales within five years. This is an example of how naïve leading figures within Plaid Cymru could be, making bold claims about their influence over and above their station. There'll be more examples of this. Kenneth O. Morgan's appraisal of Gwynfor's

44. Ibid., p. 380.

45. Pennar Davies: *Gwynfor Evans: golwg ar ei waith a'i feddwl.* Abertawe/Swansea: Tŷ John Penry, 1976, p. 43.

Gwynfor addresses a Parliament for Wales campaign 1949

contribution to the Parliament for Wales campaign is far more balanced, acknowledging Plaid's decision to join the campaign because of Gwynfor's wisdom and that he took a genuinely active part in it. There's no suggestion that Gwynfor started the entire campaign himself! The emphasis is on 'to join'.

The Parliament for Wales campaign encompassed people from all parties, including the Tories and the Communists. It was formed at a conference in Llandrindod on 1 July 1950. On stage that day were Lady Megan Lloyd George, Gwynfor Evans, Ifan ab Owen Edwards—academic and founder of Urdd Gobaith Cymru, the Welsh League of Youth and the son of O. M. Edwards, one of the founders of Cymru Fydd in 1886, and T. I. Ellis. It was agreed that they would organise a petition calling for a Parliament for Wales. But momentum was slow to gather any pace. The petition wasn't actually launched until The National Eisteddfod in Llanrwst a year later. Welsh poet Elfed was the first to put his name on the petition.

From 1950 until 1956, the campaign made a considerable impact on Welsh opinion, as Kenneth O. Morgan states. It also, however, had an almost counter-productive effect on Plaid Cymru. A significant number of its members concentrated their energies on the Parliament for Wales campaign activities, and many commentators say that this resulted in Plaid not doing so well in elections held during the campaign's tenure.

It also had another consequence for Plaid. John Davies argues that some more left-wing members thought that the party should follow a 'bolder path' than the one advocated by the Parliament for Wales campaign. Not all Plaid members signed the Petition. He says:

> *They believed that Plaid Cymru's emphasis upon the Welsh language and upon the interests of the rural areas prevented it from gaining support in the industrial south-east; they also argued that the pacifism of Gwynfor Evans... hindered the adoption of a militant stance.*[46]

The result was that fifty members left Plaid Cymru and formed the Welsh Republican Movement.

Labour and a Parliament for Wales

For all the increasing influence of Wales on the political agenda, there was no unanimity within the Labour Party to argue the cause of Home Rule for Wales. On one hand, this was a time of other divisions within the Party on matters of foreign affairs, with the pro-Soviet and pro-American factions disagreeing on foreign policy. As far as Wales was concerned,

---

46. John Davies: *A History of Wales*. London: Penguin Books, 2007, p. 604.

there was an inherent fear of anything that could be interpreted as a move towards nationalism amongst the Party's leaders. Aneurin Bevan, in particular, was strongly opposed to any measure of devolution for Wales. The key phrase of the time, and one which still has resonance today, was 'the commanding heights of the economy'. That's what was important. That was the key political philosophy. In practice, it meant both centralisation and nationalisation. This being the case, any form of devolution would weaken the central control needed to master the commanding heights of the economy. So opposition to devolution, in whichever form, could not be reduced to just being anti-Welsh. The perception was the need to stand together on other issues. It is folk-lore that they were anti-Welsh. Some were anti the Welsh language, like Leo Abse, but they were not anti-Welsh.

Keir Hardie's . . . . Confession of Faith !

Read this extract from " My Confession of Faith," a pamphlet by Keir Hardie, referring to the work of the Labour Party, he wrote:

" Those who are seeking to disrupt it, or to introduce discord into its ranks, however well-intentioned they may be, are enemies not only of the Labour Movement but of the Cause of Socialism which they profess to hold so dear."

Mrs. Bruce Glasier, who was described by Keir Hardie as the " Mother of the I.L.P.," "Urges all the Workers of the Merthyr Borough to Vote Solidly for S. O. Davies and Retain the Hardie Tradition."

G. D. Hardie, Brother of Keir Hardie, who has been speaking on behalf of S. O. Davies, gives this Message to the Workers of Merthyr:

DEFEAT THE ENEMIES OF SOCIALISM BY

Voting for S. O. Davies.

Printed by Llewelyn Davies & Co., Ltd., Merthyr, and Published by Mr. Bradley Bryson, Election Agent to Mr. S. O. Davies.

Malcolm Llywelyn

S. O. Davies aware of his heritage.

101

They certainly did have strong voices for Welsh devolution in their ranks. Five Welsh Labour MPs argued the case for devolution: Goronwy Roberts, T. W. Jones and Cledwyn Hughes, all from Gwynedd, Tudor Watkins from Brecon and Radnor and Merthyr Tydfil's S. O. Davies. These were the five who championed the formation of the Parliament for Wales Campaign within Labour. Liberal Clement Davies was the other Welsh MP who backed the campaign.

Those from Wales within the Labour party who stood against them were James Callaghan, George Thomas and Aneurin Bevan. There were calls for the five to be disciplined for going against party lines, but this action was avoided, largely at the intervention of Aneurin Bevan.

The five battled passionately within their party, but the fact they were lone voices was not only because of fears of opening the door to nationalism. Jim Griffiths's biographer, D. Ben Rees, says this of the five:

> *... prin oedd adnabyddiaeth aelodau Gogledd Cymru o fywyd diwydiannol, diwylliannol a chymdeithasol de Cymru. Roeddynt yn tueddu i fod yn groendenau, ac roedd yn hawdd ei ddigio, yn arbennig pan glywent Gwynfor Evans yn beirniadu, a hynny'n gyson, wleidyddion o fewn y Blaid Lafur oedd o Blaid Senedd i Gymru.*[47]

> *... those MPs from North Wales showed very little understanding of the industrial, cultural and social life of South Wales. They tended to be thin-skinned, and it was easy to offend them, especially when they heard Gwynfor Evans criticising, as he did regularly, those MPs in the Labour Party who supported a Parliament for Wales.*

Jim Griffiths has already been mentioned. His stance was clearly in favour of safeguarding the rights of Wales as a nation, and that's what drove his politics. But even he was not a clear advocate of a Parliament for Wales and did not join the five. Jim Griffiths stayed quiet on the whole Parliament for Wales campaign and did not refer to it in his speeches until one at the South Wales Miners Conference in 1956. On that occasion,

---

47. D. Ben Rees: *Cofiant Cledwyn Hughes.* Tal-y-bont, Ceredigion: Y Lolfa, 2017, p. 187.

he was particularly aggressive in his attack of the campaign—which was, by then, over.

S. O. Davies brought the Parliament for Wales Bill before the House of Commons in March 1955. These are some of S. O. Davies's remarks in opening the debate, as shown in *Hansard*:

> *I have Hon. Friends here who will verify my belief that never has our country been more alive, more active, more articulate and more finely organised in the demand that a substantial measure of self-government should at long last be given to Wales. I have received many hundreds of letters, postcards and telegrams. Having mentioned telegrams, I may say that I am sure that the Postmaster-General would have been delighted to have seen the scores of telegrams, in my own language, that have come to me, wishing me good luck and supporting the Bill. The telegrams have, with but one or two exceptions, been perfect in their spelling. I think that the Postmaster-General would have taken some pleasure in that, assuming that he knows a little about our country...*[48]

> *This is a modest Bill. To put it in a sentence, what is proposed is that at this stage some foundation should be laid through its provisions, on which a considerable measure of self-government could be built in the future. I am certain that what I and my colleagues are asking for on behalf of the Principality will result in efforts, particularly in Scotland, and probably in some parts of England, for a similar measure of self-government. I am not exaggerating the effect on the life of a backbencher when he senses this frustration, this stultifying effect of delegated legislation. If any Hon. Member can suggest some means of bringing back to the elected Members of Parliament powers which are increasingly being taken from them; if any Hon. Member can advance ways and means of stopping, or even retarding the withering away of our Parliamentary democracy, I and my Hon. Friends will listen with pleasure and with care.*[49]

48. *Parliamentary Debates (Hansard)*: vol. 537. House of Commons Official Report, H. M. Stationery Office, 1955, p. 2439.
49. Ibid., p. 2443.

The Bill called for specific devolved functions for Wales in industry, trade, transport, agriculture, education, broadcasting, health, housing and social services. The Bill had little support. Cledwyn Hughes, T. W. Jones, Goronwy Roberts, Tudor Watkins, backed it, the other four in the five, along with S. O. himself, with the addition of Peter Freeman. Added to this number were two legal experts, who Cledwyn Hughes, the only qualified solicitor amongst the MPs, had called upon for further advice. They were Eryl Hall Williams from the LSE, and Dewi Watkin Powell, a barrister and Plaid Cymru supporter. The Bill was drawn up by these two legal advisors, S. O. Davies, Goronwy and Cledwyn. They based it on the Government for Ireland Act of 1914. This would include a Secretary of State for Wales and an elected Assembly. The underlying principle was that Wales was being neglected while any Welsh issues were being discussed in a Parliament that had so many other matters to deal with.

Cledwyn Hughes and Goronwy Roberts had welcomed the formation of the Council for Wales at the start of the decade, under the leadership of Clement Attlee. The Council's first report, under the chairmanship of Huw T. Edwards, was presented to the Government in 1950. S. O. Davies's Bill, it was thought, would take matters much further down the road. In his Cledwyn Hughes biography, D. Ben Rees says:

> *I Cledwyn Hughes byddai mesur diffygiol S. O. Davies yn rhoddi i Gymru y statws a haeddai fel cenedl a llawer mwy o lais dros ei buddiannau, gan y byddai ganddi reolaeth dros weithrediadau ym mhob agwedd o lywodraeth bron.*[50]

> *For Cledwyn Hughes, S. O. Davies's flawed Bill would give Wales the status it deserved as a nation, and much more of a voice in its own affairs, as she would then have more control over activities in almost every aspect of government.*

This was no different to anything that Plaid Cymru had been calling for until then, or has been calling for until very recently. Way back in the

---

50. D. Ben Rees: *Cofiant Cledwyn Hughes*. Tal-y-bont, Ceredigion: Y Lolfa, 2017, p. 50.

1930s, Saunders Lewis had published his Deg Pwynt Polisi (Ten Policy Points), arguing Dominion Status for Wales, as was the situation in countries like Australia and New Zealand. By the time of the Coronation of King George VI, Dominion Status was party policy. This proved to be too much for some Plaid supporters, who formed their own republican movement, with Gwilym Prys Davies being their most prominent member. In the late 1940s, Saunders Lewis reiterated that recognising the Crown was a small price to pay to achieve Dominion Status. The message was clear from two of the party's Presidents. Plaid never stood for Independence throughout the political lives of Lewis and Evans. It's only a word that's appeared recently, as part of Adam Price's rhetoric specifically.

Back to S. O. Davies's Bill. Cledwyn Hughes and Goronwy Roberts were keen to keep the proposals in the Bill as simple as possible. S. O. Davies, however, wanted to go much further. As far as the other two were concerned, S. O.'s more militant stance angered Labour leaders and was more destructive than positive. They submitted the Bill, which went to a second reading before being rejected.

Lady Megan Lloyd George receives the Parliament for Wales petition, April 1956.

A year later, as a part of the continuing push for a Welsh Parliament within the Labour Party, Goronwy Roberts presented a petition to the Government supporting a Parliament for Wales. It had nearly a quarter of a million signatures on it, but it fell on fallow ground. The Campaign was losing momentum. It gained a little more in 1953 when one of Plaid Cymru's officers, Elwyn Roberts, was appointed its full-time secretary. Lady Megan Lloyd George made an impassioned speech at the Rhyl National Eisteddfod that year also, which succeeded in breathing some more life into the Campaign.

But it was short-lived. Labour's Deputy Leader, Herbert Morrison, concluded that the opposing viewpoints within Labour on Wales needed to be dealt with before they caused any long-term damage. On 11 November 1953, Labour announced that they did not back the idea of a Parliament for Wales. This stance had the backing of the Welsh Council of Labour, formed a few years earlier to give the Labour Party a semblance of a commitment to a separate Welsh identity. This gave the Party a new focus on the devolution issue, as summed up in *The Labour Party in Wales 1900-2000*:

If the Labour Party were to move towards devolution, it was clear that this had to be a measure of administrative devolution in the first place. Any more ambitious scheme awoke all the fears of separatism and cultural isolationism, from which the political instincts of those whose politics was based on anti-fascism and the solidarity of the Labour movement recoiled.[51]

The authors of the chapter where those words are found, R. Merfyn Jones and Ioan Rhys Jones, add in conclusion:

... it is also important to emphasise that it did open up a debate within the Labour Party, and that its chief parliamentary advocate was a left-wing miners MP... It might even be the case that this debate made it easier for less ambitious demands to be justified.[52]

---

51. Deian Hopkin; Duncan Tanner; Chris Williams (eds.): *The Labour Party in Wales 1900-2000*. Cardiff: University of Wales Press, 2000, p. 253.
52. Ibid., p. 253.

Malcolm Llywelyn

S. O. Davies

Seeds of a storm

The co-operation that the Parliament for Wales campaign had created came to an end. It was a unique movement in the way it brought people together from different political parties on one cross-party issue. Cledwyn Hughes, in particular, was annoyed at an attitude within one party involved that he saw as destructive. His biographer, D. Ben Rees explains it like this:

> *Credai Cledwyn Hughes yn ddidwyll iawn fod y sefyllfa ef ac eraill yn y Blaid Lafur wedi dioddef yn enbyd oherwydd na fabwysiadwyd idiom fwy cefnogol a diplomataidd gan Gwynfor Evans a Wynne Samuel o Blaid Plaid Cymru. Cyfeiriodd at dristwch yr ymgyrch o du gwleidyddion eraill:* 'deep resentment throughout the rank and file of the Labour movement in

Wales at the persistent and abusive attacks made by certain elements in the Principality on some of the most highly respected Welsh Labour leaders.'[53]

Cledwyn Hughes sincerely believed that his position, as those of others in the Labour Party, had suffered considerably because Gwynfor Evans and Wynne Samuel from Plaid Cymru hadn't adopted a more supportive and diplomatic idiom. He referred to sadness other politicians had expressed about the Campaign: 'a deep resentment throughout the rank and file of the Labour movement in Wales at the persistent and abusive attacks made by certain elements in the Principality on some of the most highly respected Welsh Labour leaders.'

This was a very early example of the hostilities that grew between Labour and Plaid Cymru. They came to a bitter head during the aggressive confrontations of the late sixties and the early seventies. In referring to this later period, former Head of BBC *Wales News*, Gwilym Owen, said that he could testify that such an atmosphere had never been seen in the story of Welsh politics. They sowed the seeds of that storm in the fifties, specifically during the Parliament for Wales Campaign.

Tories and a Parliament for Wales

It must be remembered, of course, that the Government from 1951 onwards was a Conservative one led by Winston Churchill. They, as dyed-in-the-wool Unionists, would not endorse any form of Parliament for Wales. But they tried to acknowledge the increasing need to recognise that Wales was different. In 1951, Churchill created the post of Minister for Welsh Affairs to work within the Home Office, a shrewd move intended, no doubt, to alleviate the calls for a Welsh Parliament.

David Maxwell-Fyfe QC, a Liverpool MP, was the man appointed. It was a controversial decision. Welsh Assembly Member David Melding, in his book *Will Britain Survive Beyond 2020?*, quotes a confidential

---

53. D. Ben Rees: *Cofiant Cledwyn Hughes.* Tal-y-bont, Ceredigion: Y Lolfa, 2017, p. 189.

Labour's Welsh MPs, 1951

internal Conservative Central Office memo on this appointment. It was sent to the party chair, Lord Wootton:

From all sides, I have heard the most alarming reaction to the appointment... These private Fleet Street reports have today been confirmed by Mr. Garmonsway, the Central Office Agent for Wales. I really do think that we cannot afford to pay (play?) a hostage to fortune of this nature. I am sure that it will have been considered already, but I believe that the position would be entirely rectified if a Welsh member were as the Under Secretary of State for Wales, with possibly the opening up of an office in Cardiff. This I would add is not my personal view, but I have had (or heard?) it from the editor of the News of the World who told me that already they were receiving more letters about this matter than any other subject since the General Election.[54]

The appointment evidently generated a great deal of letter writing!

---

54. David Melding: *Will Britain survive beyond 2020?* Cardiff: Institute of Welsh Affairs, 2009, p. 145.

Young Labour MP, and ardent devolutionist, Cledwyn Hughes, showed particular opposition to Maxwell-Fyfe's appointment. He questioned whether a Home Office Minister who also had other responsibilities could devote enough time to Welsh issues. He questioned the fact that he wasn't Welsh, and if he could, therefore, understand the way the Welsh thought and know what they wanted for their country. All Wales would get from such a situation, he said, would be 'crumbs from a rich man's table'. Maxwell-Fyfe was referred to in Wales with what Kenneth O. Morgan calls 'affectionate derision' as Dai Bananas!

Maxwell-Fyfe stayed and made a swift positive impression on two contentious Welsh issues. He refused the Forestry Commission's request to get more Forestry in Carmarthenshire, and in 1952, the War Office gave up its plans to get more land in Pen Llŷn to use for military exercises. He had shown that he could identify some main concerns of the Welsh people. He showed some influence on the Parliament for Wales campaign too. He persuaded Sir Ifan ab Owen Edwards, one of those at the conference that launched Parliament for Wales, to write a letter to Gwynfor Evans, doubting the efficacy of the Campaign.

The Conservative response to the increasing prominence of Wales as a political issue was to set about developing a Welsh Policy at the end of the forties. Following their heavy defeat in the 1945 General Election, the party set about re-organising itself. In Wales, this happened to great effect, with many improvements made, one aspect of which was to set about creating their policy for Wales. They chose someone to lead this initiative; Enoch Powell. It was not a very well-known fact at the time that he was of Welsh descent. Later on, he took the trouble to learn Welsh. None of this became known until he had finished his political life.

He travelled throughout Wales extensively in preparing his report. When he started his work, he began forming a specific policy for Wales for the first time amongst any of the larger political parties. The Labour Party was to call for a Labour Policy for Wales in 1952. *The Conservative Policy for Wales and Monmouth* was published in February 1949. It broke new ground for that party. First, it was a bilingual publication. Its new attitude to Wales as a nation reflected in the decision to publish it in both languages. This is seen clearly in this extract from the report:

A significant part of those living in Wales have kept alive the consciousness that they are a separate and distinct nation. The national individuality expresses itself in the religious and cultural life and the habit of thought and action of the people. There is no economic separateness of Wales to correspond with its national separateness. We believe therefore that the identity of Wales with England as an economic unit and its separateness as a national entity must alike be recognised.

The traditional policy of Conservatism has always been to acknowledge and to foster variety wherever found, in individuals and nationalities. Diversity in unity is our conception of society and of the nation, to which the levelling, standardising and bureaucratic spirit of Socialism is utterly opposed.[55]

The report recommended that they should create a role in the Cabinet for a minister to look after the affairs of Wales. Powell said that this was what he heard from the people of Wales.

In most parts of the area visited, the view was strongly held by Conservatives of all shades that separate Ministerial representation for Wales is a sine qua non.[56]

The Conservative AGM accepted the proposal in Chester on 28 May 1949. The response of some within the Conservative Party to this new stance had a familiar tone to it. As with Labour, so many Tories heavily criticised their own party for pandering to the nationalists and of being weakened by them! Lord Merthyr, for example, in the *Western Mail*, said that 'this document is simply a further installment of Welsh nationalism'. But the Party was clear that they were the party which had created a clear Welsh element to politics in Britain for the first time, as David Melding says, taking the argument to Labour:

---

55. Enoch Powell: *The Conservative Policy for Wales and Monmouth*, London, 1949, p. 142.
56. Ibid.

... the Conservative initiative of developing a specifically Welsh policy was weakly emulated when the Welsh Regional Council of Labour called for a 'Labour Policy for Wales' in 1952. In the post-war era, it was the Conservative Party that established a clear Welsh dimension to British politics.[57]

A couple of years after Powell's document, there was an opportunity to put the argument before the people of Wales. During the General Election campaign of 1951, two of the party's big guns did just that. Anthony Eden, Deputy Leader of the Conservative Party, said during a speech in Cardiff:

Unity is not uniformity. Wales is a nation. She has her own way of life and her own language. She has preserved and nourished over the centuries her own valuable and distinctive culture. She has her own special needs and conditions, and these must be fully recognised and met.

Party elder statesman Winston Churchill also contributed to the debate:

We shall be very mindful of the national aspirations and special problems of Wales. Unlike the Socialists, we do not believe in putting the United Kingdom in a Whitehall straight-jacket.

1951 is also the year in which it was first suggested that the Conservatives should hold their own, separate, Welsh Conference. A proposal to that end was put forward by the Llanelli Conservative Association. It wasn't immediately accepted. In fact, it would be another twenty-one years before that actually happened, the Conservatives being the last of the major political parties to hold a conference just for Wales, in 1972. When that proposal was made, the Conservative Party had no separate name identity in Wales. That wasn't suggested until the end of the decade, in 1959, when a Tom Hooson and Geoffrey Howe report, Work for Wales, suggested that in order to purposefully address their Welsh audience, the Welsh Area Council needed to change its name to The

57. David Melding: *Will Britain survive beyond 2020?* Cardiff: Institute of Welsh Affairs, 2009, p. 143.

Conservative Party of Wales. After much discussion, the principle was accepted, but it was felt that The Conservative Party in Wales was a better name. That was confirmed.

David Melding

After their Electoral success in 1951, however, as David Melding sums up, 'considerable tension existed between Central Office and the voluntary party in Wales'. Later in the decade, this showed itself in the move to create a stronger Policy for Wales. This came from the voluntary associations and from some among the party's secretariat in Wales itself. Prime Minister Harold Macmillan, it was said, was thinking about creating a Secretary of State for Wales. He decided against that, creating instead the role of Minister of State for Welsh Affairs, Henry Brooke—as opposed to the role that Maxwell-Fyfe first filled, Home Secretary with responsibility for Welsh Affairs. However, once such a post was established in 1951, from that year until 1964, only one Welshman filled the post and that was Gwilym Lloyd George. Despite being a strong advocate of recognising Welsh separateness through establishing a cabinet position for Welsh Affairs, Enoch Powell turned down such a role for himself, believing that it would be very difficult for an English MP to fulfil such a role.

The broader refusal to create a Secretary of State for Wales led to an effective ending of the Council of Wales. Its chair, Huw T. Edwards resigned as did four other members. Ironically, the withdrawal of the Council as a body that championed Wales created a vacuum that increased the calls for a Welsh Secretary of State to represent the interests of the nation.

A look back through the Fifties

The Parliament for Wales Campaign made an impression on public opinion. It also significantly kept Wales and its interests in political and public debate for most of the decade. It saw the growth in Plaid Cymru's activity and, subsequently, its profile. For the Labour Party, despite their official rejection of the Parliament for Wales Campaign, they ended the decade with a devolution-related issue on their manifesto for the 1959 General Election. It was, by then, party policy that Wales needed a Secretary of State.

The main instigator of this was undoubtedly Jim Griffiths. In 1957, the Council for Wales and Monmouth published its Third Memorandum on central government administration in Wales. Its main recommendation was the appointment of a Secretary of State for Wales. In *Labour and Devolution in Wales*, John Gilbert Evans says this:

> *The Welsh Parliamentary Party had accepted the recommendation, but the Welsh Regional Council of Labour's executive committee had not. (Annual Report 1957). James Griffiths supported the recommendation when Labour's tripartite committee, consisting of representatives of the National Executive Committee, the Welsh Parliamentary Party and the Welsh Regional Council of Labour met in 1959 (April 16) to consider a policy for Wales. Ness Edwards disagreed with Griffiths, and the committee agreed to recommend a minister without a department. However Hugh Gaitskell intervened and after he had consulted the Welsh Parliamentary Labour Party, the recommendation to the national committee*

was that a Secretary of state with responsibilities be appointed.[58]

Ness Edwards's opposition was hardly surprising. He was the one who summed up his Labour colleague's stance on devolution for Wales when he said,

If you give a sop to Nationalism, you will create an appetite for more.

But as a senior figure within Labour, Jim Griffiths had considerable influence, and particularly so on Gaitskell. The arguments coming from the other Welsh MPs on devolution issues also impressed Gaitskell. Cledwyn Hughes recalls this in an interview with R. Merfyn Jones in 1995:

I remember very well a special meeting of the Parliamentary Labour Party to discuss this and Hugh Gaitskell and James Griffiths came to listen to the debate… and we had two meetings and in the end, Gaitskell said 'well I think a very good case has been made'. And it was clear that Jim Griffiths was in favour, and that he had, I would imagine, have had a long conversation with Gaitskell and had influenced him in favour… When we were leaving the meeting Bevan was close to me and he said, 'You've got what you wanted, now you've got to make the best of it.' Jim Griffiths also emphasised the importance of Gaitskell's support.[59]

This move within Labour also emphasises that the lead came from Westminster, not from Wales.

In 1957, there was another significant change regarding Wales. Macmillan succeeded Eden in that year, and he moved responsibilities for Welsh Affairs from the Home Office. He placed them in the Housing and Local Government Department. Subsequently, Lord Brooke, the Minster of that Department, took over responsibilities for all matters Welsh.

---

58. John Gilbert Evans: *Labour and Devolution in Wales.* Tal-y-bont, Ceredigion: Y Lolfa, 2019, p. 18.
59. Deian Hopkin; Duncan Tanner; Chris Williams (eds.): *The Labour Party in Wales 1900-2000.* Cardiff: University of Wales Press, 2000, p. 255.

Aneurin Bevan supporting Cledwyn Hughes' canvassing, 1959.

But the party faithful in Wales hadn't been told of such a change. It did not go down well. The feeling was that it was easier to accept the refusal to establish a Secretary of State for Wales if the minister responsible for Wales was part of the senior governmental department of the Home Office. This perceived rebuttal triggered further calls within the Conservative Party for a Secretary of State. Colonel Llywellyn proposed a motion.

> *It is considered that the time has now come when further devolution should be given and that Wales and Monmouthshire should be granted the privilege of a Secretary of State on similar lines to Scotland.*[60]

It was passed. Brooke said that the Prime Minister was considering establishing a Secretary of State for Wales. After much consultation within

---

60. David Melding: *Will Britain survive beyond 2020?* Cardiff: Institute of Welsh Affairs, 2009, p. 149.

Wales, Macmillan decided against establishing a Secretary of State, but instead created a Minister of State for Welsh Affairs. That might have been all well and good for most in the Tory Party, but what happened after that descended into a farce. They gave the responsibility for this newly created post to D. V. P. Lewis. Who was he? A county councillor from Brecon. *The Economist* summed the story up well at the time:

> *How an obscure Brecon county councillor, visiting London (in his tweed suit) for the University Rugger match, was called to Downing Street to be made a Baron and a Minister of State, represents one of the most curious political appointments since Caligula made his horse a consul.*[61]

Soon after, the Council for Wales as good as ceased to exist. Its leader and four members withdrew from the Council because they had rejected their calls to establish a Secretary of State.

For all the advances made throughout this decade, and they are not to be dismissed even if they weren't big advances, it's equally true to say that not one political party was united in its campaigning for a Parliament for Wales. In Plaid Cymru's case, one issue arose to cause a considerable divide; pacifism. Gwynfor's opponents started to seriously criticise his solid stance on pacifism. They saw such a stance as the most visible symbol of the 'niceness' of Welsh nationalism. People who were not pacifists, Gwynfor's opponents said, felt they could not be members of Plaid. The Reverend Fred Jones and D. J. Davies were very active in the Press, articulating their opposition to Gwynfor's stance, the opposition of the former no doubt causing greater consternation because he was a man of the church. These men, according to Rhys Evans, regretted that the spirit of Penyberth had been lost. He then says that D. J. Davies had

> *revealed that Gwynfor had confided in him that he would prefer Wales to remain 'captive' if the only option were to win freedom through violence.*[62]

---

61. *The Economist*, vol. 185, December 21, 1957, p. 1034.
62. Rhys Evans: *Gwynfor Evans: Portrait of a Patriot*. Tal-y-bont, Ceredigion: Y Lolfa, 2008, p. 141.

On a broader basis, the fifties saw one other advance when Wales was recognised in a new way. 'England and Wales' was now added to Westminster legislation, instead of England only and thus not recognising Wales' separateness. No doubt this brings echoes of the old dictionary story of, 'For Wales see England'. Did this give Wales a distinctive identity, or in

Welsh politics gets TV treatment. 1955, 1959

effect, tie it more to England? The Tory government also gave Wales a capital city for the first time in this period.

The 1950s had seen four General Elections: in 1950, 1951, 1955, and 1959. They had seen the UK move from Labour to Conservative. Those within the ruling party who favoured increased devolution for Wales felt that they had been given a mandate for their cause by their results in those elections. They had won four Welsh Parliamentary seats in Wales in 1950, six in 1951 and 55 and seven in 1959. They were gaining ground.

There were a few significant individual campaigns that played into this broader party political canvas from the mid-fifties onwards. It's these campaigns we'll look at next.

7.

Furniture and Water

During that same decade, Plaid had experienced a certain maturing as a political party. In 1951, it had 0.7% of the vote in Wales. It was 3.1% in 1955 and 5.2% in 1959. There was no denying the party's upward trajectory. In terms of the Welsh Language, about 700,000 spoke the language according to the 1951 census.

While the main political parties were formulating how to deal with 'Wales' as a distinctive political issue, there were specific individual campaigns that arose which influenced the broader political debate. They varied in their nature, from what could be regarded as local issues to those that had a much broader political significance.

As the fifties began, Wales was not recognised officially by Westminster. The Welsh language had no official status within Wales and hadn't had any since the Act of Union in 1536. Business, administration, the judiciary, finance and governance were all conducted in English, with no call for use of the Welsh language in most local authorities, or cheques written in Welsh to be made legal tender, for example. There would have been very few outward public signs of the presence of the Welsh language. Some county boundaries had bilingual road signs, but most didn't.

School proved somewhat of an exception. Since the Education Act of 1870, they made English the legal language of education in Wales, whether or not every pupil in any school spoke Welsh. But after the Second World War, things began to change. Carmarthenshire local authority set up the first state Welsh-medium primary school in Wales, in Llanelli, in 1947. Some others followed in the early fifties, in various Welsh counties. In 1956, the first Welsh-medium Secondary School opened, Ysgol Glan Clwyd in Denbighshire.

In terms of the number of those who spoke Welsh, that quite simply was declining. At the dawn of the twentieth century, nine out of ten Welsh people spoke the language. By the second half of that century, Wales was losing two hundred Welsh speakers every week—which meant the number was down from nine out of ten to three out of every four. It makes one think what they could have achieved if the momentum of the latter half of the 20th century had coincided with the mass of Welsh speakers there were in Wales in the first half.

On that broader political picture, even with some devolutionary gains across all parties, it was perceived that there were no major significant gains. On that issue, Kenneth O. Morgan says:

On the whole, the thirteen years of Conservative rule from 1951 to 1964, like the Labour years of 1945 to 1951, saw no significant concession to demands in Wales for greater powers of self-government; they served merely to highlight the weaknesses -of the existing system in the principality.[63]

Many individual incidents highlighted such concerns across different areas of Wales. There was a perceived need therefore to campaign in ways other than through the ballot box. Some individuals who were not politicians campaigned in their own way. The most prominent had to do with water, which drew in all the political parties, and it's a campaign that has been remembered with renewed energy in the last couple of years. The first, however, had to do with how a family in West Wales dealt with their Local Authority's demands for their rates.

The Beasleys and their furniture

As early as 1952, one family in West Wales stood their ground on a local issue that was to take on national significance. Trefor and Eileen Beasley had moved into their first home together in Llangennech on the

---

63. Kenneth O. Morgan: *Rebirth of a Nation: Wales 1880-1980*. Oxford: Clarendon Press, 1981, p. 380.

outskirts of Llanelli. He was a coal miner and she was a teacher. When they received their demand for rates from Llanelli District Council, the form was in English only. They felt that this was unjust, as they lived in a predominantly Welsh area, where Welsh was used day in, day out in all circumstances. They refused to pay the rates unless they were sent a form in Welsh to fill in. Their battle lasted 8 years. They received 16 writs, made many appearances in court, and Trefor spent a week in prison at one point. They then sent the bailiffs to their home and removed all the furniture. They finally won their battle in 1960, and rate forms in Welsh were available in April 1961.

The Beasley family.

Such are the bare facts of the Beasley story. The impact of their stance proved to be far-reaching, but not at first. Because it was such an isolated case, in a small village in West Wales, it got little attention. The fact it took eight years in total also didn't help public awareness. The Beasleys supported Plaid Cymru—Trefor, having been won over to the party while the secretary of his local NUM lodge. That party, however, were not immediately up to speed with what the husband and wife were doing. Former President Saunders Lewis, amongst others, expressed concern that the Party wasn't supporting them enough.

Plaid Cymru did then respond. They initially, through Gwynfor Evans and J. E. Jones, tried to strengthen the Beasley's case by enlisting more people to take the same stance as they had. They set a target of 20 people. But the request fell on unwilling ears. No doubt such action was too new, too daring, and outside the way they perceived their support of Plaid Cymru. The thought of losing their furniture or being sent to prison was a step too far for the majority.

One other action taken by supporters of the family was a very practical one, especially for a family with children, as Gwynfor Evans testifies in his memoir, *For the Sake of Wales*:

> *We arranged with Dr Harry Davies of Ammanford to buy back the furniture that had been removed from their home by the local authority.*[64]

In that same volume, he gives another example of a similar stand on the availability of forms in Welsh. In 1958, a man from Bettws, Ammanford, by the name of Gwynfor S. Evans, had been encouraged to stand as a Plaid candidate in a local election. After initial unwillingness, he finally agreed to do so, on the day the forms were due in to register candidacy. He had no nomination forms in English, however, only ones in Welsh, made by Plaid Cymru themselves. Because of the lateness of the hour, they urged him to fill in the Welsh forms, which he did. He handed them in by the required time of mid-day. But because it wasn't in English, they rejected his form. Plaid Cymru saw their chance for a battle. They took the case to the High Court in London. They raised the £300 they needed for costs and engaged the barrister services of Dewi Watkin Powell, one of those who had drafted S. O. Davies' Parliament For Wales Bill a few years earlier. Gwynfor Evans says:

> *Dewi argued with uncommon skill and the case was won. The court refused permission for the County Council to appeal, and it had to pay costs. Thereafter all the electoral forms and posters in Carmarthenshire were bilingual in both local and Parliamentary elections.*[65]

Labour peer Gwilym Prys Davies comments on this court case in his book, *Llafur y Blynyddoedd* (*The Years of Labour*);

---

64. Gwynfor Evans; Meic Stephens; Steve Dubè: *For the Sake of Wales: The Memoirs of Gwynfor Evans*. Cardiff: Welsh Academic Press, 2001, p. 159.
65. Ibid., p. 160.

Gellir dadlau na dderbyniodd y Llys y gosodiad cyffredinol bod gan y Gymraeg statws swyddogol, ond credai Saunders Lewis mai "dyma'r dyfarniad pwysicaf yn yr Uchel Lys, yn Llundain, i Gymru ers dwy ganrif os nad rhagor."[66]

It could be argued that the High Court did not accept the general statement that the Welsh language had official status, but Saunders Lewis believed that "this was the most important verdict by the High Court in London, for Wales for two centuries if not more."

By the first few years of the 60s then, through these two stories, Carmarthenshire residents at least had their rate forms and the election forms available in Welsh. Such was the nature of battles for the language; individual cases here and there. There was no strategy and no national policy. The action that led to such success came from an increasing unease in Wales as to the lack of status its language had.

The drowning of Capel Celyn

There was nothing local about the main conflict of this period. The battle over the flooding of the Capel Celyn village in the valley of the River Tryweryn in Meirionnydd, in order to provide water for Liverpool, had many long-lasting effects for political parties and communities alike.

The story began quietly enough. In fact, it was so quiet that it was a well-kept secret within the Liverpool Corporation for quite some time. They had decided that they needed to increase their water supply as they were modernising their slum and heavily industrialised areas. They identified three potential sites where a reservoir could be built in order to create this new supply. Discussions with the Welsh department within the government's Housing and Local Government Ministry had identified Haweswater in Manchester, Dolanog in Montgomeryshire, and Cwm

---

66. Gwilym Prys Davies: *Llafur y Blynyddoeedd.* Dinbych: Gwasg Gee, 1991, p. 131.

Tryweryn near Bala. Liverpool favoured the Tryweryn option. Residents of both Dolanog and Capel Celyn knew nothing of these plans.

In September 1955, Liverpool said that it was considering the Dolanog option. They wanted to create a reservoir that would stretch for 4 miles up the River Vyrnwy. This area included the home and chapel of one of Wales' best-loved hymn-writers, Ann Griffiths. Both buildings would be submerged under these plans. This stirred the Welsh into opposition. The proposals were seen as an attack on the very core of Welsh culture, community, religion and language. They aimed all protesting efforts at Dolanog.

Liverpool, however, were still evaluating the Tryweryn site and another nearby, Frongoch. The Dolanog proposals worked well as a deflection from their activities in these other two areas. It might well be difficult to comprehend today, but the threat of drowning the domestic and spiritual home of a hymn-writer was a genuine threat which would have stirred up considerable opposition had it gone ahead. This is the message that was conveyed to Liverpool Corporation. With great political shrewdness, Liverpool, therefore, announced that it would not go ahead with the Dolanog proposal, heralding that it had listened to the wishes of the Welsh people in so deciding.

All it really meant, of course, was that the chances of drowning the village of Capel Celyn had significantly increased and that was, very quickly thereafter, decided upon. The residents of Capel Celyn heard of the confirmation as they read their newspapers over their morning breakfasts. They were to lose their homes, having to move elsewhere, and have their valley flooded.

In 1960, a Private Member's Bill was submitted to Parliament by Liverpool Corporation, to ask that the work go ahead. Liverpool's choice in pursuing a Private Bill had clear motives. They would not need to ask the affected Welsh local authorities for planning permission. They would also avoid any planning enquiry where opposition could be voiced. 35 of the 36 Welsh MPs voted against the Bill, with the one exception not voting. But the Bill was passed.

Reaction was swift, but not always united. Divisions surfaced much quicker than any protest strategy. On the whole, the Welsh in Liverpool, of

National Library of Wales

Protesting on the streets of Liverpool

which there were very many, saw no big issue in taking water from Wales. The people of the town of Bala, the main town nearest Capel Celyn, and those in some surrounding areas, did not think that Capel Celyn was all that special a place anyway and that there would be economic advantages to the new reservoir that would be there. Barely a month after it was confirmed that Tryweryn would be the site, Bala Town Council invited a representative from Liverpool Corporation to talk to them about the proposals. Others, however, were deeply affronted and aggrieved by a city outside Wales taking its water, with no benefit to Wales at all.

And in the middle of this stood the people of Capel Celyn themselves. They were shocked at the prospect of being uprooted. But they were also very nervous about making any protest in case that made things even worse for their future prospects. One resident wrote to the government supporting the plans to drown his own village. He argued that he had seen a decline in the community, with only 9 children going to the school there where once 50 attended. He further added that the Defence

Committee was made up of Plaid Cymru outsiders who didn't know the actual living conditions in Capel Celyn. (WJEC *Austerity, Affluence and Discontent 1951-1979*)

Initially, there was a lack of leadership to the majority opposition that was felt there, stemming, if not for any other reason, from their village life. In a letter, one of Plaid Cymru's leading lights, J. E. Jones, says this in describing Capel Celyn in the early days of the news:

> *It's true that the people of Celyn have been slow in joining the fight but this was because they lacked a leader and we didn't like the idea of doing it for them... The truth is that their poetic/musical culture has made them too dreamy and slow to deal with the whole business of Liverpool's oppression.*[67]

These community divisions, in Wales and Liverpool, were deep and heartfelt, which made the political battles, which were to follow, all the more contentious and divisive.

The broader political objection lay in two facts already stated, the obvious one being that it was a city from outside Wales making demands on Welsh territory, and then, the fact that even though not one Welsh MP voted for it, it happened anyway.

There's no doubt that for Plaid Cymru, this was a major campaign, their first large-scale operation, taking them out of the arenas they had been used to. Gwynfor Evans was widely praised for how he led Plaid's opposition to the plans, but also for the way he galvanised wider opposition and motivated public opinion. His not uncritical biographer, Rhys Evans says:

> *He did more than any other Welsh politician in his struggle to prevent Liverpool Corporation drowning the village of Capel Celyn. And no one worked harder to show how parliamentary democracy disregarded Welsh public opinion. By drawing attention to this situation in the years to come, Gwynfor created thousands of constitutional nationalists—including David Quigley, who would succeed him as President.*[68]

---

67. Rhys Evans: *Gwynfor Evans: Portrait of a Patriot.* Tal-y-bont, Ceredigion: Y Lolfa, 2008, p. 164.
68. Ibid., p. 161.

In making the same point on Gwynfor's contribution to the fight, John Davies adds a further political effect this had;

Above all, the decrease in the number of Welsh speakers and a decline in the values considered being central to Welshness fostered the feeling that uncompromising nationalism alone could save the nation from extinction.[69]

Plaid Cymru's political response when Capel Celyn first came under threat was quite clear. In 1955, its Executive Committee decided that their most appropriate response was to oppose Liverpool Corporation's plans through constitutional means and that objections within that framework should be on economic grounds.

In his dealings with Liverpool Corporation, Gwynfor argued that the city should turn to Manchester for its water needs. He further accused them of exaggerating, if not falsifying, reports that its slums were rotting as a justification for needing the new water supply. He reminded them that there was a newly developed sense of Welsh identity in Wales which would not let them have their own way there. As the campaign momentum increased, and the protest grew, it had a definite effect on Plaid as a party, as Rhys Evans says:

Very gradually, Tryweryn began to transform Plaid Cymru's activities as the party channelled more and more of its efforts into saving this remote valley.[70]

It did, initially, maintain other campaigns, including holding meetings to discuss the viability of starting a Welsh language commercial television production company, but Tryweryn took over.

Plaid's stance became all-consuming then, but it was not entirely harmonious. On one hand, it brought an issue to the fore that would not go away for decades, if it has at all. Were constitutional methods enough to fight the plans for Tryweryn? Or was it time to consider more direct action

69. John Davies: *A History of Wales*. London: Penguin Books, 2007, p. 640.
70. Rhys Evans, ibid., p. 165.

to oppose such a serious issue? The same Executive Committee meeting that adopted a constitutional fight also decided to prepare a confidential report on the potential use of law-breaking methods in their protesting. This was in 1955. This tension between constitutional and law-breaking means to achieve their goals is a tension that has consistently blighted the nationalist cause as it is under Plaid's banner. It was not a new emphasis that rose out of the 1960's revolutionary spirit.

But these weren't the only divisions in the campaign. Locals, who would be displaced by the dam-building, weighed up principle against compensation. In the wider county, Merioneth, there was a growing conviction that the area would benefit from the increased jobs brought in by the project and their opposition dwindled. The Conservative Party had a clear view, as outlined by David Melding, in summing up Brooke's position.

Brooke felt the interests of Liverpool outweighed those of a small Welsh-speaking rural community. Unfortunately for Brooke, the issue was taken as a proxy for the government's general attitude towards Wales.[71]

Cofiwch Dryweryn

But the village was drowned. Twelve houses and farms ended up under the new lake, Llyn Celyn, created by the dam. 48 people of the 67 who lived in the valley lost their homes. 3.2 km2 of land were submerged. They moved 8 bodies from the chapel cemetery to a new one. The total cost of the project was £20 million.

Cofiwch Dryweryn are the words painted on a ruin of a stone wall on the side of the road between Llanrhystyd and Aberystwyth. Remember Tryweryn. It's been there since the 1960s and any attempts since then to erase the message have been quickly dealt with and the message re-painted. Tryweryn is not going to go away.

---

71. David Melding: *Will Britain survive beyond 2020?* Cardiff: Institute of Welsh Affairs, 2009, p. 150.

National Library of Wales

Protesting on the day the reservoir was opened, October 1965.

But what was its legacy after the village of Capel Celyn was eventually drowned? It would seem that for all their active leading from the front in the campaign, Plaid Cymru didn't gain any political advantage. Kenneth O. Morgan says:

> *… such strength as this brought the party was transient. Its share of the poll in Merioneth in 1959, where Gwynfor Evans was again the candidate was, at 22% virtually identical with that of 1955. The big battalions won their inevitable victory over local sentiment. The reservoir at Tryweryn was built just the same.[72]*

Gwynfor Evans, however, saw it differently. In referring to the campaign to oppose Liverpool's plans, and the awakening of a Welsh consciousness occasioned by it, he says:

---

72. Kenneth O. Morgan: *Rebirth of a Nation: Wales 1880-1980*. Oxford: Clarendon Press, 1981, p. 382.

Plaid Cymru has carried out this essential work, which no other party has attempted, not only by conventional electoral politics but also by unceasing effort in trying to create national public bodies, many of them in the economic sector.[73]

Understandably, one of those national public bodies, which Plaid Cymru campaigned for, was a Welsh water authority that could challenge any future Tryweryn scenario. But to claim again that they were the only party to do so is wide of the mark. Former party leader Dafydd Wigley went further:

> *… Tryweryn… showed how impotent Welsh MPs were when all but one voted against Liverpool Corporation's Bill, but of course MPs from the other parts of these islands outvoted them. That drove the growth of Plaid Cymru at that time, there is no doubt about it, and it was a factor in the mindset that enabled Gwynfor Evans to win the 1966 by-election, which then enabled Winnie Ewing to win the Hamilton by-election the next year for the SNP in Scotland and triggered the whole period that we've lived through.*
>
> *You can say that Welsh politics and perhaps even Scottish politics wouldn't be the same today had it not been for that.*[74]

Labour and Liberal figures opposed the plans for Tryweryn, as did some Tories. But the campaign highlighted the tension between Labour and Plaid Cymru. MPs such as Cledwyn Hughes felt affronted when his love for his country was questioned by Plaid Cymru when that party said that they were the only ones doing anything for Wales.

On the other hand, leading Labour figure Huw T. Edwards, the North Wales' trade union organiser and Labour baron, left his party to join Plaid Cymru. *The Labour Party in Wales 1900-2000* says that he:

---

73. Gwynfor Evans; Meic Stephens; Steve Dubè: *For the Sake of Wales: The Memoirs of Gwynfor Evans*. Cardiff: Welsh Academic Press, 2001.
74. David Williamson: 'The story of the outrage that has shaped Welsh politics for more than five decades,' *WalesOnline* 14.11.2016, https://www.walesonline.co.uk/news/politics/story-outrage-shaped-welsh-politics-12173216 (visited 09.04.2021).

... left the party when it failed to oppose the flooding of the Tryweryn valley in 1956.[75]

It then says:

Plaid's inability to reconcile linguistic nationalism with radical policies led him to return shortly after. Such doubts were not uncommon. Others sympathised with nationalist views but remained with Labour. Gwilym Prys Davies, for example, a deeply patriotic Labour activist who in his youth had flirted with the Welsh Republican Movement, felt Plaid was 'too negative, that they weren't lively enough to the needs of the person travelling on the bus in Pontypridd'.[76]

The 1950s then highlighted the tension between Plaid and Labour on whose the most patriotic when it comes to Wales.

As far as the Tryweryn story itself goes, to round it off, Liverpool Corporation issued an official apology in October 2005. It was voted for unanimously, including full backing by the Labour party on the council who were in charge at the time of the drowning.

We realise the hurt of forty years ago when the Tryweryn Valley was transformed into a reservoir to help meet the water needs of Liverpool. For any insensitivity by our predecessor council at that time, we apologise and hope that the historic and sound relationship between Liverpool and Wales can be completely restored.[77]

---

75. Deian Hopkin; Duncan Tanner; Chris Williams (eds.): *The Labour Party in Wales 1900-2000.* Cardiff: University of Wales Press, 2000, p. 268.
76. Ibid., p. 268.
77. "Official apology over Tryweryn," *BBC News*, 19 October 2005, http://news.bbc.co.uk/2/hi/uk_news/wales/4354256.stm (visited 09.04.2021).

Rhodri Morgan

It was an apology that was warmly welcomed by Welsh First Minister Rhodri Morgan and Plaid Cymru alike. The apology came about because of intervention by Liberal peer Lord Roberts of Llandudno. There was no lack of political unity decades later.

8.

An Office and a Secretary

The battle for Tryweryn still raged as the first years of the Sixties rolled on. No water had yet been spilled in Capel Celyn, and the residents were still in their homes, but the battle was in full flow. As well as the two local and national major thrusts of the battle itself, the fight also highlighted the opposite ends of the approach the broader nationalist cause should take in the name of its political cause. Was it to be direct action or peaceful resistance? We have already heard that it was not a new confrontation. But by 1962, it had come to a head, as Martin Johnes sums up in *Wales Since 1939*:

> *Flirtations with explosives or roadblocks won little support among most nationalists in the early 1950s but Tryweryn raised the stakes for a handful, leading to open discussion of extra-parliamentary action.*[78]

In terms of the Tryweryn campaign itself, Plaid's leadership followed a non-violent path in their opposition to Liverpool's wishes for Tryweryn, but that decision didn't last long. *Baner ac Amserau Cymru*, an influential and long-standing Welsh weekly, published an anonymous article in July 1960, arguing that the weapon of reasoned argument had proven to be a blunt one, not respected by anyone. The closing battle-cry of the article asked the rhetorical but heartfelt question; can we leave the old nation to be murdered without striking a blow for it? Striking a blow is hardly a pacifist posture.

---

78. Martin Johnes: *Wales since 1939*. Manchester: Manchester University Press, 2013, p. 220.

135

1960 wasn't a good year for Gwynfor Evans. In the party's annual conference that year, things didn't go the leader's way. As his biographer says of that year and that conference,

For most of the younger generation, Plaid Cymru had lost its way.[79]

He quotes one young delegate, Gerald Morgan, as being flabbergasted that with

... Soviet-like obedience, numerous resolutions were carried 'like sausages and emerged in hygienic plastic jackets full of breadcrumbs'. No one dared challenge the annual report and neither Gwynfor nor anyone from among his inner circle made the least attempt to explain why the election has been such a washout... Following the 1960 annual conference, some of the younger members became increasingly critical of how the party saw its future direction, and since Gwynfor seemed so bereft of ideas, they filled the vacuum with their own.[80]

This increasing internal unrest gave rise to one leading individual dissenting voice, and three leading fractions of opposition to the Plaid leadership, each known by a house name associated with their prominent members. The one voice in 1960 was John Davies. He would go on, a couple of years later, to be the first joint secretary of the newly formed Cymdeithas yr Iaith Gymraeg, the Welsh Language Society. He called for an organisation that could campaign for the refusal to pay licenses of various kinds that were in English only, thus freeing Plaid Cymru from having to carry out such campaigning.

Harri Webb, a leading poet and activist, lived in Garth Newydd in Merthyr Tydfil. He called for law-breaking as a political weapon, such had been used by Gandhi and would later be used in United States' civil rights campaigning. Emrys Roberts stood with Harri Webb on this and

---

79. Ibid., p. 204.
80. Ibid., pp. 204-205.

had considered for the consideration of the possibility of breaking the law during the Tryweryn campaign.

The Belle Vue group, mostly centred on Aberystwyth, and comprising predominantly students, also called on Plaid Cymru to use unconstitutional methods. The third group were the Garthewin people, who were led by Richard Wynne, referred to by Rhys Evans as a 'Catholic squire'. He was happy with armed rebellion, and we'll hear more of him later! Needless to say, Saunders Lewis was supportive of this group and subsequently, this is the faction that Gwynfor and his followers feared the most.

Little wonder then, that in such a climate, there was an escalation of more direct action in the early Sixties. Gwynfor Evans knew beforehand of the plans to vandalise an electricity transformer in Tryweryn, and he had no inclination to oppose the action. Martin Johnes says this of Gwynfor's stance:

Evans was left saying that he did not morally disapprove of all violence, but that he did reject it as a political weapon.[81]

A statement by the Merionethshire county committee of Plaid, to the Plaid Cymru Executive Committee, shows these dualities clearly, made even more relevant of course because Tryweryn was in Merionethshire. In a lengthy statement, summarising their response to the campaign as a whole, they say:

Gan gredu'n gydwybodol y byddai gweithredu anghyfreithlon yn peri colli cefnogaeth i'r Blaid, yn creu gelyniaeth,—a chredwn hyn wedi ystyriaeth yn ddwys pob agwedd i'r mater—credwn o hyd mewn parhau'r frwydr yn erbyn cynllun Lerpwl ymhob dull mewn gwleidyddiaeth a chyfraith.

Believing conscientiously that illegal action would lead to the loss of support to Plaid, and would create enmity,—and we believe this following sincere consideration of every aspect of the matter—we still believe in

---

81. Ibid., p. 220.

continuing the battle against the plans of Liverpool, in every possible way within politics and law.

The statement then says, immediately:

Bu i Mr Gwynfor Evans ac eraill o swyddogion y Blaid geisio ein per-swadio fod angen gweithredu anghyfreithlon. Efallai nad yw'n wybyddus i amryw eu bod wedi annog hynny. Fodd bynnag, ni chawsant ddim cefnogaeth i'w hannogaaeth yn ein plith ni, nid yn unig yn ein Sir ni, ond hefyd mewn cylchoedd uwch yn y Blaid. Gwelsom i Mr Gwynfor Evans ac eraill o swyddogion y Blaid gael ei beirniadu ar y mater hwn o weithredu, o rai cyfeiriadau.

Mr Gwynfor Evans and other Plaid officers tried to persuade us that there was a need to act illegally. It may not be clear to many that they had encouraged us in such a way. However, their pleas had no support amongst us, not only in our County but also within higher circles within Plaid. We see that Mr Gwynfor Evans and other Plaid officials have been criticised on this way of acting, from some quarters.

The statement then moves on to two underlined sentences, increasing the emphasis:

Eithr gwybydded pawb mai plaid wleidyddol ddemocrataidd yw Plaid Cymru. Nid unbenaethiaid yw ei harweinwyr.

But let everyone know that Plaid Cymru is a democratic political party. Its leaders aren't dictators.

They argue this argument against the backdrop of the opening para-graphs, which not only state that Tryweryn was in Merionethshire, but,

... ym Meirion y mae Plaid Cymru gryfaf o unrhyw etholaeth yng Nghymru; y mae dwy fil aelodau, a bu cyfraniad y Blaid yn y Sir yn gyfraniad pur nodedig yng ngwaith y Blaid yn gyffredinol.

... in Merionethshire Plaid Cymru is at its strongest amongst all the constituencies of Wales; there are two thousand members here, and the county's contribution has been a particularly significant one to Plaid generally.

The battle lines weren't only drawn on constitutional or non-constitutional lines. Not all the pro-constitutionalists thought that Plaid should fight every General Election. In a statement they put out in May 1962, Plaid set out as their second of ten points for the Sixties.

The main activity of all branches to centre around fighting local elections... members are asked to make local elections their main sphere of activity and the main object of their financial contributions.

This unrest and disagreement also showed itself in internal disciplinary matters that surfaced in 1962 and the following year. Neil Jenkins was an active and vocal Plaid member. He had consistently accused Gwynfor of being a 'pacifist coward'. For this and many other comments, a sub-committee was asked to look at his case and they subsequently asked him to apologise. When he refused, there were calls for his party membership to be taken from him. This triggered a further division in Plaid, with some thinking it despicable that such a loyal nationalist was being asked to leave the Party. They further pointed out that there were other individuals in Plaid who could be considered as subversive as some thought Neil Jenkins was. Their stance against him was therefore inconsistent in their eyes.

The meeting, at which his case was discussed, expelled him from the party, by 50 votes to 8. Gwynfor Evans didn't speak at the meeting but he was clearly in favour of removing a disruptive force, someone he had called 'a nasty boy'.

But that was only the beginning of the troubles. Following the result, Saunders Lewis wrote to Gwynfor Evans telling him that the decision was 'another example of mimicking the English Labour Party'. He then said that he would resign publicly if the decision was not overturned. Gwynfor faced a new dilemma which had many faces. He was keen to keep such dispute from the media. He wanted Neil Jenkins out but realised how real a threat Saunders Lewis' resignation would be; he didn't want to be seen to defer to Saunders' threat either. Neil Jenkins himself, in one sense, was of no consequence; an errant party member. But it pitted the two men, Lewis and Evans, against each other. Gwynfor believed that the root cause of Jenkins' discontent was Catholicism, thinking that Jenkins and his supporters were increasingly impatient with the Nonconformist control of Plaid Cymru. Jenkins was not a Catholic, but was perceived to be a leading light of a Catholic conspiracy or a Papist plot within Plaid.

Both Evans and Lewis remained intransigent for quite a period. As befitted their relationship, exchanges weren't usually cordial. Saunders wrote to Gwynfor urging him again not to expel Jenkins, as it was men like him who were Plaid's only hope. Rhys Evans mentions the end of that letter:

> *And he closed with the coup de grâce: '... you know that it is in spite of the Executive's policy that I have remained a member of Plaid. It was Plaid Cymru's executive that betrayed the cause at Tryweryn. I cannot forget that. Forgive me for troubling you, Saunders.*[82]

Neither letter worked, and Jenkins' expulsion stood. Lewis withdrew any prior threat he had made. This victory boosted Gwynfor's confidence and standing at a time when Plaid were facing what Rhys Evans calls a civil war, not only on this issue but on others as well.

1962 was a pivotal year in this broader debate.

Other waters

The Tryweryn battle was still raging. But they weren't the only waters that were troubling. On 16 March 1960 the people in a quiet Carmarthenshire valley read their *Western Mail* newspaper at breakfast time and found out that there were plans to build a reservoir where their homes stood. The papers headline couldn't be more stark: *'A Welsh valley faces death by*

---

82. Rhys Evans: *Gwynfor Evans: Portrait of a Patriot.* Tal-y-bont, Ceredigion: Y Lolfa, 2008, p. 223.

drowning'. This dam was to provide water for the large town of Swansea, not far away from the village of Llangyndeyrn, Carmarthenshire. Just in Capel Celyn, the residents were to protest against the proposal. It mattered not if the water was to quench the thirst of people the other side of Offa's Dyke or fellow country men thirty miles east. The homes were not for drowning. Following a long campaign, the villagers of Llangyndeyrn won their battle and saved their homes.

The relevance of their victory, at a time when Tryweryn was still raging, is two fold. Firstly, it played into the broader debate about the use of either violence or direct action during a campaign. The people of Llangyndeyrn achieved their goal without using any form of violence. Second, in a wider context, it is noteworthy that the defeat of Tryweryn is called upon to be remembered far more vociferously than the victory at Llangyndeyrn.

Remember Tryweryn. Remember Llangyndeyrn, on a Llangyndeyrn bus stop 2020

The Fate of the Language

But Wales wasn't only about water. The plight of the Welsh language itself was also causing considerable concern for many people. It was not an easy time for those who championed the nationalist cause, as Siôn Jobbins outlines in his book, *The Phenomenon of Welshness 2*:

> *The late 1950s was a frustrating and heartbreaking time for the supporters of the language. It was becoming patently obvious that Welsh was losing ground quickly... Welsh was a language for the old dusty chapel and the boring old days. With Plaid Cymru's inability to take an effective stand against the drowning of Tryweryn, young nationalists were looking for other avenues to save the language.*[83]

Rhys Evans is quite clear.

> *Plaid Cymru was in ferment by 1962, and it was against this background of administrative and ideological confusion that Saunders Lewis decided to save his party from oblivion.*[84]

This was achieved through a radio lecture on the BBC, broadcast on Tuesday 13 February 1962. Called 'Tynged yr Iaith', the 'Fate of the Language', it clearly demonstrated the battleground for the nationalist cause—the Welsh language. *In Trwy Ddulliau Chwyldro...?*, the history of the organisation that would be born from that lecture, *Cymdeithas yr Iaith Gymraeg*, Dylan Phillips says:

> *Nid bwriad Saunders Lewis wrth draddodi ei ddarlith radio oedd ffurfio mudiad iaith o'r newydd, ond yn hytrach annog swyddogion Plaid Cymru i wneud y Gymraeg yn brif ffocws ei strategaeth wleidyddol. Er gwaethaf hynny, canlyniad y ddarlith oedd ysbrydoli criw bychan o aelodau cangen*

83. Siôn T. Jobbins: *The Phenomenon of Welshness 2, Or 'Is Wales too poor to be independent?'*. Llanrwst: Gwasg Carreg Gwalch, 2013, p. 84.
84. Rhys Evans: *Gwynfor Evans: Portrait of a Patriot*. Tal-y-bont, Ceredigion: Y Lolfa, 2008, p. 216.

tref Aberystwyth o Blaid Cymru i lunio cynnig i'w osod gerbron Ysgol Haf y Blaid ym Mhontarddulais, ym mis Awst 1962, yn galw am ymgyrch ddifrifol o blaid yr iaith.[85]

It wasn't Saunders Lewis' intention, in broadcasting his lecture, to create a new language movement, but alternatively to encourage Plaid Cymru officials to make the Welsh Language the main focus of its political strategy. Despite that, the consequence of the lecture was to inspire a small crew of Plaid Cymru members in Aberystwyth to formulate a proposal to put before Plaid Cymru's Summer School in Pontarddulais, August 1962, calling for a serious campaign for the Welsh language.

The broadcast in print in the Welsh weekly, *Y Faner.*

In that broadcast lecture, Saunders Lewis was as equally damning of his fellow Welsh speakers for their part in the languages' demise as he was of the English. His argument was that Welsh would not exist as a language at the beginning of the twenty-first century, because it faced the double death-blow of politics and economics. His answer to his perceived analysis was simply that they could only avoid the situation through 'revolutionary methods'. He didn't even think that self-government was an

---

85. Dylan Phillips: *Trwy ddulliau chwyldro...?: Hanes Cymdeithas yr Iaith Gymraeg, 1962-1992.* Llandysul: Gomer, 1998, p. 79.

answer to the problem, as in his eyes, self-government without Welsh being recognised as an official language would only hasten the demise of the language and all that it stood for.

Cymdeithas yr Iaith Gymraeg was officially formed in October 1962. It continues to be active and a force for pressure within the nationalist cause. As Martin Johnes says of their continuing existence:

> *... it completely undermines historians' claims that the British student protests of the 1960s were ineffective and unimportant.*[86]

The society's activities from those formative 1962 days, move on to very active campaigns for bilingual road signs, Welsh television programmes and official documentation in Welsh for everything from rates to dog licences.

As far as Plaid Cymru was concerned, there were now two organisations campaigning on nationalist causes, thirty-seven years after Plaid was formed.

The broadcast on vinyl.

---

86. Martin Johnes: *Wales since 1939*. Manchester: Manchester University Press, 2013, p. 222.

On the broader political spectrum, the next General Election was to prove an acid test for Plaid. This surge of nationalist spirit, albeit along two different lines of how to approach their goals, would be tested in 1964. The result was that of the twenty-three Plaid candidates who stood in that election, twenty-one lost their deposits. As Tryweryn hadn't bolstered their fortunes in the 1958 election, so the formation of a nationalist pressure group hadn't bolstered their fortunes in 1964.

Politics and scheduling

We haven't forgotten about Labour! It may well be surprising to some that they have a direct contribution to the debate outlined above about the future of the Welsh Language. And it's one of those quirks of history that it is Saunders Lewis' lecture that's remembered, not a Labour politicians—and BBC scheduling has a major part to play in that quirk.

Two days before Saunders Lewis walked into the BBC studios to record his talk, another politician had done the same for the same reason.

Labour MP Jim Griffiths had gone to the BBC studios—the TV studios in his case, not the radio studios, to record a programme in the series Dylanwadau (Influences) On that programme, he was asked by Aneurin Talfan Davies what the main problem facing Wales is today. His reply is noted in D. Ben Rees' biography of Jim Griffiths, *Arwr Glew y Werin*:

'Mae problem cael gwaith, problem cael cynhaliaeth yn bwysig,'. Ond y syndod mawr i lawer ohonom oedd ei glywed yn dweud hyn. Prif broblem Cymru heddiw yw achub yr iaith—rwy'n credu mai dyna'r brif broblem dros y deg i'r ugain mlynedd nesaf.[87]

'The problem of having employment, the problem of being sustained is important.' But the big shock for many of us was to hear him say this.

---

87. D. Ben Rees: *Cofiant Jim Griffiths: Arwr Glew y Werin*. Tal-y-bont, Ceredigion: Y Lolfa, 2014, p. 215.

'Wales' main problem today is to save the language—I think that will be the main problem over the next ten, twenty years.'

That programme was recorded on 11 February, two days before Saunders' talk was broadcast, but Griffiths' programme wasn't broadcast until 21 March. Two leading Welsh politicians had identified the same issue as the most important that Wales was facing at the beginning of the Sixties, and would still face for years to come. It was an accident of scheduling that meant that Saunders Lewis' talk was broadcast first. Jim Griffiths was from a different party, but he said the same thing. Lord Gwilym Prys Davies' response to that is quite clear in *Cynhaeaf Hanner Canrif:*

Ateb chwyldroadol gan un o arweinwyr y Blaid Lafur. Credaf y gellir dweud nad oedd yr un arweinydd Llafur wedi dweud peth fel hyn erioed o'r blaen... dengys ei ateb y newid cywair a chyfeiriad yr oedd ef am ei weld ar ran Llafur o 1962 ymlaen.[88]

A revolutionary answer by one of the leaders of the Labour Party. I believe that it can be said that no other Labour leader had said anything like that before... his answer shows the change of emphasis and direction he wished to see in the Labour Party from 1962 onwards.

These words were spoken four years before Gwynfor Evans' success in the Carmarthen By-election in 1966—the significance of which we shall return to.

A new office

The 1964 General Election saw the first manifesto for Wales from the Conservative Party. In it, they affirmed their decision not to create a Secretary of State for Wales.

---

88. Davies, Gwilym Prys: *Cynhaeaf Hanner Canrif: gwleidyddiaeth Gymreig 1945-2005*, Llandysul: Gomer, 2008, p. 57.

We believe that the interests of Wales are best safeguarded by attachment to a department of state whose minister is in the Cabinet and has a powerful influence on national policy.

But the Election saw the return of a Labour government after many years out of power. They had many UK wide priorities, of course, but they took this opportunity to fulfil one long-standing promise to Wales. They established a Welsh Office. The Labour Party had rejected the idea for decades, as we've heard. Even post-war, Attlee had stated that such n establishment would be an 'unnecessary duplication' of administration. Others, such as Herbert Morrison, Attlee's deputy leader, echoed Labour objections of previous generations when he said:

Wales could not carry a cadre of officials of the highest calibre, and the services of high English officials would no longer be available.

But there had always been a strong, influential minority of Welsh Labour MPs who had championed the cause of a Welsh Office from 1945 onwards, especially during the 1950s' campaign for a Parliament for Wales. They had convinced Jim Griffiths to change his mind and support their campaign too. This was a significant step, as Jim Griffiths was to be a pivotal player in Labour's shaping of devolutionary policy for Wales. The book that gives the history of The Labour Party in Wales 1900-2000 says:

Resolutions had been passed at the WRCL conference stating clearly the call for a Secretary of State or minister with a seat at Cabinet in 1954, 1957, and 1958. That this became party policy was largely the result of the efforts of James Griffiths. He persisted with the demand for a Secretary of State and it was his influence on Gaitskell, which was crucial in getting the manifesto pledge through the NEC, although Gaitskell also appeared to be impressed by the support of Welsh Labour MP's.[89]

---

89. Deian Hopkin; Duncan Tanner; Chris Williams (eds.): *The Labour Party in Wales 1900-2000*. Cardiff: University of Wales Press, 2000, p. 254.

Labour's plans for Wales were put together in a booklet, Signposts to the
New Wales, published in 1962. It was effectively the party's manifesto for
Wales ahead of the 1964 General Election.

Outside the Labour Party, other forces moved that were also influencing the devolution debate. Historian John Davies suggests:

> The Labour Party's readiness to advocate a substantial measure of admin-
> istrative devolution arose in part from the realization that Plaid Cymru
> was winning support.[90]

Although the point has been made that Plaid gained no parliamentary
success on the back of Tryweryn, for example, John Davies says that their
support had been growing. He cites the example of an increase of candidates put forward by them for General Elections—4 in 1951, 20 in 1959.

> In 1959, Plaid Cymru polled 77,571 votes and its candidates got quite
> respectable results in some constituencies of the industrialized south-east,
> where an indigenous nationalism, different in its emphasis from that of
> the Welsh-speaking districts of the north and west, was striking roots.[91]

Labour were not in power during this time and for all the Labour MPs
that were in Wales, they had no voice in government for 13 years. Plaid
could have been seen to offer another alternative, albeit not an equal one.

The promise that Labour actually fulfilled in their first year back in
government was the establishment of a Secretaryship for Wales. Jim Griffiths was inaugurated in that role on 17 October 1964. But that could
have been done without establishing a Welsh Office as well. The Secretary
of State for Wales could have administered his duties within the existing parliamentary administrative structures. But Jim Griffiths was determined to secure more meaningful power for the new role he was about to
fill. A Welsh Office was also founded. Its inaugural responsibilities were

---

90. John Davies: *A History of Wales*. London: Penguin Books, 2007, p. 639.
91. Ibid.

Jim Griffiths, First Secretary of State for Wales, 1964

limited, having jurisdiction over policy in housing, local government and roads. However, the first step had been taken.

A year into his new job, Jim Griffiths took receipt of a parliamentary committee report, commissioned a year before they established the Welsh Office. In 1963, a report by the Council for Wales was published. It was presented to the government to show ways in which the Welsh Language could be strengthened. Some months later, Sir Keith Joseph, the Welsh Affairs Minister in the Conservative government, announced the establishment of a committee to outline the legal status of the Welsh language and to suggest possible changes that could be made to that status. Sir David Hughes Parry chaired the committee, and he presented the findings, The Legal Status of the Welsh Language, to Jim Griffiths in October

Welsh Office staff, 1964

1965. The report outlined the need for a new law to establish the equal status of Welsh and English, and it recommended removing ten relevant laws from the statute books. This report, now driven by Jim Griffiths in his new role and office, formed the basis of the Welsh Language Act of 1967: the Act which established that legal equality for the first time in Wales.

Jim Griffiths had achieved much within his party to increase recognition and establish an identity for Wales and the language. His biography quotes Ioan Matthews, in an article that appeared in *Planet* August/September 2000:

> *Under Griffiths' leadership, the Labour Party in Wales came close to becoming a genuine national movement that would be accepted as such in Welsh-speaking rural areas.*[92]

Many in the Conservative Party had not turned away from their policy for Wales, made in 1949, even if it had decided against establishing a

---

92. D. Ben Rees: *Cofiant Jim Griffiths: Arwr Glew y Werin.* Tal-y-bont, Ceredigion: Y Lolfa, 2014, p. 223.

Secretary of State for Wales. Sir Charles Hallinan, chair of the WMCUC, stated in 1964:

> ... if the Party cannot accept that Wales should have a secretary of State... then it should agree that the Welsh Office at Cardiff, which is now attached to the Ministry of Housing and Local Government, should be given complete independence and be wholly responsible for redevelopment in Wales and all Welsh Affairs.

Remembering Carmarthen

When the David Hughes-Parry report appeared, it received widespread support in Wales. Jim Griffiths, as has been said, picked up the gauntlet and championed its cause to good effect. Within the nationalist cause, Plaid Cymru and Cymdeiths yr Iaith were forging different emphases in the championing of their cause, as we've outlined. Gwynfor Evans, in those early years of the Sixties, had the increasing emphasis of the need for direct action from Cymdeithas yr Iaith on one hand, and on the other, the seeming success of the Labour Party establishing not only a Secretary of State but a Welsh Office too. His biographer, Rhys Evans sums up his predicament:

> These tendencies left Gwynfor in no-man's-land: he could not speak out in favour of irreverent acts by the younger generation, but he also knew that it was unwise to be kind about any Labour government.[93]

It was from this kind of backdrop that Gwynfor stepped into the electoral battle for the Carmarthen seat in the 1966 General Election.

Labour, at the time, was in a honeymoon period. In Wales, it had a definite Welsh presence, in the shape of the Office it had just established. Gwynfor Evans was not having an easy time. In March 1965, a bomb

---

93. Rhys Evans: *Gwynfor Evans: Portrait of a Patriot.* Tal-y-bont, Ceredigion: Y Lolfa, 2008, p. 255.

exploded at Clywedog reservoir, another incident in the growing use of direct action in the nationalist cause. Again, Gwynfor was asked to condemn such action. He refused, saying that people would continue to turn to violence if Plaid Cymru's voice wasn't listened to, in terms of the status of Wales and its language. In the run-up to the April General Election, all talk was of an easy Labour win. In the constituency itself, Labour Candidate Megan Lloyd George was a popular charismatic figure, who also, of course, brought the myth and aura of the Lloyd George name with her.

John Morris campaigning, 1962

When she was chosen as a candidate for Carmarthen in the 1957 Election, she had only just left the Liberal Party. She won the nomination for candidature by only one vote. The person who came so close to being chosen in her place was John Morris, who was to be MP for Aberavon for over 40 years, as well as Secretary of State for Wales and the Attorney General. Carmarthen is well used to close votes. How different the story would be if John Morris had succeeded.

That becomes even more pertinent when we get to 1966. Megan Lloyd George was popular. But she was also unwell in the run-up to that election. She did not appear in the early weeks of campaigning. The story was that she had a virus infection. She would, it was promised, be back for the last week of campaigning. It was left to her nephew, Benji Carey-Evans, and Gwilym Prys Davies to run the campaign. It worked, and she secured a victory of over nine thousand votes. Because of her absence, the campaign lacked any spark, however. Gwynfor, on the other hand, did well, increasing his party's vote from 5,495 in 1964 to 7,416. It was enough to make him declare that he would win next time. But it was Labour's night. Throughout Wales, they took 32 of the 36 Welsh seats. Plaid's vote fell in fifteen constituencies.

Megan Lloyd George's story wasn't over. Everyone believed that she had a virus—she had failed to turn up at the announcement of the result. But one person, who campaigned for her in 1966, has difficulty in accepting the story that Lady Megan had a virus. It was an open secret, says Gwynoro Jones, before the General Election, that Lady Megan was ill, with rumours of cancer and that she was terminally ill. It was the kind of story, he recalls, that was discussed in the shops and the streets of his home village, Cefneithin. He refutes accounts in at least three books that the exact nature of her illness was a huge shock to everyone when it was actually announced. Lady Megan's death was announced on 15 May 1966.

Gwilym Prys Davies himself writes,

Pan gyhoeddwyd dyddiad etholiad cyffredinol 1966 gofynnodd Cliff Pro-theroe a awn yn ôl i Gaerfyrddin gan nad oedd Megan wedi gwella'n llwyr o'r saldra fu'n ei meddiannu ar hyd y gaeaf, ac na fedrai fod yn bresennol i agor yr ymgyrch.[94]

When the date of the 1966 General Election was announced, Cliff Pro-theroe asked me if I would return to Carmarthen because Lady Megan hadn't recovered from the illness that she'd had throughout the winter, and she wouldn't be able to be present to open the campaign.

---

94. Gwilym Prys Davies: *Llafur y Blynyddoeedd.* Dinbych: Gwasg Gee, 1991, p. 53.

During the election campaign, Megan Lloyd George phoned her constituency office, and Gwilym Prys Davies himself, regularly to enquire how the campaign was progressing. Gwilym Prys Davies says that he didn't realise that Megan Lloyd George would not recover until the night of the count itself. Her nephew, Benji Carey-Evans, informed him, he says.

So it was known for months she was ill. So much for it being a shock after the General election to Gwynfor's agent, his biographer and Jim Griffiths' biographer too. Plaid said that they first knew of Lady Megan's condition at the end of April, and set about preparing for a by-election, whenever that would be.

Those who knew of her actual illness say that she should not have stood in the March General Election. The leaders of her party in the constituency, however, could not or would not bring themselves to tell her as much. It's easy to hear the conversations 'Which one of us is going to tell Lloyd George's daughter that she should step down?' Gwynoro Jones, in *Gwynoro a Gwynfor*, thinks that this unwillingness was very costly for Labour:

> *Gyda gwell cynllunio, a mwy o rhagweld gofalus ar ran y Blaid Lafur, a falle mwy o hyder i drafod y sefyllfa gyda'r Fonesig ei hun, ni fyddai angen yr ail etholiad hwnnw yn 1966 o gwbl, un a brofodd i fod mor hanesyddol i Plaid Cymru.*[95]

> *With better planning, and with more careful foresight from the Labour Party, and maybe more confidence to discuss the situation with Lady Megan herself, there would have been no need for that second election in 1966, one that proved to be so historical for Plaid Cymru.*

But a second election was needed, and it was called for 14 July. Plaid had their candidate, and they had started to put their campaign together. Labour needed a new candidate, of course. They had two to choose from; Gwilym Prys Davies and a young local man, Denzil Davies. The Labour machinery was behind Gwilym Prys Davies. Locally, Denzil Davies was

---

95. Gwynoro Jones; Alun Gibbard: *Gwynoro a Gwynfor*. Tal-y-bont, Ceredigion: Y Lolfa, 2019, p. 23.

very popular in his own right, but also because of his stark contrast to Gwilym Prys Davies. He came from North Wales and was, at the time, a solicitor in Pontypridd. He was a gifted, intelligent man but was not very good with people. Denzil, on the other hand, was known, local, personable and because he was local, they understood his accent. Many in that selection meeting, including Gwynoro Jones, felt that they had chosen the wrong person.

I have vivid memories of Gwilym Prys' hands shaking badly as he held his notes. He was incredibly nervous. Denzil, the young solicitor, was full of confidence and very knowledgeable of the constituency and very polished in addressing those present.

Opposition to Gwilym Prys Davies, within his own party, hung on his past political life. As Rhys Evans summarises:

... Gwilym Prys Davies was also a square peg in a round hole... some in the party were suspicious of him because he had left Plaid Cymru for the Republicans before coming to his senses.[96]

Prys Davies' selection adds a third tale to Labour candidate choices in Carmarthen. Lady Megan herself was only chosen in 1957 by one vote. How different it would have been if they had chosen John Morris. The same Lady should not have stood in March 1966 and if she hadn't, there would have been no need for the July By-election. When that had to be called, the wrong candidate was chosen, in the eyes of many, and that election was lost. How would it have gone if Denzil Davies was chosen, they surmise? On such narrow threads, fortunes turn.

There were other issues, of course, not least of which was the state of the economy. Things had turned for Labour after a very short honeymoon. A series of resignations based on Labour's stance on the Vietnam War and a strike by seamen split the party. A third issue, Labour's policy

---

96. Rhys Evans: *Gwynfor Evans: Portrait of a Patriot.* Tal-y-bont, Ceredigion: Y Lolfa, 2008, p. 261.

on Prices and Income, led to the resignation that proved a huge blow, especially in Wales. Frank Cousins stood down as Technology Minister. He was the former Secretary of the Transport and General Workers' Union, a powerful force in Labour politics. For Trade Unionists of any Union, his stance was very influential in spreading dissatisfaction with Harold Wilson and his government.

Gwilym Prys Davies recalls canvassing in such a climate, one which, he says, was transformed within two months of the General Election. He recalls a letter from Jim Griffiths:

> *I am sorry that your campaign has to bear the strain of the rifts and resignations. This is political life—one can never be sure what may happen any day... Do concentrate on the areas where our vote is strongest to get our full vote there.*[97]

Things weren't any better locally. The Labour-led Local Authority had announced plans to close some rural schools. Canvassing in those rural areas proved difficult for Labour and was made worse by unrest amongst farmers at Labour cuts in their sector. While not in the heartland of the South Wales' coalfield, the constituency included the anthracite coalfield of the Gwendraeth Valley and rumours that Labour had plans to close coal mines added to the unrest and dissatisfaction.

Plaid, on the other hand, were putting together an efficient campaign. They had a well-oiled publicity machine, led by author Islwyn Ffowc Elis. They took advice from the SNP's tactics in Scotland. This campaign was the first time that Gwynfor was 'sold' as Gwynfor, not as Gwynfor Evans, with the obvious emphasis on getting people to respond to the man, not the policies.

Tryweryn wasn't mentioned. Independence wasn't mentioned. Purist nationalist policy wasn't the plan of attack. Plaid, in those two months of '66, practised what Richard Nixon's campaign manager was to say years later; 'Get the people to like the guy and the battle's two-thirds won'. It worked in the USA for a while; it certainly worked in Carmarthen.

---

97. Gwilym Prys Davies: *Llafur y Blynyddoeedd*. Dinbych: Gwasg Gee, 1991, p. 54.

Alan Evans photography

Campaign HQ 1966.

Before the result, the bookies were offering odds of 2000-1 for Gwynfor to win. When the result was announced, he'd won by 2,436 votes. The scenes were riotous, passionate and emotional on Guildhall Square when that was declared.

As Martin Johnes says,

Welsh nationalism had come of age, and Gwynfor was its icon.[98]

Johnes quotes a cartoon from the *Daily Express*, which is a response to the victory.

---

98. Martin Johnes: *Wales since 1939*. Manchester: Manchester University Press, 2013, p. 224.

A jubilant crowd in Guildhall Square, Carmarthen.

... a Daily Express cartoon showed people leaving a floundering ship called the UK in a lifeboat labelled 'independence for Wales', with James Callaghan, then Chancellor of the Exchequer, telling the captain, Prime Minister Harold Wilson, 'you can hardly blame them for wanting to take to another boat'.[99]

Within the Labour Party, Plaid's victory led to Labour MPs, who had championed the Welsh cause and increased devolution, being viewed with deep suspicion. There was a mistrust of their fellow Labour MPs

99. Ibid.

who spoke Welsh for this reason. The nationalist upsurge, it was claimed, was only a distraction from economic issues.

Kenneth O. Morgan says of Plaid's victory in 1966:

Henceforth, Plaid Cymru became credible, an appealing alternative to an apparently ageing, timorous, and entrenched Labour Party, which showed all the symptoms of too long a monopoly of power. Gwynfor Evans himself, once an indulgent Speaker had allowed him to take his oath in Welsh, proved to be an effective spokesman for Wales, dignified, courteous, but with a shrewd eye for the prospects of ventilating the manifold grievances of his nation.[100]

Things weren't seen quite the same within Wales. The response in the Welsh nation wasn't as positive as it was outside Wales—as illustrated by the *Express* cartoon! Martin Johnes mentions two examples of the prejudice experienced after July 1966:

When Gwynfor Evans was invited to speak on Welsh history at a Workers' Educational Summer School in a local authority building in Ferryside (Carmarthenshire) the Labour-controlled council insisted that the event be cancelled unless the invitation was withdrawn. The Western Mail was also hostile to Plaid Cymru, and its news editor of the 1960s remembers that the paper actively 'sought to suppress the party's rise to prominence'.[101]

So, however it came about, Plaid's victory in July 1966 proved to be a watershed in the politics of Wales. There was now a Plaid Cymru MP. There was also a Welsh Office and a Secretary of State for Wales. The Conservative Party felt the need to reassess its relationship to Wales at such a time. In 1968, they commissioned a survey, Scope for Conservative Advance in Wales. It confirmed that the Party was overwhelmingly

---

100. Kenneth O. Morgan: *Rebirth of a Nation: Wales 1880-1980*. Oxford: Clarendon Press, 1981, p. 386.
101. Martin Johnes: *Wales since 1939*. Manchester: Manchester University Press, 2013, p. 225.

considered to be an English Party for England. An internal Conservative Central Office memo saw it in this way:

> *Have we been anti-Welsh? There is only one major snag, and that is, however competent Welsh people consider us, they do not think we are the right ones for Wales. This is rather vital.*

The story moves on.

PART TWO:

The Carmarthen Cauldron
1966–1974

This next section of the book is a continuation of the preceding narrative, but from a different perspective. The story of the cross-party battle for devolution in Wales will continue, and continue chronologically. However, it will be told as an account by someone who was directly involved at the front line of this battle, not only in Carmarthen but within the Labour establishment in Wales. He was the research officer for the party and one of the key architects of preparing the party's evidence to the Kilbrandon Commission on the Constitution of the UK. In 1967, Gwynoro Jones was chosen as the Labour Party's candidate for the Carmarthen Constituency for the General Election that was to be the next one after 1966. That would turn out to be in 1970. He, therefore, was to be the first to challenge Gwynfor Evans' first defence of his seat. The battle between Gwynfor and Gwynoro, and therefore between Plaid Cymru and Labour, would rage in this one constituency for more than a decade. Carmarthen became the cauldron for the broader devolution debate—and it was a fiery one at that!

9.

Into Battle

We have seen that there had been many battles between different parties in the genuine desire of each one to secure some form of devolution for Wales. I entered this arena when the political climate was changing significantly. But don't just take my word for it:

> *I can testify from firsthand experience that the period in question was one of the most volatile and bitter ever experienced in Welsh politics, and certainly Welsh-speaking Wales never saw a period like it and hasn't since then.*

That's the account of Gwilym Owen, a journalist who was a reporter, presenter and editor of political television and radio programmes for TWW, HTV and the BBC in the period under consideration here, and for many years after as well. He then goes further:

> *It was in the Sixties and Seventies of the previous century that the foundation stones were laid for Wales to step towards the independence that is slowly developing in Cardiff Bay.*

It was a seminal period, and I was fortunate enough to be involved in it, however bruising a time it was! When I was chosen as the prospective candidate for Carmarthen for the General Election, the date of the election was unknown. But it was more than certain that whenever that election would be, I had a battle on my hands. It would not be easy.

Plaid confident, Labour reeling

Plaid Cymru had just won their first-ever seat, in Carmarthen in 1966. Naturally, their confidence was high. This had consequences for the party I was standing for. There was an obvious need for re-evaluation after such a defeat. There was a real and perceived need to restore a party that had been beaten soundly by Plaid. Having secured my nomination in my first speech, I said that I was confident that we could win the seat back.

> *This is a seat that can definitely be won back, and given the energy, enthusiasm and will to do so, we will win this setback for Labour. The battle is on from now on, without a doubt.*

That was part of the account the *Evening Post* newspaper gave on October 30th, 1967, of the speech I had just delivered. I believed that, but I also knew that they were difficult days for the Labour Party outside the Carmarthen constituency too.

The young candidate meets the elder statesman, Foelgastell 1968.

In the year in which I was nominated, Labour had a significant scare when Plaid came so close to taking a Labour seat—in the Rhondda, of all places! Plaid came within two thousand four hundred and sixty-seven votes of taking Rhondda West from Labour. Traditionally, Labour in the Rhondda had enjoyed victories by majorities of between sixteen and twenty-three thousand. 1967 was a real scare!

This was followed a year later by a very similar scare in equally Labour Caerffili. Plaid candidate Phil Williams came within one thousand eight hundred and seventy-four votes of defeating Labour, who previously had a majority of over twenty thousand.

In summing up the success of Plaid Cymru between 1966 and 1968, Phil Williams has a definite view. He argues that 1966, gaining its first-ever MP, was not in fact the turning point for the party. He says that if he had to choose such an occasion, it would be the General Election of 1959, when Plaid contested more than half the seats in Wales, therefore becoming more of a political party than a pressure group. In his book, *Voice from the Valleys*, a title which in itself is a statement, he says:

> *Caerfyrddin was not the turning point; it was instead the first real product of a turning point that had already occurred. Between 1959 and 1966, Plaid had been totally transformed into a political party.*[102]

How Gwynfor Evans could have benefited from such hindsight in the wake of the 1959 General Election. This was the exact period that Rhys Evans refers to as a civil war within Plaid. One of Gwynfor's inner circle, D. J. Williams, says that failure in 1959 was a blow from which he wouldn't easily recover. It led to Plaid questioning its own direction. It would lean more to the left. Rhys Evans:

> *With Labour now powerless, Gwynfor concluded that devolution would be 'more attractive' and that it would be Plaid Cymru's task henceforth, to turn Socialists into Welsh Home Rulers. By meeting these Labour supporters 'personally and in groups', Gwynfor was sure that Plaid Cymru could steer a rather different political course from the one his Party had*

---

102. Phil Williams: *Voice from the Valleys*. Aberystwyth: Plaid Cymru, 1981, p. 69.

taken between 1955 and 1959. Hope, he told D. J. Williams, 'still sprang eternal' under his 'wounded breast'.[103]

Phil Williams could look back at this period in a different way to how Gwynfor saw it.

Following Plaid's achievement in 1967, Phil Williams developed his argument further:

The Rhondda by-election was—in its way—even more sensational than the result in Caerfyrddin. The political commentators had explained away the result in Caerfyrddin. It was a Welsh-speaking rural constituency; Gwynfor had an enormous personal vote; it had never really been a safe Labour seat... The Rhondda was an even larger swing to Plaid Cymru, was English-speaking and industrial... the Rhondda was the citadel of the Labour Party.[104]

These were troubling times for Labour. In three successive years, '66, '67 and '68, they had suffered a defeat and two real scares. It was a serious triple whammy! Andrew Edwards, in his book *Labour's Crisis: Plaid Cymru, the Conservatives and the Decline of the Labour Party in North West Wales 1960-1974*, says this of the period:

Plaid Cymru, while still retaining the energy of a protest movement, had, by the end of the decade, developed realistic political aims, a credible economic policy and a robust local organisation. Emerging figures such as Dafydd Wigley and Dafydd Elis Thomas represented a new realism... In some senses, the 1960s marked Plaid Cymru's coming of age as a political party. The work of its general secretary, Emrys Roberts, contributed to modernisation at a national (Welsh) level, while the emergence of the radical Cymdeithas yr Iaith Gymraeg (The Welsh Language Society) allowed Plaid to focus on less controversial and more politically inclusive issues than the Welsh language. At a local level—in contrast to the Labour

---

103. Rhys Evans: *Gwynfor Evans: Portrait of a Patriot*. Tal-y-bont, Ceredigion: Y Lolfa, 2008, p. 198.
104. Phil Williams, ibid., p. 73.

Party—Plaid was vigorous. The party strengthened its branch structure, developed a more active social calendar and focused upon the recruitment of the young, while the adoption nationally of a range of populist, social- istic policies allowed the party to challenge Labour on its own ideological ground. This is not to mention, of course, the impact of Gwynfor Evans' spectacular election victory at Carmarthen in 1966. Considered together, these developments suggested that by the end of the 1960s, Plaid Cymru was breaking out of the culturally exclusive mould within which it had been confined since its foundation in the 1920s.[105]

That's the situation I faced when my campaigning began in the Car- marthen constituency. Whilst being aware of this, I also knew that my real opponent was Gwynfor Evans, of course, the sitting MP in the con- stituency. I wasted no time in attacking him either. On 17 November 1967, I responded to comments made by him about his vision of an independent Wales. He had said that there were definite signs that the next Westminster Parliament would contain a significant number of nationalist MPs from Wales and Scotland. I couldn't see that happening. However, I didn't only attack his viewpoint; I gave my view of what I thought Wales needed, which can be summed up by this quote from a speech I gave at the end of 1967:

... my personal belief was that the Welsh people need more control over their affairs and should have an Elected Council and greater decentrali- sation of authority.

What Gwynfor saw confidently happening didn't happen, of course. That was my first introduction to the over-promising and the hyperbole that characterised his politics.

I did not foresee one aspect of Labour feeling the full effect of the Plaid ascendancy, however. It gave me a battle I was not prepared for. In what I thought was a separate issue, not wholly linked with any attempt

105.Andrew Edwards: *Labour's Crisis: Plaid Cymru, the Conservatives and the Decline of the Labour Party in North West Wales 1960-1974*. Cardiff: University of Wales Press, 2011.

to respond to the Plaid attack, I made my case for a clear identity for the Labour Party in Wales. The *Carmarthen Times* headline *'Gwynoro's Broadside'* sums it up well. They were reporting on a speech I had given in Llandeilo on Friday 1 December 1967, in which I called for the establishment of a Wales Labour Party, separate from the UK Labour Party. The comments caused quite a stir and a lot of media attention. This quote sums up what I said:

> *In accordance with my aim of voicing the claims of Wales within the Labour movement, I believe it is important that an official Welsh Labour Party is established.*

That was it, simply put. I suggested four benefits of establishing a Welsh Labour Party. First, it would enable the Labour Movement to hold an annual conference, where it would be possible to discuss matters relevant only to Wales. Second, it would then be possible to pass motions relating to Wales and third, such activity would promote socialism throughout Wales, leading to the last point of giving Wales a voice in the Labour Movement throughout Britain.

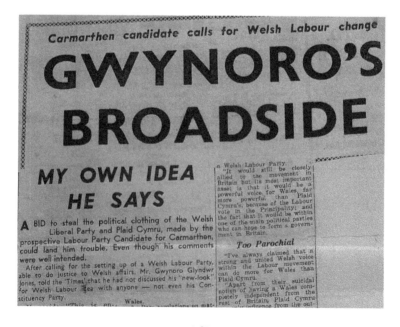

Carmarthen candidate calls for Welsh Labour change

GWYNORO'S BROADSIDE

MY OWN IDEA HE SAYS

A BID to steal the political clothing of the Welsh Liberal Party and Plaid Cymru, made by the prospective Labour Party Candidate for Carmarthen, could land him trouble. Even though his comments were well intended.

After calling for the setting up of a Welsh Labour Party, Mr. Gwynoro Glyndwr Jones, told the 'Times' that he had not discussed his "new-look" for Welsh Labour idea with anyone — not even his Constituency Party.

"This is an... Wales.

a Welsh Labour Party.

"It would still be closely allied to the movement in Britain but its most important asset is that it would be a powerful voice for Wales, far more powerful than Plaid Cymru's, because of the Labour vote in the Principality; and the fact that it would be within one of the main political parties who can hope to form a government in Britain.

Too Parochial

"I've always claimed that a strong and united Welsh voice within the Labour movement can do more for Wales than Plaid Cymru.

"Apart from their suicidal notion of having a Wales completely independent from the rest of Britain, Plaid Cymru... dependence from the out-

The Labour Party had a regional office and organised an Annual Rally in Wales. But to me, that was far from enough. Labour in Wales needed its own voice. I made sure that my comments didn't mean that I wanted to see any form of schism within British Socialism, and that unity within that field was essential. My aim was to secure a clear, powerful voice for Wales in the broader Socialist world. This was the period when I first met Harold Wilson. He asked me to speak at one Annual Welsh Rally which was always held in Newtown.

Plaid Cymru were part of my argument. Establishing Welsh Labour, I argued, would secure a stronger voice for Wales than Plaid Cymru ever could, based on the strength of the Labour tradition and vote in Wales, and consequently the number of Welsh MPs in Westminster. The parties most likely to form a Government were the ones with the best hopes of securing Welsh interests. Plaid Cymru had no hope of doing so. This is another quote from the speech:

Apart from the suicidal notion of having a Wales completely independent from the rest of Britain, Plaid Cymru can only influence from the outside, and their interests are too parochial.

But I also had some comments to make about the Labour Party too. One journalist, from the *Carmarthen Times*, asked me if I knew anything about the structure of the Labour Party in Wales. This was my reply:

To be absolutely honest, I don't know, and I believe that very few people do. More should be done anyway to give Labour supporters in Wales a unified voice… Revising the system as well as the name is essential. We must look closely at the organisation, the officers and policy… At the moment, nobody knows what goes on in the Labour Party in Wales.

My speech ended by summarising the principle behind my comments, in the widest context possible:

The aims of the official Wales Labour Party would not be narrow nationalism, but it would aim at furthering the needs of Wales, remembering

that Socialism involves far wider horizons. I believe that the vast major-
ity of people in Wales are Socialist and have their country's interest at
heart. I again reiterate, nationhood is above politics.

And then came the response! The editorial in the *Carmarthen Times* was
clear enough. Referring to Prime Minister Harold Wilson, it says:

The statement he made last week is certainly not from the readings of
King Harold. And it is more than likely to upset others who view the
movement through rose-tinted spectacles... is this not what Plaid Cymru
are seeking? Is this not in keeping with the policy of Welsh Liberalism? A
rose by any other name, perhaps? The idea may sound fine, but Socialists
generally will sink it without trace. They will want nothing to do with
any schemes which even skim the surface of those already advanced by
other political organisations.

And of course, the Labour Party itself responded. The first to do so was
Emrys Jones, the Labour Party's organiser in Wales. He asked to see me
and made it clear that he wasn't happy at all with my comments. I reiterated that I didn't think that the Labour Party in Wales was obviously a
party that could safeguard the interests of Wales. For me, I said, it was a
regional party, not a national one. The interests of Wales were very close
to my heart. I was a nationalist by instinct, but I didn't think that it was
through Plaid Cymru that they could fulfil any nationalistic aspirations.
Gwynfor had become popular since 1966, of course he had. But it was
a small proportion of the Welsh population that knew much about him,
and he only had influence over a small proportion too. For me, it was
more possible to argue the Welsh cause within a party, which was bigger
than Plaid Cymru and had more MPs.

But I knew equally that not everyone in the Labour Party saw things
my way. Many, a significant number, were anti devolution of any kind. In
fact, they were anti-Wales and anti the language as well. It was going to be
a tough nut to crack. This would be especially true in the industrial areas
of south-east Wales, where there were up to 20 Labour MPs who stood
against devolution and all things Welsh. The two of the most vociferous

opponents were Neil Kinnock and Leo Abse. Further west, Swansea's Alan Williams was equally opposed to devolution. And of course, there was George. No one was more vocal and nastier in his opposition to devolution and almost everything Welsh than the former Speaker of the House of Commons and former Secretary of State for Wales, George Thomas. He was particularly nasty to those of us within the Labour Party who were pro-devolution, calling us crypto-nationalists and spreading rumours about us to discredit us within the party framework. I was told, later on in my political life, after becoming an MP, that he, George, had blackened my name with Harold Wilson in order to ensure that I would not have any junior ministerial post. According to George, I would be divisive because I was a nationalist. I was told this by Fred Peart, the Minister for Agriculture.

In saying what I had said, I had in effect struck a double blow. First, I had criticised the Labour Party for how it was run in Wales, and second, I had made observations that could be interpreted as nationalistic when Plaid Cymru was in the ascendancy. Little wonder then that dyed-in-the-wool Labour members thought that Plaid Cymru had corrupted me. I was called to Labour HQ in Transport House, London. I was to explain my comments. They asked me if the broader political climate had influenced me. Not at all, I said. But there was obvious concern that I was following the same course as the man I would fight against in the next General Election. Their questioning of me was obviously very nervous and suspicious. My reply was clear. Wake up! We are the Party of Wales. There's no need for Plaid Cymru. I wasn't disciplined officially, and I wasn't reprimanded. But I knew I was in the minority. Only about a tenth of the Labour Party in Wales saw things as I had outlined them. Amongst them, MPs such as Cledwyn Hughes, Goronwy Roberts, John Morris, Elystan Morgan, Tom Ellis, John Morris and Will Edwards were the leading lights. The first two were leading figures in the battle for a Parliament for Wales in 1956/57, along with Merthyr Tydfil MP S. O. Davies who presented the Bill.

All this happened at the end of 1967, only a few months after they chose me as a candidate for Carmarthen. I was convinced that this was the right thing to say. I still don't regret what I said in Llandeilo. In fact what I called for is what happened about 20 years later.

I made my comments at the beginning of an election campaign. It was an example of the battles to be fought in years to come. This is how the man who lost to Gwynfor Evans in Carmarthen in 1966, Gwilym Prys Davies summed up the campaign leading up to the 1970 General Election:

... campaigning in the by-election had very little to do with traditional nationalist issues, but instead was a battle between two different types of Welsh nationalism, one housed in the Labour Party and the other in Plaid Cymru.

For the record, Plaid Cymru themselves were silent on the whole content of my speech in Llandeilo.

I didn't relent in my attempts to reform the Labour Party in Wales. In 1968, following the third big blow, the Caerffili Election result, John Morris, MP for Aberavon and then Parliamentary Secretary to the Minister of Transport, summed up the situation in this way:

The nationalists had become a looming danger on the political horizon. New thinking was needed for making governmental Wales more democratic and accountable.[106]

I wrote a letter to the Carmarthenshire newspapers calling for a specific response from the Labour Party to the same events. The heading was 'What Labour Must Do'. I started by saying that as well as they had done, if Plaid Cymru had failed to win Caerffili with so many economic and political factors in their favour, then they had no hope of winning in a General Election there. I then offered a word of advice to the Labour Party. I called for definite clear and positive response, not resting on any laurels, in the belief that the voters would come back to us come election time.

... the Labour Party should implement the policy outlined in its Election Manifesto, that is, give control for health, agriculture and education in

---

106. John Morris: *Fifty Years in Politics and the Law.* Cardiff: University of Wales Press, 2013, p. 88.

Wales to the Welsh Office. Alongside this, there is a need for an Elected Council, thus ending the farce of numerous nominated committees. The Labour Party need not fear change, but rather provide the people of Wales with the ability to influence the system of government in relation to aspects of Welsh Affairs.

The end of the article is more emotive in its appeal. It clearly shows that my call for a Wales Labour Party came from a deep-seated awareness that I am a Welshman and one who loves his country.

Hence, as a Welshman within the Labour movement, we must start a dialogue with our fellow countrymen—especially the younger generation, so that the appeal to emotional patriotism poured on them, is countered or mixed with reason. What is needed is an open debate before it is too late—for Wales.

But as there was a debate within Labour about our perception and expression of Welshness, the same debate existed within Plaid Cymru. In a 1968 BBC programme called A Disunited Kingdom?, broadcast throughout the UK, the cause for nationalism in Wales, Scotland and Northern Ireland was debated at length. Presented by a young Robin Day, each nation explained the reason and vision for their nationalism. Welsh international rugby player Carwyn James argued Wales' case. He presented a seven-minute film outlining Welsh nationalism. They introduce him as

Carwyn James, former rugby international for Wales against Australia in 1958. Now a House Master at Llandovery College, Carmarthenshire, he's a man dedicated to the idea of a Wales governed by the Welsh. He wants dominion status for the Welsh nation.

Carwyn was a close confidante of Gwynfor Evans and there is no doubt that Carwyn's contribution to that programme was worked on by himself and Gwynfor. This was, after all, the closest Plaid Cymru would get at the time to a party political broadcast. In outlining the roots of Welsh nationalism, Carwyn says this on film:

General Election pamphlet, 1970

To be Welsh today is to be aware of an old vital tradition that has survived. It is also to feel a new sense of nationhood, which is at last finding full expression… The spirit of Wales is born in the mountain farmhouse, in the cottage by the brook, in the coal miner's home, and if it be not fostered, the Welsh nation will become merely derivative and second rate. The proud possessor of the oldest living language in Europe, the Welsh nation must guard her soul and then she has it within herself to make a contribution among the leaders of the world.

He says that he himself is more at home in the coal mining villages of East Carmarthenshire than in the more agricultural area of North Carmarthenshire. But he was a product of the traditional Welsh heritage he outlines in his film. The images are of rural farming Wales, and include a conversation between Carwyn and a sixth-generation descendant of Welsh hymn-writer, William Williams Pantycelyn, on the eponymous farm itself. Any economic argument that is made is made against this backdrop.

It is interesting to compare this vision of Welsh nationalism, that Plaid showed the rest of the UK, with the view that was outlined by another of its leading lights, Phil Williams. In his book, he says:

> *For many people, the emotional roots of nationalism can be found on a small farm in North Carmarthenshire, or on the shores of Llyn Tegid; for me, nationalism began in Cardiff Civic Center. Indeed the recognition of Cardiff as the official capital in 1955 came as a complete shock; it had never occurred to me that Cardiff was anything but the Capital of Wales.*[107]

For many, Plaid's emphasis on locating the spirit of Wales concentrated too much on the mountain farmhouse and not enough on the mining village or the Civic Centre.

---

107. Phil Williams: *Voice from the Valleys*. Aberystwyth: Plaid Cymru, 1981, p. 58.

10.

Enemies Within and Without

We certainly needed a dialogue. But there were cross words that were also loud and distracting from finding that clarity of dialogue. As Gwynfor Evans' time as MP continued, there were more and more comments and actions by him that drew both myself and other Labour MPs into strong disagreement with him. Equally, there were increasing critical noises coming from some other fellow Labour MPs, who were judging me and some of my colleagues, for our perceived stance on devolution. In my case, this significantly escalated after my speech in Llandeilo. No wonder the period immediately after Gwynfor's triumph in 1966 was the beginning of the most volatile period in Welsh politics.

Anti-Labour

As the new year of 1968 arrived, there was another move to debate a Parliament for Wales, this time put forward by the Liberal MP Emlyn Hooson. He put forward a Private Member's Bill in January 1968. Seven months later, Labour's Lord Ogmore proposed the same Parliament in the House of Lords. Both failed. Cledwyn Hughes' influence on these debates, in supporting them, was clear enough. But even though he was Secretary of State for Wales, he had two formidable opponents within the Cabinet, Richard Crossman and Tony Crosland. Crossman in particular, was not only strongly opposed to any devolving of power to Wales, he also had little regard for Cledwyn Hughes, as he showed in his diary entry for 30 November 1966. For example:

It made me furious that little Cledwyn wanted to publish his own White Paper on local government reform and even to legislate on it for Wales in this Parliament before our Royal Commission for Wales had reported—absolute nonsense.

A clear enough view and clear enough in his disparaging of a Cabinet colleague. In his own diaries, Cledwyn Hughes was equally clear.

He was naïve and shrewd in his own interest, clever yet lacking in judgment: he could bully yet cave in under attack... in a way, he is a sad figure, for he never achieved anything in spite of his considerable intellect.

It's easy to forget that such inter-personal factors more than play their part in political decisions too!

Unfortunately for Cledwyn Hughes, his two main foes on the Cabinet were friends of Harold Wilson. Cledwyn Hughes was replaced as Secretary of State for Wales after only two years in the job. George Thomas took over.

Cledwyn was a man of clear political vision, as he himself summed up succinctly enough:

Mae'n anghenreidiol i mi sefyll yn gadarn dros resymoldeb a Chymreictod fel yr wyf fi yn eu deall: fy nghefndir yw radicaliaeth anghydffurfiol—ac ni ellir newid hynny.

It is essential for me to stand firm for reasonableness and Welshness as I understand them: my background is radical nonconformism—and that can not be changed.

Others saw the full measure of his contribution, maybe best summed up by the front-page story on the *Liverpool Daily Post*:

He has received little credit for his efforts to advance the Welsh cause and had been belaboured for his inability to produce instant changes towards self-government. Little credit has been given to the man who has suffered a bed of nails in the last two years.

The famous and influential political columnist of the time, Andrew Roth, referred to George usurping Cledwyn in a *Manchester Evening News* column, some years later, on 19 November 1974:

Cledwyn Hughes could not help hating the idea of turning over Wales to George Thomas, a chirpy South Wales sparrow in Mr Wilson's palm.

Many claimed that's why he was only Secretary of State for Wales for two years. His successor George Thomas wasted no time in attacking his own, devolution-backing MPs as crypto-nationalists. He even accused the BBC of championing the nationalists' cause in Wales, and that light entertainment programmes were being used for propaganda. The battle lines were drawn.

In his published dissertation, *The Labour Party in Wales and the 1979 Referendum*, Hubert Gieschen summarises this move:

With devolution off the agenda in 1968, it seemed appropriate to replace the pro-devolutionist Cledwyn Hughes with an anti-devolutionist MP for Cardiff West, George Thomas, as Secretary of State for Wales. They moved Cledwyn Hughes to Secretary of State for Agriculture. While George Thomas always prided himself on his Welshness, he only Supported Welsh devolution temporarily for the sake of party unity.[108]

Gwynfor and Gwynoro

When 1968 began, I had still not met Gwynfor personally. Exchanges until then had been through the newspaper articles we exchanged, and the subsequent letters of our respective followers. I continued in that vein in the first month of that year. In an article on 5 January, in the *Carmarthen Times*, I went on the attack. The headline summed it up succinctly: *'Gwynfor and I are poles apart'*.

---

108. Hubert Gieschen: *The Labour Party in Wales and the 1979 Referendum*. Frankfurt: Haag and Herschen, 1999, p. 11.

Recently, letters have been directed at some of my latest comments in the Press and reference has been made to the fact that Plaid Cymru is not anti-Labour, but it seems peculiar to me that people are able to state this and yet feel unable to give public praise to the Labour Government's achievements in Wales.

Gwynfor is not one of those who made such claims that Plaid was not anti-Labour. He never ever gave such a reassurance. And to me, that's what counted. He was their only MP, after all. In the article, I list many things that Labour had achieved for Wales until that point. I mention various grants Wales had received, improvements to hospitals, amongst other things. I then turn back on Plaid Cymru:

Finally, an article appeared in the Carmarthen Times, stating that Gwynfor Evans and I appear to be almost on the same wavelength. May I state that this inferred that both of us want the best for Wales and for Carmarthenshire, then hence the reference is correct. But Plaid Cymru and I are poles apart on the best way to achieve this.

To have complete political separation, which would have economic consequences, is not the best way of attaining a better Wales. Those who do call for a Free Wales should have a look at the hard realities of economic life.

That was my stance, and it put clear waters between me and Gwynfor.

With such an article in mind, it's interesting to note a conversation I have had with Lord Elystan Morgan on more than one occasion since then. Elystan said that he had asked Gwynfor many times what he thought the Labour party had done for Wales. 'Nothing at all' was his reply every time. That is a very strange comment.

Later that same month, John Morris, MP for Aberavon, and a Parliamentary Secretary in the Ministry of Transport, said what he thought of the increasingly loud call for devolution. He wanted change, but:

Throughout my life, I have worked for the right kind of constitutional and administrative machinery for whatever the need is, but a separate parliament for Wales, with or without dominion status, does not of itself solve our problems.

Later on, that same year, referring to a speech by Enoch Powell, he makes a similar statement, elaborating a little:

He warns us if Wales and Scotland pulled out of the Union it would be on an all-or-nothing basis... the basis of our future prosperity is partnership not separation, but partnership based on a full recognition of the needs and aspirations of all partners.

In March 1968, Llanelli MP Jim Griffiths was speaking at a meeting in Maes yr Yrfa School, Cefneithin, Llanelli. These are three extracts from his speech.

A combination of socialism and nationalism provides the best way forward for my native land.

*The other day someone described me as a Nationalist with a small 'n'
and I accept that description if it means that I am proud of my country
without hating any other, of my language and culture.*

*In the 1966 by-election, Gwynfor Evans won by gathering the protest
vote against the difficulties which beset us, and his vote was made up of
a majority of electors who, whilst registering their protest, do not support
the policies of Plaid Cymru.*

Devolution was rapidly becoming a leading topic for the Labour Party
within Wales, at least in terms of defining its idea of devolution compared
to Plaid's. It had for years before that, of course, argued for increasing
devolved powers to Wales. He went further, calling for a democratically
elected Council for Wales:

*Such a Council with real authority and resources can do much more than
a second class mini-Parliament of the model of Ulster's Stormont.*

As we walked into the School Hall, having just been introduced to Jim
Griffiths, I turned to him and said, 'Jim, these are difficult times'. He
turned to me with the wisdom of experience and said, 'Gwynoro bach, I
remember difficult years!' No doubt he was referring to the locust years of
the 1920s. That put this young 25-year-old candidate in his place!

The voices calling for changes in and for Wales, Jim Griffiths, Cledwyn Hughes, John Morris, Elystan Morgan, myself and many others,
were continually moving the debate forward. And as we've said before,
this was often in the face of opposition within our own party. Cledwyn
Hughes refers to this opposition in the late Sixties:

*They would never admit it even to themselves, but they regard those who
spoke Welsh as fellow travelling Nationalists more often than not. They
forget that we have fought the Welsh Nationalists longer and harder than
they have, and that the Nationalists, in fact, made dramatic gains in two
seats, Rhondda West and Caerffili, where the members, Iori Thomas and*

Ness Edwards had been consistently hostile to progress in Welsh matters.[109]

Cledwyn is making a fair point there that the stance taken by Edwards and Thomas had not proved popular in their constituencies, which could not be regarded as being in the Welsh-speaking heartland of Plaid Cymru.

In summing-up the effects of '66, '67, '68 on Labour and Plaid, historian Martin Johnes, in *Wales Since 1939*, says:

> *Those votes owed much to dis-satisfaction with the Labour government, but the fact that large numbers of working-class voters were willing to turn to Plaid Cymru to make their protest was an indication that the sands were shifting, and that popular patriotism could become political. But among the masses, nationalism still had a long way to go.*[110]

As far as my belief was concerned, I made a clear distinction between self-government and separation at this time. In April 1968, I went on the offensive.

> *Wales depends on capital and industry from outside the Principality, and we are in no position to shout for separation. In order to attract industry to Wales, we must control growth in the Midlands and southeast of England... Then when we add to this that, since 1959, more has been spent in Wales than taken in taxes from Wales and that grants to persons, local authorities are greater per head than any other part of Britain... Separation will create problems in Wales not yet fully discussed.*

In that same article I quoted some relevant statistics:

> *A recent opinion poll showed that 40% of people in Wales wanted self-government, and six out of ten of them were not in favour of separating from the rest of the UK.*

---

109. D. Ben Rees: *Cofiant Cledwyn Hughes*. Tal-y-bont, Ceredigion: Y Lolfa, 2017, p. 125.
110. Martin Johnes: *Wales since 1939*. Manchester: Manchester University Press, 2013, p. 225.

Within my own Gwendraeth Valley, two labour MPs made similar statements. In a meeting of the Lower Gwendraeth Labour Party, in Bancffosfelen in December 1968, Ivor Davies said:

> *The Labour government had been confronted with such vital and extreme changes in both the economic and social life of the nation. Despite this, only the most extreme and biased person would deny the great advances that had been in recent years in industry and social security.... Wales was in no position to advocate economic separation. Wales was dependent on capital and industry from outside the Principality. It was useless pretending little would change economically if we severed our relationship with the rest of Britain. A separated Wales could not have much influence. The government is allocating 20% of the monies available under Local Employment Acts to Wales and an additional sum of £25m in investment grants to firms in Wales"*

In a meeting in Llandeilo, in May 1969, Will Edwards said:

> *The Welsh dairy farmer of Carmarthen entirely depends on the centralised control of a collective milk market and a Milk Marketing Board. How could a separatist Wales deal with this sort of situation? All the military establishments in Wales would be closed down because their role could not possibly fit in with any military policy which a Welsh Stat would have. So, what kind of society is Gwynfor Evans crusading for in Wales?*
>
> *He either does not know or does not care about the direction in which he is channelling the national fervour in Wales. His whole concern is to sink the British ship of state in order to grab a small boat for himself and a few of his colleagues...... It will be a boat without the means to sustain its passengers.*

And in his first Party speech after becoming Secretary of State for Wales, George Thomas said this in a meeting in Cefneithin:

> *Wales has never had a better friend at No 10. Since Labour has come to power more was being spent on roads, housing, education, health and*

Mr. Wilson: 'The best friend of Wales'

MINISTER HITS OUT AT 'CHARACTER ASSASSINATION'

200 PEOPLE attended a public meeting at Maes-yr-yrfa school, Cefneithin, where the Secretary of State for Wales, the Rt. Hon. George Thomas, made his first Party speech following his new appointment to Cabinet rank.

At the outset of his speech, Mr. Thomas referred to the constant attack on the Prime Minister in the daily press which, he said, was nothing short of character assassination.

The Secretary of State stated that "Wales has never had a better friend at No. 10," and he used as the basis of this contention that since Labour had come into power more was being spent on roads, housing, education, health and welfare, hospitals, and ports in Wales than ever before.

Mr. Thomas said that a re.............

BLATANT UNTRUTH

Mr. Gwynoro Jones also referred to the constant attack on the Prime Minister which was disgusting.

"To state that the Labour Government has broken all its promises is a blatant untruth," he said.

From Leasehold Reform to the Rent Act and Rate Rebates; from vast increases in Social Service expenditure to expenditure on education; the Government was meeting its promises.

"Obviously there the things left undone, and there are problems to be solved, but let us not give the impression that these have only appeared since 1964.

"The Welsh people had realised the danger of separation to the Welsh economy. While Labour lost many seats

welfare, hospitals and ports in Wales than ever before…. A record number of houses were built in 1967 in Wales, expenditure on roads had increased by over 30%, capital expenditure on hospitals had increased by over 70%'…. The Government policy of moving Government offices to Wales, such as the Royal Mint to Llantrisant, Motor Taxation to Morriston and the Inland Revenue to Cardiff would involve 11,000 new jobs'

Such a stance was not, contrary to popular perception, far removed from Plaid Cymru's. They did not use the word independence themselves, and neither did they do so throughout the following decade. The focus was very much on self-government. The 'I' word wasn't mentioned.

Westminster moves

The initial response within the government—to the broader situation not so much my letter!—was to concentrate on more administrative issues to do with devolution as opposed to moving any government functions to Wales. But there were many of us in the party who called for more, many of them MPs as well.

The Home Secretary, Jim Callaghan, in the summer of 1968, proposed the idea of a constitutional commission. His aim was to see if any changes were needed to the functions of central government in different parts of the UK. By October, he reiterated that he thought that such a commission was the only answer as the government hadn't offered any credible alternative to the situation.

John Morris took the unusual step, in June 1968, of writing a memorandum to Prime Minister Harold Wilson, in order to give his thoughts on the Draft Conclusions of the Ministerial Committee on Devolution. Having reassured the Prime Minister that he had studied the document, he introduces his argument with this summary:

> *This is a sad document, not only for its conclusions, but worse, for its sheer argument on and lack of philosophy. There appear to be colleagues who do not wish to do anything, and others, who, when specific proposals are put, albeit on functions or decentralisation of administrative centres, if their own departments are affected, seek to reject them.*

Later that summer, in August, John Morris and Elystan Morgan discussed this constitutional situation while their families were on holiday together in Cornwall. John Morris recounts the story:

> *... he told me, coming up from the beach one day, that he believed the answer to our problems was a Royal Commission for Wales and Scotland. It could consider whether any major changes were desirable for the fundamental reform of government. I immediately warmed to the suggestion, which was completely new to me.*[111]

In his autobiography, *Atgofion Oes Elystan*, Lord Elystan Morgan recalls two meetings that have a significant role to play in this debate. He does not claim so himself; he never would. All he says is that in leaving both meetings, he felt satisfied that he had been true to his convictions. The first meeting was with Prime Minister Harold Wilson when Elystan had just been appointed as a Minister in the Home Office. He says that the meeting began with him reiterating his belief in the need for Home Rule

---

111. John Morris: *Fifty Years in Politics and the Law*. Cardiff: University of Wales Press, 2013, p. 88.

and Dominion Status for Wales. He then quotes from some of that conversation:

> *Even though there is clearly a very considerable feeling of disaffection*
> *towards the Government, I don't pretend to you that there is a pulsating*
> *power in Wales at the moment that represents a deep desire for a Parlia-*
> *ment—I only wish there was. Plaid are being opportunistic and, like the*
> *Liberals in England, are exploiting a political vacuum.*[112]

Wilson's response was to say that he realised that, but then asked Elystan
Morgan what he should do in such a situation. The response outlined
that the feelings of the people of Wales were far from insubstantial, even
if there wasn't so much emphasis on a parliament for Wales. He emphasised that there was a layer of sincere patriotism on many levels in Wales
that it would be foolish for the Labour Party to ignore.

> *If you give them the impression that you are totally intransigent, then*
> *that power may well rise against you. How exactly you do it is a matter*
> *for you—I can suggest two or three things, but I believe that a credible*
> *elected body for Wales is an absolute must.*[113]

The second meeting was with Jim Callaghan, the Home Secretary. Elystan Morgan says that he was unaware that they had discussed the idea
of a Commission prior to his meeting with Callaghan. He says that he
outlined his arguments one by one and that Callaghan was particularly
knowledgeable in his replies. The discussion had been ongoing for some
time before Callaghan asked Elystan Morgan:

> *Well, what would you like to see?*
> *Policy A would be to block everything forever and pretend that Welsh*
> *nationhood does not exist—not my favoured option and one I believe*
> *that would be disastrous for the Labour Party, and unworthy of it, in*

---

112. Elystan Morgan; Huw L. Williams: *Elystan: Atgofion Oes.* Tal-y-bont, Ceredigion:
   Y Lolfa, 2012, p. 177.
113. Ibid., p. 177.

light of its history.

Yes, and your next point?

The other extreme, of course, would be to plan immediately for a Welsh Home Rule Parliament, if not for Welsh independence. A middle course would be to show imagination, progressiveness and understanding of Welsh nationhood that would carry with you the majority of opinion in Wales and Scotland, and possibly in England as well. That would be the course that I would counsel.

Oh, and how do you achieve that?

By setting up a Royal Commission to study that question.[114]

By the October of that year, Callaghan had said that he saw no alternative to establishing a commission, as the government had not come up with an alternative and that the administrative and parliamentary devolution that had been discussed were insufficient by themselves. In his memoirs, John Morris reflects on this move:

In my view, it could act as a catalyst for fundamental constitutional changes for Wales that we could hardly dream of. If the evidence went well, there could be immense changes. Looking back onto my interest and discussions in the early 1950s, we were now in a new field—or perhaps better expressed, on a 'new planet'... Here, to me, was a practical way forward with immense potential.[115]

He is clearly enthused by such a prospect. Not all were, of course. As we have seen, Morris himself had commented on the effect of Plaid Cymru gains between 1966 and 1968, calling them a 'looming danger'. Critics of a constitutional commission saw that calling for such an enquiry was a reaction to nationalist success. But Morris rejected this:

So it might appear. To me, it was different.[116]

---

114. Ibid., pp. 177-178.
115. John Morris, ibid., p. 89.
116. Ibid.

Gwynfor's biggest enemies are his own friends

27-1-68

HOME RULE SOLVES NO PROBLEMS

KEY to the future prosperity of Wales, Scotland and the North of England was the control of industrial growth in the Midlands and the South East.

Mr. John Morris, M.P. for Averavon, Parliamentary Secretary to the Ministry of Transport, said this to members of the Labour Party in Carmarthenshire at the weekend.

Speaking at the annual dinner of the Upper Gwendraeth Labour Party at the Smiths Arms, Voelgastell, last Saturday, Mr. Morris said the separation of Wales would not solve Welsh problems.

"Throughout my life I have worked for the right kind of constitutional and administrative machinery for whatever the need is, but a separate Parliament in Wales, with or without dominion status, does not of itself solve our problems," said Mr. Morris.

British problem. As we are slowly being carried nearer to the main stream of Europe, our challenge is to ensure that there is prosperity in Wales at the same time as in the Midlands.

"We share this need with Scotland and the North of England."

STRONG AFFINITY

Commenting on the failure of Mr. Gwynfor Evans, Plaid Cymru M.P. for Carmarthen, to get into Vietnam, Mr. Morris referred to the "fantastic statement" from the Welsh Nationalist Leader that there was a strong affinity between the N.L.F (National Liberation Front) of Vietnam and Plaid Cymru. This had been said because both were fighting for self-government.

In view of this statement, it was an opportune time to examine what underlay Plaid Cymru's current objectives, said Mr. Morris who added, "Re-

Socialists as Mr. Goronwy Roberts and Mr. George Thomas, Ministers at the Foreign and Commonwealth Offices, there is no monopoly in this.

"And, it was Mr. Harold Davies, a Welshman with a lifetime's experience of the Far East, who last got into Vietnam."

Mr. Morris said the theory dominating the activities of the Nationalists, was that there was a conspiracy threatening the need to separate Wales.

He said: "Every Welsh Labour leader is believed to be conspiring against Wales's interests. Some pretty extravagant things have been implied from time to time.

INTOLERABLE

"The bomb outrages and threats that have taken place over the last few years have been said to be the work of the enemies of the nationalist party —the Government somehow or other have some responsibility. In any adult society are we really to believe this?

"It is intolerable in a peace loving country that there should be a pattern of lawlessness and a condonation of it by those who should know better. And, I am sure that on reflection the nationalist leader would prefer to consider that he was mistaken in suggesting affinity between his party and the N.L.F.

the other measures."

Mr. Jones also expressed the hope that the cuts would not have too adverse an effect on the roads programme in Wales. He added: "To attract industry to Wales we must have strong lines of communication."

JANICE SEES THE WORLD

When Miss Janice Williams of Tyllwyd, Llangendeirne, says that she has seen a bit of the world, she is being modest.

Actually Janice has covered a large slice. More perhaps in a short space of time than many would in a lifetime.

It was in April, 1966, that Janice waved farewell to her friends in the tiny Carmarthenshire village and sailed out from Southampton on the S.S. Franconia, arriving eight days later at Montreal.

During her stay in Canada she was employed at Expo '67 as a secretary.

This, of course, was exciting enough but when her duties had ended, she and a friend decided to travel for three months before coming back to the comparative tranquility of Wales.

In Canada she saw the Niagara Falls, the Prairies, Rocky Mountains and other places of interest. From there she boarded the S.S. Cleveland and globe-trotted to places such as San Francisco, Japan and Hong Kong.

By air she went to Calcutta from where she travelled over

John Morris joins the press attack.

Prime Minister Harold Wilson announced the forming of the Commission in October 1968, led by Lord Crowther. He died soon after, and Lord Kilbrandon took his place.

This is when the devolution issue became an active part of my political life. It landed on my plate with a vengeance when I was asked to chair a working party to prepare the Labour Party's evidence to the Kilbrandon Commission. It was also the time I met up with the key people in the party in London—Sir Harry Nicholas, Gwyn Morgan, Ron Hayward and Margaret Jackson (later Beckett).

We were a team of seven and we worked exceptionally diligently for months. It was an interesting group—Paul Flynn, Alun Michael, the lecturer and broadcaster Barry Jones. Bruce George, who at the time was a farmer near Monmouth and eventually became a West Midlands MP, Wyn Thomas much later of Swansea Sound fame and Gareth Howell who was the son of Lyn Howell of the Wales Tourist Board.

189

There were monthly reports to the Welsh Executive and a few meetings with the Welsh Labour group of MPs. Most of them were heated discussions and I remember George Thomas and the South Wales Valley MPs getting very animated and hostile. The reality was that the party in Wales just did not wish to go down this road. But there were good allies on the executive, Jack Brooks being one, and since he was Callaghan's agent, I got the sense of what the then Labour government was expecting from our evidence. However, the records will show that the group recommended an all-Wales body much stronger than the actual evidence presented to the Kilbrandon Commission and included in its report when it was published in October 1973.

The group was in favour of a legislative body, but opposition was strong in both the Welsh Labour executive and the Welsh Labour Group of MPs. The final report *Reform of the Machinery of Government* was presented to the Welsh Executive and MPs in August 1969.

The general principle was that those powers residing in the Welsh Office at the time and those of Welsh departments within other ministries should become the responsibility of an elected Welsh Council, which would have 72 members for a fixed term of 4 years.

They also proposed shared responsibility between the Council and Westminster—on economic planning and industrial development, social security, water resources and agriculture, for example. It was suggested that a Joint Committee should be established with Westminster on future devolution operations.

While Prime Minister Harold Wilson was on his holidays in 1969, in his favourite Scilly Isles, he received a letter from George Thomas, who wanted to outline his thoughts on increased powers for Wales. As John Morris says:

George was seeking to exploit what was understood to be his special relationship with the Prime Minister. He certainly believed that he had such a relationship.[117]

---

117. Ibid., p. 90.

George Thomas called for an elected, or partly elected, Welsh Council, with members being paid.

> *The functions of the Welsh Council could be partly executive and partly advisory. The following responsibilities are amongst those that could be administered by the council, namely: the Health services in Wales, the Welsh Arts Council, the Welsh Committee of the Forestry Commission, The Welsh Committee of the Countryside Commission, the Welsh Joint Education Committee, the present advisory responsibilities of the current nominated Welsh Council, the Welsh Committee of the Water Resources Board, the Central Training Council (Welsh Committee), the Youth Employment Council (Welsh Committee).*

He ends his letter to the Prime Minister calling for administrative devolution, not parliamentary devolution.

With Gwynfor Evans in Westminster by now, he was, of course, able to have discussions with Ministers and MPs he otherwise wouldn't have been able to have. There's a record of meetings he had in 1968 in Plaid Cymru's Executive Committee's minutes. They were meeting he had with the Conservative Party. He had several meetings with Willie Whitelaw, the Tory Chief Whip, and Keith Joseph, who, in the previous government, was Minister for Housing and Local Government. A copy of the memo written to summarise one of the meetings between Gwynfor and Willie Whitelaw is included with Plaid's minutes and marked Completely Confidential.

> *Three significant points have emerged from the Evans/Whitelaw meeting.*
>
> a. *Whitelaw states his opinion that Wales and Scotland are nations in a sense that England is not.*
> b. *Gwynfor Evans emphasised that it is essential for the London Government to manifest some response to political and constitutional nationalist activity if the conclusion that Westminster will only respond to unconstitutional or violent action is to be avoided. The failure of Westminster to respond to political and constitutional pressure in the case of Tryweryn—and much earlier, the failure to*

> respond to constitutional demands by Irish nationalists in 1912 *(which would not have led to the violence of 1916/22) was discussed. Whitelaw conceded that authority must respond to political pressure as well as to violence.*
>
> c.   *Whitelaw did not see the English consenting to Plaid Cymru's demands in toto, although he conceded the reasonableness of our British Common Market Policy. Gwynfor Evans related how he found MPs on both sides of the House accepting that if the people of Wales wanted full self-government, then they should be given it. Granted that Plaid Cymru would accept nothing less than its ultimate goal, Whitelaw enquired whether an elected Council for Wales would be acceptable as an interim measure, Gwynfor Evans said that the opportunity for such a development had been lost by the Labour Government and nothing short of a Parliament would now be acceptable (as a 'step in the right direction') A discussion followed on the nature of such a Parliament.*

The memo confirms that a meeting with Mr Heath, party leader Edward Heath, is in the offing. The minutes end in this way:

> *Conclusion: Mr Gwynfor Evans is of the opinion that the Tories are now willing to think seriously in terms of a Welsh Parliament.*

This was when the Tories were still saying they were opposed to a Secretary of State for Wales. It's another example of Gwynfor's dreaming— that's the only way he could have gone from the discussions outlined in the memo to concluding that the Tories were now thinking of a Parliament for Wales.

Vietnam and some bombs back home

The Vietnam War was evidently one of the main world news stories. Officially, it was a war between Communist North Vietnam and non-Communist South Vietnam. The USA, fearing the spread of Communism, ploughed money and arms into South Vietnam, to help the fight against the north. Up to a quarter of a million South Vietnamese lost their lives, with up to 60,000 USA soldiers killed or missing in action. Gwynfor Evans decided that he wanted to play his own part in the almost world-wide protest against the USA's involvement in a war that wasn't theirs. He thought that the voice of the Welsh people should be added to that opposition, and in doing so, add support to the innocent people of Vietnam who were casualties of that war. That was admirable enough a sentiment, but the way he expressed it caused much consternation. He set out on a trip to Vietnam as part of a peace delegation, in their midst, Welshman Emrys Hughes, a left-wing MP for a Scottish constituency. His own party weren't united behind him in his decision to go on the journey. Many naturally feared for his safety. On a more ideological issue, those on the right-wing of the party feared that the visit would align Plaid Cymru with Communist supporters. For me, in the Carmarthen constituency, my thought was that such a gesture was underlining the increasing claim that Gwynfor saw himself as the Member for Wales, that he felt the need to champion Welsh issues above those of concern to his constituency.

Despite the opposition, Gwynfor left the UK on 3 January 1968. He landed in Phnom Penh, the capital of Cambodia. The plan was to get visas there to go into Vietnam itself, but the visas were refused. They never arrived in Vietnam. While they were abroad, chapels back in Wales would pray for his safety in war-torn Vietnam, without ever realising that he never got there.

This visit gave me a new opportunity to attack Gwynfor, especially as he then made speeches about Vietnam, including in Westminster. Two comments of his annoyed me immensely. First, he said that the Vietnam War was the fault of the Americans. That was said in one of his House of Commons' speeches. Second, he then compared Plaid Cymru to the National Liberation Front of South Vietnam. To me, both comments were bonkers.

In December 1967, before Gwynfor went to Cambodia, I replied to a letter in the *Carmarthen Journal*, asking me for my views on the Vietnam War. I began my reply by saying that I was strongly opposed to what was happening in that part of the world and that it was a tragedy that so many innocent people were being killed. I then said that neither side was likely to win, and any talk of victory was nothing more than empty words. I was also critical of America's role;

> *America has lost the aim stated by the late President Kennedy when he said in 1963, "In the final analysis it is their war".*

I emphasised that blame lay at the feet of both sides of the war. In referring to wider support given to both sides, I then said:

> *But having expressed my opposition to the war and a condemnation of the extension of North Vietnamese cities, let me hasten to add that both sides are at fault. Let those people who march and demonstrate outside the Russian and Chinese Embassies, both of which supply North Vietnam with weapons and technical aid for the continuation of the war.... It is useful to remember that in December 1965 the Americans stopped bombing for 36 days in the hope there would be some response from North Vietnam, but this never materialised.*

Many joined in the criticism of Gwynfor for his stance. John Morris, for example:

> *I am sure that on reflection the nationalist leader would prefer to consider that he was mistaken in suggesting affinity between his party and the N. L. F. which has been involved in a great deal of sheer terrorism.*

Gwynfor was clearly out of his depth. He was also given a rap on the knuckles by his own Party. In fact, the Regional Committee of Plaid Cymru issued him with an official reprimand. That same reprimand included another concern felt by the Party; they felt that he was out of his constituency too often and that such wider travel needed to be curtailed as the General Election drew closer.

I was also aware, on that point, that Gwynfor's voting record in the House of Commons was appalling. In his first stint as MP, '66-'70, there were 955 votes in Westminster. Gwynfor only took part in 155.

Temple of no peace

Another area of conflict between Gwynfor and myself was on the use of violence by a minority of more radical Welsh Nationalists. Throughout the Sixties, there had been a steady increase in using violence in the name of the nationalist cause, but not directly in the name of Plaid Cymru, it must be said. The issue with them was their response to it.

The fire at the Bombing School on the Llŷn Peninsula in the Thirties was the first incident of direct action in the name of Welsh nationalism, in recent times at least. The three perpetrators were active in Plaid Cymru, one being one of its founders and first President. Subsequent bombing attacks, in the Fifties and Sixties, were not in the name of Plaid but the differentiation between the bombers and Plaid was lost under the umbrella of nationalism. How Plaid was to respond to the bombs and other direct-action protests was an ongoing confrontation, both within Plaid itself, and between Plaid and Labour in particular.

Before looking at that confrontation, an indication as to the extent of the campaigns that used varying degrees of violent action. The Tryweryn protest saw the first bombings of the Sixties, when there were two attacks on the building works at the site of the dam. That was in 1963. Then there was an attack on the reservoir in Clywedog, in 1966. The following year saw the beginning of bombing attacks on buildings, especially as the Investiture of the Prince of Wales drew closer. In addition, civil disobedience and direct action that didn't involve bombs also became part of the nationalist fight. 1965 saw a campaign to refuse to pay road tax, leading to the first imprisonment of a Cymdeithas yr Iaith member. Then came the campaign to either remove or paint over the English-only road signs; for example, they defaced over 100 road signs in Ceredigion in one week during February 1969. There was also a campaign to attack television masts in the name of calling for a Welsh language TV channel.

They did none of this in the name of Plaid Cymru. But, as the causes championed by the more violent action were causes they believed in, inevitably, Plaid were tarred with the same brush, or at least called upon for a reaction to the direct action.

Gwynfor was repeatedly called upon to denounce the use of violence in the name of nationalism. He refused to do so for a very long time, as I referred to in another newspaper article:

> *An instance of this was the reported interview in The Times national newspaper in July 1966, by the President of the Nationalist Party, Mr Gwynfor Evans—the day after the Carmarthen by-election. In this interview, Mr Evans was asked if he thought the extremists would stop their activities since he had won Carmarthen.*
>
> *Surely, here was an instance for Mr Evans to express his view on bomb outrages. But no! The answer was, 'It is up to the government'. Mr Evans then stated that '... the government does not think anyone is serious until people blow up things or shoot others...' Maybe someone has taken these words literally?*

That might well not have been a direct endorsement of such action, but he did not distance himself from it either. In the same article, I draw attention to Plaid activist Richard Wynne's comments, when he said that history shows that constitutional methods alone are not enough to enforce any change. He went further when asked;

> *I ask is Mr Wynne still a member of the Nationalist party whose leaders speak a different language on the extremist issue?*

Richard Wynne was interviewed about the bombing on the *24 Hours* current affairs programme. He was asked, considering his stance on non-constitutional methods, if he too would plant a bomb. This was his reply:

> *Well, I am getting a bit old for that sort of thing: but I suppose that if I felt that it was my duty and that it was necessary, I would have to pull up my socks and do something.*

Saunders Lewis welcomed Richard Wynne's comments. He also made some comments himself in the Welsh language monthly magazine, Barn,

that said a stance that depended on constitutional change alone was
'… unrealistic dreaming, childish and impolite'! I responded:

> *Surely, if the Nationalist Party leaders' words are to mean anything,
> such an utterance, even though it came from the founding father of their
> movement, merits the question whether Mr Lewis is also still a member
> of the Nationalist party?*

I remember many an occasion when Elystan Morgan told me a story
relating to his time as a Minister in the Home Office. He told me of a
body being discovered in Foulness, on the Ministry of Defence land near
Shoeburyness. This man was involved in meeting boats that came to the
shore to offload drugs. Gwynfor held the Home Office responsible for
the man's death. But worse than that, remembering the close association

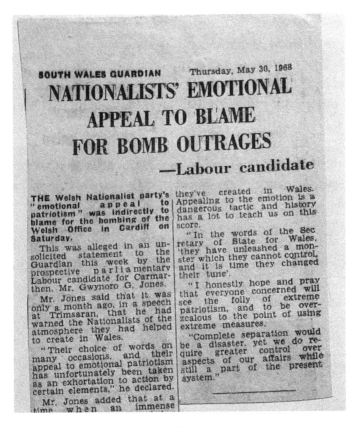

SOUTH WALES GUARDIAN   Thursday, May 30, 1968

NATIONALISTS' EMOTIONAL APPEAL TO BLAME FOR BOMB OUTRAGES
—Labour candidate

THE Welsh Nationalist party's "emotional appeal to patriotism" was indirectly to blame for the bombing of the Welsh Office in Cardiff on Saturday.

This was alleged in an unsolicited statement to the Guardian this week by the prospective parliamentary Labour candidate for Carmarthen, Mr. Gwynoro G. Jones.

Mr. Jones said that it was only a month ago, in a speech at Trimsaran, that he had warned the Nationalists of the atmosphere they had helped to create in Wales.

"Their choice of words on many occasions, and their appeal to emotional patriotism has unfortunately been taken as an exhortation to action by certain elements," he declared.

Mr. Jones added that at a time when an immense they've created in Wales. Appealing to the emotion is a dangerous tactic and history has a lot to teach us on this score.

"In the words of the Secretary of State for Wales, 'they have unleashed a monster which they cannot control, and it is time they changed their tune'.

"I honestly hope and pray that everyone concerned will see the folly of extreme patriotism, and to be overzealous to the point of using extreme measures.

"Complete separation would be a disaster, yet we do require greater control over aspects of our affairs while still a part of the present system."

between Gwynfor and Elystan when he was in Plaid Cymru, Gwynfor accused Elystan of being a part of a plot to keep the incident quiet. Plaid Cymru distributed hundreds of leaflets in Ceredigion, Elystan's constituency, accusing him of being part of this conspiracy. My response, on hearing this story, every time, was, 'what does this say about Gwynfor?'

A common tactic of Gwynfor, in response to any bombing incident, was to say that MI5 were responsible for them, in order to discredit nationalism. I responded to that comment, again in the Carmarthen press:

> *To seriously suggest that the government finances Secret Agents to blow up its own offices in order to do the maximum damage to Plaid Cymru is irresponsible behaviour from a public figure... only a month ago, in a speech in Trimsaran, I warned the Nationalist party of the atmosphere they have helped to create in Wales where extremism and stronger action could materialise. Their choice of words on many occasions and their appeal to emotional patriotism has unfortunately been taken as an exhortation to action by certain elements in Wales.*

I was surprised that the only thing about any bombings that concerned Plaid was the effect it had on them. They thought of no other implication or anyone:

> *They should have been aware in the first place of the damage, not to a party but to a nation; a smear on the character of a great and proud nation.*

Cledwyn Hughes also shared his view on Gwynfor's stance on the role of the secret services. This is part of a statement he released from the Welsh Office, where he was Secretary of State at the time:

> *Mr Evans and other members of his party have been making increasingly wild statements, but this is the worst of them all. That it is entirely unfounded is shown by the prosecution that followed earlier explosions.*

"ATMOSPHERE NATIONALISTS HAVE HELPED TO CREATE"

Produce evidence or withdraw allegation

Outrages must cease or lives will be lost, says Labour Candidate

TO seriously suggest that the Government finances Secret Agents to blow up its own offices in order to do the maximum damage to Plaid Cymru is irresponsible behaviour from a public figure, says Mr. Gwynoro Jones, prospective Labour candidate for Carmarthen.

That Secret Service agents could be responsible for the recent bomb attack on the Welsh Office at Cardiff was the suggestion made by M.P. Mr. Gwynfor Evans.

"Mr. Evans will have to produce evidence of his Secret Agents charge or withdraw his allegation," declares

made after the other outrages recently.

"Like other public figures I am astounded at this statement, and I can only reiterate what I said of his statement following the Temple of Peace incident. This is one of the most amazing utterances ever made by a Welsh M.P.

"To seriously think that the Government finances secret agents to blow up its own offices in

GWYNORO JONES

my knowledge—that the Government does not think anyone is serious until people blow up things or shoot others.

"Well someone has taken that statement seriously and has put it into

The bombings were first discussed in Parliament in 1968. On 27 May that year, a debate on the matter was opened by the then Secretary of State for Wales, George Thomas.

It is clear that these outrages have been committed for political reasons. The House and the people of Wales will roundly condemn this attempt at political terrorism.

Liberal MP Emlyn Hooson and Labour MP Ted Rowlands asked what was being done to find the bombers. They said that efforts up to that point had been insufficient. They also added that such violent protest was not supported by the majority of the people of Wales. In response to them, George Thomas said, as *Hansard* shows:

I do not know whether the hon. and learned Gentleman expects my right hon. Friend the Prime Minister to act as Sherlock Holmes [Laughter.] It is patently absurd to try to criticise the Government because the police have not found the criminals. Unfortunately, on the last occasion when a man was found guilty, and sentenced to 12 months' imprisonment, the hon. Member for Carmarthen (Mr. Gwynfor Evans) issued leaflets outside the court in which he said: "Although we do not agree with the action they have taken, we cannot condemn them." Any statement that encourages people to political violence is to be deplored.

Gwynfor was in Westminster that day, and he took part in the debate:

Is the Minister aware that Plaid Cymru has condemned without reservation these outrages? [HON. MEMBERS: "Oh."] It has done so consistently. Is he aware that it condemns his own verbal explosion over the weekend, in which he said that Plaid Cymru had wrought havoc in the life of Wales? Will he withdraw that and apologise? Is he prepared to face the fact that the havoc has been in the Labour Party in Wales?

George Thomas: The hon. Gentleman must have forgotten the leaflets he distributed at the time of the Tryweryn explosion. The leaflet he issued whilst the case was being tried said that those who blew up the transformer "... have merely tried to implement the wishes of the people of Wales..." I believe that statements of that sort have led on to these bomb outrages.

Gwynfor and Plaid took far too long to get to this point of condemning without reserve. This was in 1968. The sound of the first bombs had been heard years earlier at the beginning of the decade. I challenged him personally, many, many a time on this issue and never received an answer that was a clear denouncement of the bombing. When he made the above statement, I responded in a memorandum to George Thomas, called *Extremism in Wales*.

Whilst it is true that the Welsh Nationalist Party have condemned vio-
lence and have said that they disassociated themselves from the extremists,
the following points must be borne in mind:

1. *The seeds for discontent and the potential atmosphere for extreme*
   action to take place have already been planted before last year or so.
2. *Is Saunders Lewis—the founder member of the movement—still in*
   the Party? If so, all people who call for extreme action have not been
   ostracised from the party.

I also said that:

The continual emphasis of the Nationalists on the 'London' or 'English'
Government does create the wrong atmosphere. Such emotive words do
not help... The use of statements like 'freeing' Wales also lends itself to
various interpretations.

Jim Griffiths, amongst others, would say that Plaid's insistence on referring to those who opposed them as 'enemies of Wales' did their own cause
no good, let alone the cause of Wales itself.

The response of the people of Wales to this increased direct-action
activity was lukewarm, to say the least. In Wales Since 1939, Martin Johnes quotes a survey held in the Welsh-speaking heartland of Ceredigion,
which shows that only 19% of Welsh speakers and 9% of non-Welsh
thought that the pulling down of road signs was justified as protest.

So, it isn't as straightforward as saying that this was a boom time
for Plaid Cymru; nor is it fair to say that it was a time in which Labour
did nothing to advance the cause of Wales. Both parties continued their
championing of their particular visions for Wales. Both faced internal
battles as well as their battle against each other. And through it all, the
battle to win the hearts and minds of the voting Welsh public raged on.
All these battles came to a further head in 1969, the year of the Investiture of the Prince of Wales in Caernarfon Castle. That ceremony was
a battleground all of its own, and one which saw Gwynfor and I clash
further in the Carmarthen constituency.

11.

A Dual Carriageway and a Messiah

At the beginning of 1969, my focus was very much on the constituency. I wrote a few articles on local issues, keeping my arguments and my presence in the shop window. On a broader scale, I expressed my annoyance at Plaid Cymru's constant belittling of anything that the Labour Government had achieved in Wales. Under the heading '*Druids of Despair*', I wrote:

> *I am sure that the people of the Principality are fed up with the politically motivated opportunists who are not prepared to concede that the Government has done more for Wales than any previous administration.*

I believed that to be true at the time and I still believe it now, even though my relationship with the Labour Party has completely changed. Wales, in those years, received a lot of attention from Labour Ministers, including Harold Wilson as Prime Minister. George Thomas was correct in describing Wilson as Wales' best friend. So many improvements were made in Wales under his guidance, and it seemed churlish for anyone to suggest otherwise because they were blinkered by their own ideology.

The dual carriageway

My first major step at the start of 1969 was to write a report on every aspect of life in Carmarthenshire. This twelve-page report involved looking at the economy, health, transport, agriculture, tourism, schools, etc.

My aim was to see how the situation in each individual sector affected the collective life of Carmarthenshire. This was me in my element, doing market research, which was my field. The first section highlights the four main problems in the area—the road infrastructure, tourism, agriculture and jobs. I suggested the building of small industrial units to offset any job losses in the coal industry, for example. Agriculture was an obvious need in such a rural constituency, as I wrote in another article in the *Carmarthen Times* in February 1969.

> *Coming from an agricultural background with many relatives closely connected with farming, I am becoming increasingly aware of the fact that Agricultural policy will be one of the most important issues of the next election.*

I also addressed what effect Plaid's nationalism would have on agriculture:

> *I recently cited the case of the milk transport costs problem as an excellent example as to why Wales should not be independent from England. Welsh farmers are able to object vigorously to the claims of South East England, but a separate English government would automatically give preference to the South East.*

But the roads issue was one which grabbed the most headlines. Everyone of a certain age who tried to drive through Carmarthen in the Sixties and early Seventies remembers only too well how bad the town's traffic was. It could take an hour to drive from one end of this small town to the other. This now might appear to be a very local issue, as important as it was to the constituents, but it is another example of where Gwynfor and I clashed. For me, it is also another example of how Gwynfor postured as a champion of something he did very little about. When a dual carriageway was finally opened around the town, Gwynfor was referred to triumphantly as Gwynfor Dual Carriageway. This name has grown to be part of the Gwynfor Evans myth, with Plaid leaders very recently using that description. It is a good example of Gwynfor creating a name for himself for no apparent reason. He certainly didn't do any detailed work offering proposals to deal with the problem.

Following my report on the constituency, I wrote another report containing proposals for the road infrastructure of Carmarthen and the surrounding area. This was submitted to George Thomas in August 1969. He was then Secretary of State for Wales. I outlined a 10-year plan, costed at £30 million. It included suggested improvements not only in Carmarthen but also in Pontarddulais, St Clears, Llandeilo, Llandyfri and Ammanford. Later that same month, following a visit by Harold Wilson to Carmarthen, it was announced that they would build a Bailey bridge over the river to ease town-centre traffic.

On the streets of Carmarthen with the Prime Minister.

I gave my report on the economic situation in Carmarthenshire to Harold Wilson. I am certain that the constituency MP at that time had done nothing similar to that report, looking at life in his own area, as he had proposed no specific plan to deal with the road infrastructure specifically. Latching on to the dual carriageway issue was Gwynfor, seeing an opportunity to keep some hold on constituency matters, instead of his first love, which was to be the Member for Wales! This reminds me of an amusing but telling quote that one Carmarthen resident said in a story that Dennis Johnson of the *Guardian* wrote on the Carmarthenshire Constituency. Referring to Gwynfor, he says:

We didn't get ourselves a local MP. We got ourselves a bloody Messiah!

Unexpected allies

March 1969 saw a big change for me. I was called in to see the chair of Wales Gas, Mervyn Jones. People on my level in the company didn't get a call to see the chair that often, so I was a little apprehensive in going to see him, to say the least. It turned out that Jim Callaghan, a Cardiff MP and the Home Secretary in Wilson's Cabinet, had contacted him. Callaghan had asked Jones to release me from my job because he wanted me to work for the Labour Party in Wales, as a research and public relations officer. The reason for contacting Jones directly was for Callaghan to ask him to keep my job open, should I not win in the next General Election. Everything was agreed, and I left Welsh Gas.

My new role was a joy to me. Strangely, it was an important step towards what I'd called for on being chosen as a candidate, the need for a Wales Labour Party. Thankfully, Callaghan didn't pay any attention to some of my fellow Labour colleagues when they accused me of being far too influenced by the nationalists in calling for such a thing.

Right at the start of my new job, I saw that the Labour Party in Wales, in South Wales at least, was not in a good state. I decided to visit every Labour Party Executive Committee in every constituency in industrial South Wales. It was evident that the party had been sitting on its backside for far too long. At meeting after meeting, I would be lucky if six people attended, where there should have been 30. It was an eye-opener and a huge disillusionment for me. The memberships seemed apathetic and the

MPs were growing older. A new emphasis and a new image were needed, so we could promote the party.

Part of this process was visiting George Thomas fortnightly in order to gather information for articles and pamphlets. I drew up a list of 200 people in the 36 constituencies who could write to the newspapers, on a range of topics, whenever the need arose. I also started a new quarterly publication, *The Radical.* The party itself showed no interest at all at the time in doing any public work or attracting new members. As far as they were concerned, they didn't need to. 32 of the 36 constituencies in Wales were theirs. But that was a short-sighted approach, which Callaghan had identified.

Back in the Carmarthen constituency, I adopted the same approach of being very active throughout the area and being very visible. I visited every fair, jumble sale, dinner and carnival that I could! My campaign received an unexpected boost from an unexpected direction. It was announced that year that the Liberal Candidate for the General Election was to be Huw Thomas, *ITN News* main newscaster, the Huw Edwards of his day. In his very first speech, with about 300 people present, he laid into Plaid Cymru uncompromisingly, with Gwynfor firmly in his sights:

How dare this man say that he speaks for Wales; how dare he speak on behalf of all Welsh people.

That was the beginning of his direct confrontations with Gwynfor. It wasn't only me from then on. In that same speech he added:

'Who do these people think they are? You get the same symptoms wherever you have nationalism. You have only got to look back to Nazi Germany to see the same sort of thing. The Nazis were arrogant and intolerant of everybody... Violence is to be seen in Wales at the moment, and the violence we are experiencing is going to get worse. These violent people are Welsh Nationalists. They are not Liberals, Tories or Socialists.'

In light of such attacks, Gwynfor changed his usual tactic of letting other people answer for him. He replied directly to Huw Thomas in a *Car-*

The newscaster turned politician.

marthen Times article. Huw Thomas replied in a letter under the heading '*Slanging Match Continues*':

> *I am encouraged that my first attack on the Nationalists should have caused Mr Gwynfor Evans to break his usual practice of 'not replying in the press to vulgar abuse by opponents'. It must surely mean that those of my points reported in the Press must have been true and the truth hurts, otherwise, why did he not leave it to the intelligence and experience of Carmarthenshire people to determine whether I was 'violent and extreme' or whether, in fact, what I said was worth saying.*
>
> *It has bought forth another spate of his usual arrogant misstatements, and I will not allow a foreigner—a Barry man—to hoodwink my fellow county men and women.*

He says the only people who put loyalty to Wales first are those who chose to live in Wales. Where do I start to deal with this further example of arrogance?

Very few Welshmen, including myself, would choose to live in a grim industrial city like London. Even Mr Evans was heard to remark recently that he much prefers to spend his time in Carmarthenshire. Who can blame him for saying this? Nearly every Welshman, wherever he has had to find a job outside Wales, would willingly change lots with Mr Gwynfor Evans. A wonderfully big modern house with a lovely view of the Towy Valley and a prosperous pleasant market gardening business. If all Welshmen would have been in a position to do this—what heddwch!

Huw Thomas' comments, certainly the reference to arrogance, struck a chord with what had been my experience during my canvassing. I found it to be particularly so in the village where Gwynfor lived, Llangadog. I found very little support for him on the council estate there, where many houses had my posters in the window. These houses were homes to many of those who worked for Gwynfor in his market garden business. It's true to say that a significant number of villagers who worked for him told me to my face they had no respect for Gwynfor as an employer. It became clear around this time that the business was in financial difficulty again, as many workers told me. I did not feel it appropriate to use that fact as part of my campaigning.

Many others joined in the criticisms of Gwynfor's policies and approach. But perhaps the most memorable was the comment made by Merionethshire Labour MP, Wil Edwards. In a speech in Llandeilo, he referred to Gwynfor as '… the ageing Bernadette…', a reference to the young Irish politician and campaigner, Bernadette Devlin, who sympathised with the aims of the IRA.

CARMARTHEN TIMES, Friday, May 16th, 1969

M.P. Lashes Welsh Nationalists

Gwynfor: the ageing Bernadette

A PARTY WITHOUT ONE COMPETENT ADMINISTRATOR

Plaid are on the run

IN a scathing attack on Welsh Nationalism at Llandeilo last week, Mr. William Edwards, M.P. for Merioneth, referred to Mr. Gwynfor Evans as an "ageing Bernadette."

Said Mr. Edwards: "Gwynfor Evans has now made his position clear. He has come to bury the Government, not to praise it. It is quite obvious that his philosophy is destructive rather than constructive."

THE people of Wales have enough of emotional appeals that have no economic reality. And they have said so. Through the ballot box.

This is how prospective Labour candidate for Carmarthen, Mr. Gwynoro Jones, summed up the dismal Plaid Cymru results in the recent local elections.

Speaking at Llandeilo last week, Mr. Jones said: "I suppose that the Nationalists will start claiming that next year

12.

A Prince in Wales

The main event of 1969 was the Investiture of the Prince of Wales in Caernarfon Castle on 1 July. Having stated that one major feature of this era was the intensity of the political activity in the newspapers, it's remarkable to note that in Carmarthenshire at least, the Investiture was prominent by its absence in the newspapers. It didn't seem to exercise people greatly. There was plenty of talk on the roadside, but few letters in newspapers.

Politically, there's no denying that the Investiture was significantly advantageous to the Labour Party. The nationalist claim was that the Investiture was a tool used to re-enforce Britishness at a time of increasing Nationalism. There's no doubt that George Thomas would have seen it in that way. It was, after all, the Labour Government who had approached the Palace to suggest such an Investiture. It was then announced in May 1967 that the Investiture would take place. This works some way against the claim that the Investiture was a reaction to nationalism. At the time of the announcement, Gwynfor had won Carmarthen but the other two by-elections in Labour heartlands hadn't taken place.

Once the announcement was made, there was, of course, reaction. There were sit-ins and protests of various kinds. There were also bombing campaigns. The FWA (the Free Wales Army) and MAC (Mudiad Amddiffyn Cymru, The Movement to Defend Wales) had been responsible for bombing campaigns during the Tryweryn protests. They planted a bomb at Clywedog Reservoir in 1966 and then five more bombs in 1967 and 1968, one of which was in the Welsh Office.

Such activities continued the debate within Plaid Cymru about the use of violence in the name of their cause. Martin Johnes:

The extremists put Plaid Cymru in a difficult position, especially since Labour did its best to associate the Party with the violence. Despite the very strong sympathy for their objectives, there was a strong feeling within the Party that both the language campaigners and the bombers were alienating potential support.[118]

Gwynfor Evans expelled some FWA members from Plaid and did then condemn the use of violence as a campaigning weapon. But this did not stop Special Branch agents following Plaid Cymru members. Gwynfor thought that this Special Branch involvement was a trap to lure the nationalists, and he accused Special Branch agents of being agents provocateurs, luring Plaid members to perform illegal acts. He even thought that they had prepared a honey trap for him, to lure him into a sex scandal.

National Library of Wales

Anti investiture protest, Caernarfon, March 1969

118. Martin Johnes: *Wales since 1939*. Manchester: Manchester University Press, 2013, p. 234.

The Government were more than aware that they had a situation to deal with. The Welsh needed to be placated and made to feel significant in such a prestigious event as the forthcoming Investiture. They made Swansea a city, even though towns in England met the criteria and Swansea didn't.

But the big move was to send the soon-to-be Prince of Wales to Aberystwyth to learn Welsh. The choice of Aber was significant. It was a very Welsh University in a very Welsh town. There was no shortage of Welsh nationalist enthusiasts there, as members of both Plaid and Cymdeithas yr Iaith Gymraeg. In fact, the Society's first two protests were in Aberystwyth. But even though there were protests in the town when the Prince was there, he also received a great deal of support. Charles endeared himself to many in Wales when he said that it was understandable that people were objecting to his Investiture, as he was an outsider who had hardly been to Wales. This, to some, was far too accommodating, as Martin Johnes says:

> ... Charles' determination to recognise the National question worried George Thomas enough for him to write to the Prime Minister with his fears that the Prince had come under too much nationalist influence at Aberystwyth. He suggested the Queen have a quiet word with her son.[119]

But the vast majority of people in Wales supported the Investiture, and people of all political shades. A *Western Mail* survey showed that three-quarters of the nation backed the Investiture. With such a strong backing, it's no surprise that there was also an opposition to the nationalists' opposition. Dafydd Iwan, Welsh language activist who had released two singles about the Investiture received some death-threats in the mail. A newspaper article at the time sums up the general majority attitude to the Investiture. It was in the *Argus* newspaper.

> ... the inbuilt tension cannot disguise the fact that for the vast majority of the people in Wales, the investiture is a joyful and memorable occasion. For the ordinary man and woman in the street, the abstract polit-

---

119. Ibid., p. 235.

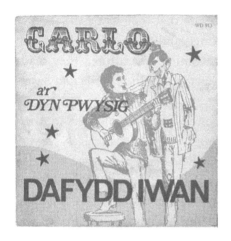 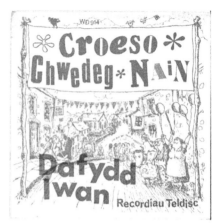

Two protest singles—Carlo and Croeso Chwe Deg Nain.

ical arguments are less imposing than the reality of a colourful ceremony involving a young prince and his family who, in the past week or two, have come to be more intimately alive and real, thanks to film, photographs and interviews in the press and broadcasting media.

Plaid and the Prince

Plaid were evidently divided on the Investiture issue. Young Plaid activists, such as Dafydd Elis Thomas and Dafydd Wigley, were opposed to the Investiture. Along with the third Dafydd, Dafydd Iwan, they were very influential on the minority within Plaid who wanted to actively oppose what was planned for Caernarfon in July 1969.

Officially, Plaid remained neutral, neither opposing nor endorsing. Their stance is summarised by J. R. Jones in *Gwaedd yng Nghymru* (*A Shout in Wales*), a collection of essays by the philosopher and Nationalist which evaluates the political climate of the Sixties.

I gyfiawnhau cadw allan o'r brotest, y mae Plaid Cymru'n dadlau fod seremoni'r urddo yn amherthnasol i'w hymgyrch hi I ennill annibyniaeth i Gymru; ni pheidiai 'Cymru rydd' â chydnabod sofraniaeth y goron.

I berswadio Cymdeithas y Iaith i beidio ag ymyrryd yn y brotest, dadl ychydig yn wahanol a ddefnyddir, sef nad yw'r Arwisgiad yn berthnasol I faes gweithrediadau protestiadol y Gymdeithas gan mai yr iaith Gymraeg fel y dengys ei henw swyddogol, yw hwnnw.[120]

To justify staying out of the protest, Plaid Cymru argue that the investiture ceremony is irrelevant to their campaign to win independence for Wales; a 'free Wales' would not cease to acknowledge the sovereignty of the crown. In order to persuade Cymdeithas yr Iaith not to interfere in the protesting, a slightly different argument is used, that the Investiture isn't relevant to the area in which the Society protests, as it's the Welsh language, as their name shows, that is that area.

If, as has been stated, Plaid stood for Dominion Status, there was no need to protest against establishing a Prince of Wales. As J. R. Jones says, there was nothing inconsistent in not protesting against Prince Charles. In fact, some argued even more strongly. The ceremony would draw more attention to Wales and, politically, it was a clear recognition that Wales existed as a nation.

Charles learned enough Welsh in Aberystwyth to ask his tutor one day, 'Ydy Gwynfor Evans yn mynd i Gaernarfon?' Is Gwynfor Evans going to Caernarfon? Charles was aware enough of who Gwynfor was to ask the question, and also that it wasn't certain if Gwynfor would be there. The answer was no. Gwynfor decided not to accept the invitation, as a sitting Welsh MP, to go to Caernarfon. This decision caused a mix of responses. To many, it was an embarrassing decision. That's what the Principal of Aberystwyth University, Thomas Parry, felt. He attempted to bridge the gap between the Prince and Gwynfor by suggesting the two should dine together in the University. Gwynfor refused, 'in case one of our lads heard about it'. He then suggested that the Prince should go to his house in Llangadog for supper. That didn't happen!

---

120. John Robert Jones: *Gwaedd yng Nghymru.* Lerpwl, Pontypridd: Cyhoeddiadau Modern Cymreig, 1970, p. 39.

Druids and Beefeaters in the Investiture procession.

In May 1969, there were Local Government elections. The predictions were good for Plaid Cymru. The Party fielded a hundred candidates, the largest number they had ever fielded. The *Western Mail* wrote that Plaid were likely to make substantial gains. As it turned out, it was the Conservatives that made the gains. Plaid won only seven seats. A report was written by two Party Central Office workers:

In the Investiture's year, further bomb outrages, the FWA trial, sign-daubing, canvassers from all areas reported that the public raised these matters frequently during the campaign. There can be little doubt these things affect Plaid Cymru's progress.

Such a situation made many within the Party fear that Gwynfor would not hold on to his seat in Carmarthen. Those fears became more real because of something that happened in Carmarthen itself after the Investiture. Having refused to go to the Investiture, Gwynfor then accepted an invitation to meet Prince Charles on his post-Investiture tour of Wales. This was received with total incredulity! For me, this was one of Gwynfor's biggest political mistakes. People accepted that he would not be involved in the ceremony, but they were completely unprepared to accept that he would then accept an invitation to meet him in Carmarthen. Calls of hypocrisy and double standards were common from more than one political corner. There's no doubt that Gwynfor lost a great deal of respect because of that decision. Some of his own fellow nationalists were calling him Sioni-bob-ochor, Johnny two-sides. Gwynfor, no doubt, had by then seen how the Investiture had been received by the people of Wales and that it would be good for him and his cause to be a part of that. But that's not how it was perceived by the people of Wales. Personally, I had no interest in the Investiture. I didn't watch it, and I didn't go to Carmarthen to see the new Prince of Wales. I had no issue at all with Gwynfor's stance on not going to the ceremony. It was his hypocrisy afterwards that annoyed me.

In his biography, Rhys Evans tells of a letter written by Gwynfor to Harri Webb, evaluating the Investiture and its impact. In his letter, Gwynfor says:

... that we shall see six months down the line that the Investiture has done us more good than harm, especially by the fillip it has given the Welsh language (which is so closely associated with us) and the jolt it has given to the national identity of half-hearted Welshmen.

Rhys Evans, in response, says:

With the benefit of hindsight, it can be seen that Gwynfor's attitude towards the Investiture was an eccentric one, but most of the leadership of Plaid Cymru concurred.[121]

Looking back at that year, on one hand, I can see Gwynfor's dilemma clearly. Many argued that he would have benefited greatly by going to the Investiture ceremony in Caernarfon. It was, after all, an extremely high-profile event, with Wales in the shop window. Others said that he had stood by his principles and refused to play the popularity game by going to the ceremony, even though plying it in such a way would have been of benefit to him. But I don't see it in that way. He was a politician, an MP, and therefore he had a political game to play—within his own Party and with the public. Going to the Investiture would have meant standing against influential members of his own Party and against Cymdeithas yr Iaith. There's no way he would have done that. His mistake, as I've said, was going to meet the Prince in Carmarthen having not gone to the Ceremony.

What this did in effect, as well as the impact of the individual decision itself, was to add to previous stories that undermined his credibility, Vietnam and the denunciation of violent protest in particular. I have no doubt that he made my work a lot easier as the canvassing intensified from 1969 onwards. My employment within the Labour Party in Wales meant that as 1969 drew to a close, I could see that it was looking increasingly likely that the General Election would be in the following year. The momentum given by the Investiture was going to be a boost for me as the campaigning began in earnest.

---

121. Rhys Evans: *Gwynfor Evans: Portrait of a Patriot*. Tal-y-bont, Ceredigion: Y Lolfa, 2008, p. 305.

13.

The Battle for Carmarthen

Prior knowledge of when the General Election was likely to be might well have been of personal benefit to me in the constituency, but it is also true to say they weren't good days for the Labour Party. That was a definite disadvantage, which added to the battle. There were three specific areas that caused difficulties for Labour.

First, the farmers weren't happy with their lot. In Carmarthenshire, that is a major consideration. Their concern was for the prices they were paid for their produce. Tensions were high, as was demonstrated when Home Secretary Jim Callaghan visited Pembrokeshire and Ceredigion. As he addressed one particularly stormy meeting, some rotten tomatoes were thrown at him. Fortunately, Employment Secretary Barbara Castle was on official duties in West Wales some five weeks later. She took a different approach to Jim when she was confronted by farmers. The *Western Mail* headline for the story on her visit couldn't be clearer; *'Farmers Fall for Barbara'*. In March 1970, over 200 farmers attended a meeting she held in Carmarthen. Many had gathered outside the Ivy Bush Hotel in the town as she arrived. They shouted, 'We want Barbara!' Her response was brilliant. 'Ok, let me just put some lipstick on'. She won them over, and it was a peaceful meeting with no rotten tomatoes. That was a clear example of how two leading politicians from the same party could address the same issue, in the same part of Wales, but with opposite effects.

This was consolidated when she held her next meeting in Carmarthen, where she chatted further with some more farmers. She told officials from the NFU that there was a future for small farms, as were the majority in Carmarthenshire. She reassured them that the Government would support them as much as they could. Thank goodness she intervened in this debate.

The other issue facing Labour was in Defence. There were plans to move the MoD's Military Base from Shoeburyness to the site of the Pembrey Firing Range near Llanelli, in Carmarthenshire but not directly in the Carmarthen constituency. The Llanelli MP, Labour's Denzil Davies, and Gwynfor Evans were opposed to such a move. I, however, supported it. My argument was that it would be beneficial for the area in terms of jobs and the economy. It would also secure the future of the Firing Range itself. It employed 600 people at the ammunitions testing and manufacturing centre in Pendine. The economy of West Carmarthenshire depended heavily on these jobs. The MoD said that constructing the Gunnery on the eight-mile coastline stretch between Pembrey and Cydweli would create 1500 jobs, and they would employ 1000 there once it was operational. It would also secure the future of Pendine. In April 1970, residents heard that hundreds of troops were on their way to their Pembrey village. They quickly set up a protest campaign.

I wrote an article for the *Carmarthen Times* on the matter. The headline was one I'm particularly pleased with: '*We want bread and butter before buckets and spades*'. The headline shows clearly the main argument of those who opposed the plans, that such a base would damage tourism. In the article I said:

> We have heard a lot of talk about estuarine barrages, about the conservation of beauty, about the potential of Pembrey as a tourist attraction. In fact, we have heard a lot of pie-in-the-sky talk... Let those who object to the Pembrey gun range give viable alternatives. It is their moral duty.

Gwynfor was one of those who I called upon to offer better alternative proposals. Having visited the Firing Range many times, I came to a definite conclusion:

> ... I am of the opinion that there is not sufficient evidence to oppose the proposed Pembrey range... I am not prepared to throw away 530 jobs at Pendine. Let us not throw away in Carmarthenshire over 1000 permanent jobs between Pendine and the Pembrey proposal, plus 1000 construction jobs for at least five years without making sure there is alter-

native employment... I for one will not be a party to throwing away valuable jobs and see the depopulation of West Carmarthenshire unless there are overpowering reasons for the Pembrey proposals. As yet, I am unaware of such reasons.

The protestors organised a petition, which was presented to the public enquiry called to look into the proposals. It had 27,000 names on it. The MoD plans were rejected, and they were criticised for not considering the local impact of their Gunnery proposals.

Druids of despair

The Welsh Language was the third contentious issue facing Labour. These were the days of active and ferocious campaigns for bilingual road signs, for example. English-only signs would be painted green or removed completely, and there would always be confrontation and many arrests.

This issue meant that Jim Callaghan had a far quieter time from farmers in the town of Ammanford in Carmarthenshire than he had in Haverfordwest. In the Amman valley, he was quizzed far more about the law-breaking methods of Cymdeithas yr Iaith, the imprisoning of Dafydd Iwan, folk singer and leading language activist and the claims of the alleged involvement of Special Branch in nationalist protests. Because of these issues, Denzil Davies and I had a far more difficult time in that meeting than Callaghan had, no doubt because we both were Welsh-speaking Carmarthenshire boys. Our presence highlighted the long, ongoing battle between Plaid and Labour on being Welsh.

In the following months, the language became a prominent topic in the battle between Gwynfor Evans and me. My comments were increasingly attacking Plaid Cymru. That's how the year had started. On 8 January, a story based on comments I'd made in a local Labour Party meeting was printed in the *Carmarthen Times* and the *Carmarthen Journal*. The headline was: *'Nationalists have not shown they can run a parish council'*.

CARMARTHEN TIMES, Friday, January 9th, 1970

Nationalists not capable of running parish council

—LABOUR CANDIDATE

MR. Gwynoro Jones, prospecive Labour Candidate for Carmarthen, took another swipe at Plaid Cymru last week, when he addressed a General Management Committee meeting.

Druids of despair

The Editor, Carmarthen Times.
    Sir,
    Mr. Dafydd Williams, in a letter to your paper last week, referred to statistics concerning jobs in prospect for Wales that appeared in the last issue of the Welsh Digest of Statistics.
    The Welsh Digest of Statistics shows that from 1965 to 1968 60,000 jobs were envisaged by industrial Development 'Approvals.' During the same period, only 19,000 jobs were showing in the 'completions' table. There are valid reasons for this difference.
    1. The figures for 'APPROVALS' (60,000) are a record of ALL Industrial Development Certificates issued. They relate to projects of every kind, even where no new building is involved, only the change of use of existing buildings. 'COMPLETIONS' on the other hand,

Addressing his party's constituency management committee, Mr Jones said that since July 1966, too much talk about Wales had been heard from Carmarthen MP Gwynfor Evans and not enough about the constituency. This was reflected in the type of question he asked in the House of Commons. 'Let Mr Evans tell us the number of questions he has asked specifically about the constituency' challenged Mr Jones.

That set the tone for what they then confirmed as General Election year, but the intensity increased. Some weeks later, I was on the attack again, revisiting a theme that had been a very prominent one from the day they chose me as a Labour candidate—Gwynfor Evans' stance on the use of violence and law-breaking protests by nationalist protestors.

It is high time Mr Evans realised that he just cannot say he deplores violence on the one hand, and continue to make irresponsible, emotive statements on the other. He has compared Wales with Lithuania—'oppressed', then that Wales is in a state of 'near ruin' and being 'whipped' by the English. He has even expressed the viewpoint that only when someone is 'shot or blown up' will the government listen…

The fact is that too many Plaid Cymru leaders refuse to accept that this Government has done anything worthwhile. They depict this Gov-

ernment as plotting to 'kill' the Welsh Language. Let him admit that many measures have been taken to foster the language.

The suggestion that Labour Party members were killing the Welsh language really hurt those of us within the party who loved the language and fought for it. We were as Welsh as anyone in Plaid Cymru. Reading the Welsh language press in those days, it was easy to get the impression that nationalists not only believed that the Government had done nothing at all for the language, but that it was actually doing as much as it could to actively kill the language.

Gwynfor Evans was asked more than once what he thought the Labour Party had done for Wales. His answer was almost always, 'Nothing!' It was really difficult to accept such a stance in a period when it was the Labour Party that had established the Welsh Office, a Secretary of State for Wales, and passed the Welsh Language Act of 1967. Plans were also underway to allow local authorities to erect bilingual road signs, and this happened before any road sign campaign by Cymdeithas yr Iaith had taken any significant hold. These are Labour achievements on Welsh language-related issues only. There are also so many other things the Labour Party introduced that benefited Wales. Let's just mention the NHS.

I regularly criticised Gwynfor's tendency to discredit the Labour Party. As far as I was concerned, when he said as much, he was discrediting Wales as well. His constant and consistent stance of painting a bleak picture of Wales was anti-nationalist. This is when I accused Gwynfor and anyone else who stood with him on this kind of interpretation as *'Druids of Despair'*. They didn't do Wales any favours by continuously criticising the nation.

By the end of February 1970, I turned my attention to the young people of the constituency. It was a bold enough headline, along with a photograph of me, that was in the *Carmarthen Times* on Friday 27 February 1970.

Gwynoro Jones—a Welsh-speaking Welshman—says:
  Young people are being exploited

There was a quote from the article in a box by the side of the photograph:

High time so-called lovers of Wales realised that recent antics are driving people further away from the language.

I argued that young people were being misled by middle-aged men who had failed to do what they wanted to do and were now calling on young people to act. I also said that such an approach would cause a rift in Wales as religion had done in Northern Ireland.

The lesson of Northern Ireland has been that religion has so divided its people that they have been unable to unite to solve far greater problems— bad housing and social conditions.

A road-sign protest

The article also contained a quote from a *Hansard* report on the debate about the Welsh Language in Parliament 16 February.

*18. **Mr. Gwynfor Evans** asked the Secretary of State for Wales if he will now seek to raise the Welsh language in Wales to a status of equality with English in Wales.*

*§**Mr. George Thomas** The Government has already raised the legal status of the Welsh language in Wales to that of equality with English.*

*13 §**Mr. Evans** Is the Secretary of State aware that some people may admire the lion-hearted way in which he has stood up, with nothing more formidable than the British Government behind him, to the great bully the Welsh Language Society and the way in which he is resisting any advance in Wales to national status? Is he also aware that I am not among his admirers?*

*§**Mr. Thomas**, I feel heartbroken by the hon. Gentleman's last remark. I am well aware that the hon. Gentleman does what he can to stir up members of the Welsh Language Society to indulge in the sort of hooligan exercises which we have recently witnessed. I share the opinion of Lord Justice Arthian Davies that they can do nothing but bring shame and disgrace to Wales.*

*§**Mr. William Edwards** Is my right hon. Friend aware that the implicit misrepresentation about the status of the Welsh language in that supplementary question is typical of the kind of misrepresentation taking place in Wales by people who should be more responsible and which is leading young people who are misrepresented to take unjustifiable and unwise actions?*

*§**Mr. Thomas** My hon. Friend speaks for a very wide representation of opinion in the Principality. Major constructive steps have been taken in an endeavour to succour the Welsh language, and no good at all will ensue from the sort of militant action of which the hon. Member for Carmarthen (Mr. Gwynfor Evans) is so proud.*

Gwynfor's early stance on the role of direct action in language protests was still very much an issue. During his campaign for the same General Election, in Llanelli, Denzil Davies also contributed to the debate and to the attacks on Gwynfor. Again in a newspaper article, he criticised Gwynfor for comparing Wales to another country, yet again.

> *Mr Gwynfor Evans has gone so far as to compare the fate of the Welsh with that of the Lithuanians, who were massacred by Stalin.*

This was another example of Gwynfor seeing the germ of a point and turning it into a complete argument.

Gaining ground

As far as Plaid Cymru were concerned, the General Election of 1970 was an opportunity to prove that 1966 wasn't a fluke and that they had built on the resurgences in Caerffili and Rhondda West, besides Local Authority successes in parts of Wales. But as early as March 1970, the newspapers were talking in terms of a Labour victory in Carmarthen. *'People Tired of Plaid's Unrealistic Outbursts'* is how the *Carmarthen Times* saw it at the end of March, adding,

> *Increased enthusiasm and the unrealistic outbursts of Plaid Cymru has made Labour the strongest political force in the county.*

And this when the Labour Party were facing some big difficulties. From then on, headlines such as *'Labour Will Win Back Carmarthen'* were far more frequent.

The Labour Party in Wales held their Annual Conference in May 1970, in Llandudno. On the Friday night, the national organiser, Ron Hayward, came up to me. I was half expecting him to ask me to lead the singing, as a singsong was a strong last-evening tradition. But no. He asked me why I was still in the Conference. He explained that Harold Wilson was about to announce the date of the General Election on the following Monday. Early the next morning, I left for home. On the Sunday morning, we called a campaign team meeting, where I could strongly suggest that a date was due to be announced. On 29 May, Parliament was dissolved, and the Election was set for 18 June.

I had been campaigning non-stop since October 1967. There were letters or articles by me in local newspapers every week. I had been to every fair, carnival and agricultural show in the constituency. I had shaken thousands of hands and kissed hundreds of babies! It became apparent to me early on that it was essential to re-connect with the people in the constituency and that there was only one way to do that; meet them face to face.

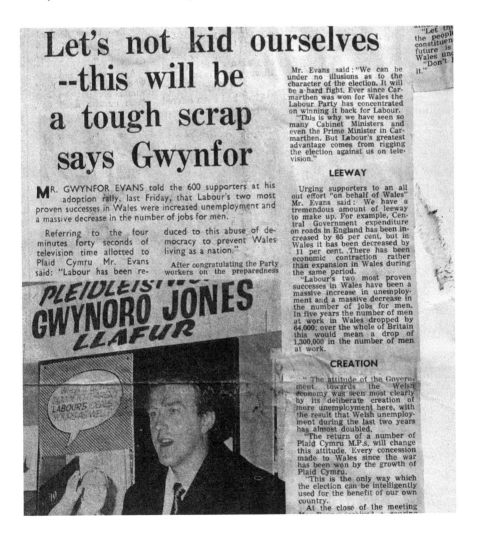

Let's not kid ourselves --this will be a tough scrap says Gwynfor

MR. GWYNFOR EVANS told the 600 supporters at his adoption rally, last Friday, that Labour's two most proven successes in Wales were increased unemployment and a massive decrease in the number of jobs for men.

Referring to the four minutes forty seconds of television time allotted to Plaid Cymru Mr. Evans said: "Labour has been re- duced to this abuse of democracy to prevent Wales living as a nation."

After congratulating the Party workers on the preparedness

Mr. Evans said: "We can be under no illusions as to the character of the election. It will be a hard fight. Ever since Carmarthen was won for Wales the Labour Party has concentrated on winning it back for Labour.

"This is why we have seen so many Cabinet Ministers and even the Prime Minister in Carmarthen. But Labour's greatest advantage comes from rigging the election against us on television."

LEEWAY

Urging supporters to an all out effort "on behalf of Wales" Mr. Evans said: We have a tremendous amount of leeway to make up. For example, Central Government expenditure on roads in England has been increased by 65 per cent, but in Wales it has been decreased by 11 per cent. There has been economic contraction rather than expansion in Wales during the same period.

"Labour's two most proven successes in Wales have been a massive increase in unemployment and a massive decrease in the number of jobs for men. In five years the number of men at work in Wales dropped by 64,000; over the whole of Britain this would mean a drop of 1,300,000 in the number of men at work.

CREATION

"The attitude of the Government towards the Welsh economy was seen most clearly by its deliberate creation of more unemployment here, with the result that Welsh unemployment during the last two years has almost doubled.

"The return of a number of Plaid Cymru M.P.s. will change this attitude. Every concession made to Wales since the war has been won by the growth of Plaid Cymru.

"This is the only way which the election can be intelligently used for the benefit of our own country.

At the close of the meeting

But now, there was a need to pick up the pace and change my plan of attack. The political temperature had gone up a good few degrees since I had been chosen. On the evening of his official selection as a Plaid Candidate for Carmarthen 1970, Gwynfor Evans saw it in this way:

> *We can be under no illusion as to the character of the election. It will be a hard fight. Ever since Carmarthen was won for Wales, the Labour party has concentrated on winning it back for Labour. This is why we have seen so many Cabinet Ministers and even the Prime Minister in Carmarthen. But Labour's greatest advantage comes from rigging the election against us on television.*

And true to form, this was another occasion for him to roll out one of his famous unfounded sweeping statements:

> *Every concession made to Wales since the war has been won by the growth of Plaid Cymru.*

Absolute nonsense! One only needs to study Plaid's election performances in the 1950s and early 60s until the by-election to see that the party was of no consequence electorally.

But it wasn't only me who had Gwynfor in my sights. Tory candidate, Lloyd Havard-Davies and Liberal candidate, broadcaster Huw Thomas, turned their attacks on Gwynfor in their formal adoption meetings. Lloyd Havard-Davies first:

> *If his record since his arrival at Westminster is any guide, then we can truthfully assume that no journey in Welsh history was as purposeless as this.*

Huw Thomas:

> *The Welsh Nationalists think with their blood instead of their heads.*

The spirit in which the campaign ahead would be fought was clear enough.

There was an interesting and historical paragraph in the *Carmarthen Times* right at the end of May:

Carmarthen Labour Club was granted an extension of licensing hours until 2 am on election night, June 18th, by Carmarthen Magistrates on Monday. The application was made for members wishing to follow the election broadcasts on the club's colour television.

14.

The Big Night

There was considerable political and media attention on the Carmarthen constituency from the day the election date was announced. Would Gwynfor keep his seat? That was the big question. Amongst the endless column inches and airtime given to pre-election analysis of the Carmarthen constituency, one stands out. Dennis Johnson from the *Guardian* newspaper spent some days in the constituency in June 1970. The heading of the article he wrote as a result of his visit was *'Plaid Cymru's magic may have faded'*. He really captured what type of constituency it was and what the issues were for the 1970 General Election. He began by summing up the significance of Gwynfor's victory in 1966.

> *Thousands of delirious supporters gathered to cheer Mr Evans in what the Nationalists have now come to regard as those rather magical early hours of July 15, 1966… Nothing would be the same again for Wales or Carmarthen said the bright-eyed victor who had even surprised himself. Almost four years later, things don't seem to be quite the same at all.*

He then says that Gwynfor

> *… shot his bolt with too much protesting and too little influence on mainstream politics at Westminster… No one, however, is suggesting that the Nationalists have lost their appeal. They made a profound impact on the intellectuals, with much of the teaching profession totally committed, and much of this influence remains. West Wales still has, at the very least, a passionate interest in devolution and detests remote control.*

He could see that the election would be a close three-horse race, with the Liberals and Plaid Cymru getting many votes, but that Labour would win.

> *Carmarthen had still not shaken free of Lady Megan, whose brinkmanship between Liberal and Labour had the constituency confused right to the end. Because of what happened at the by-election, no one still knows for sure how much of her vote was Labour, how much Liberal (many old Lloyd Georgians still cannot believe she was anything else) and how much Lady Megan.*

Another consideration, as a backdrop to Johnson's comments, was the nature of the constituency itself. Slender majorities are part of Carmarthen's historical, political fabric. In the seven elections between 1928 and 1951, for example, the largest majority secured by any candidate was 1,279. The majority was less than a thousand in four elections and the lowest majority was 47. I would take that figure to the extreme in years to come! Also, more than one party had represented the seat over the years. This is in stark contrast to the neighbouring constituency of Llanelli. They will be marking 100 years of having a Labour MP in 2022 and more often than not they returned the candidate by one of the largest majorities in Wales, and sometimes the UK.

Johnson's article also included two stories that are more anecdotal, but which capture the colour of the constituency. One has been mentioned already, when a local referred to Gwynfor as the Messiah. The second tells of a conversation Johnson had with a councillor.

> *I'm on the Borough Council and I was given a lift to some meeting by a colleague who turned up in a Rolls Royce and said, "Here, man, let me shift this straw out of your way first." Folk tale or not, that's Carmarthen.*

On the campaign trail

Because of my employment as marketing officer with the Labour Party, I had regular opportunities to attend meetings with political campaigners far more experienced than I was. This included regular meetings with George Thomas as Secretary of State for Wales and with other senior politicians and party organisers in Transport House, London. There's no doubt that this helped me understand the political process better as well as learning about campaigning.

It was through such experiences that I became aware of the election campaign of a candidate in Scotland. He used campaign leaflets that were particularly striking. I decided to do the same thing. I prepared two leaflets on the form of a supplement in a newspaper. One was slightly larger than the other and concentrated on the policies and successes of the Labour Party. I called this the *Labour Election Special*. The other concentrated on me and my vision for the constituency, and was called *Your Labour Candidate*. Such publications were comparatively new. I remember emphasising the importance of having a red strip across the front page of both publications. *Your Labour Candidate* had more than one red strip on the front. I had learned of the importance of using colour in campaigning, and red in particular. Both publications were also bilingual, but not 50:50. Using Welsh was a must for me, and, in *Labour Election Special*, there was also a section on the Welsh Language. This is its opening paragraph:

Yn Rhagfyr 1965, dywedodd Mr James Griffiths, yr Ysgrifennydd i Gymru ar y pryd, wrth yr Uwch Bwyllgor Cymreig, y byddai'r llywodraeth Lafur yn gwneud yr hyn oedd yn rhesymol ac yn ymarferol i roi dilisrwydd cyfartal i'r Iaith Gymraeg. Yn ddistwr bu'r Llywodraeth Lafur wrthi'n dawel yn cyflawni'r addewid hwn.

In December 1965, Mr James Griffiths, the Secretary of State for Wales, told the Welsh Grand Committee that the Labour Government would do what was reasonable and practical to give the Welsh Language equal status. Quietly and without fuss, the Labour Government has been working towards fulfilling this promise.

I then outlined specific examples of what Labour had done for the Welsh language, beginning with the Welsh Language Act of 1967. The big step forward that the Act achieved was to lift legal restrictions on the use of the Welsh language. It was, after 1967, possible to use the language in legal cases in Wales, for example. Other examples have been referred to earlier in this book. By the year of the election, 230 Government leaflets were in Welsh or were bilingual. In the April of that year, the car tax disc was also bilingual. In the *Labour Election Special*, I noted more specific financial investment in Wales.

Dros y bedair i bum mlynedd ddiwetha mae y Llywodraeth Lafur wedi bod yn hael iawn gyda'i grantiau i'r Urdd—dros £70,000. Yna rhoddwyd dros £28,000 i Gyngor y Celfyddydau er mwyn hyrwyddo llenyddiaeth Gymreig.

Over the last four or five years, the Labour Government has been extremely generous with its grants to the Urdd (The Welsh League of Youth)—over £70,000. The Welsh Arts Council received £28,000 in order to further Welsh literature.

I closed this section by saying:

Yn y pen draw nid y llywodraeth ond agwedd y bobl yng Nghymru fydd yn penderfynu dyfodol yr iaith.

In the end, it's not the government but the attitude of the people that will determine the future of the language.

It was essential for me to include such a section in my campaign literature because it angered and hurt me that Gwynfor and his people gave the impression that it was only them who loved the language. Labour had done a great deal for it as well. It also flies in the face of Gwynfor's constant claims about what Labour had, or as he said, had not done for Wales.

Battle plans

It's worth noting how we campaigned in the run-up to the General Election, if only to show how much the process has changed since then. Campaigning was centred on the use of newspapers in the constituency, as was a great deal of political activity when it wasn't election time. We had a team of twenty-one; one campaign leader and twenty people who worked in every area of the constituency. Every campaign day followed the same pattern; distribution of leaflets and canvassing in about six areas and then three public meetings in the evening. Every party would buy a full page in the local newspapers every week in order to announce the locations and times of their public meetings. In the small villages, there would be about a hundred people at each of my meetings. In the larger villages and the towns, we could expect three to four hundred. Gwynfor would attract similar numbers, as would Huw Thomas. Towards the end of the campaign, Huw Thomas and I shared the same platform and audience occasionally. For example, he would address a meeting in Carmarthen, and I would address a meeting on Llandeilo. When we both had finished, we would go to the other location to address the same people, made up of his followers and mine. For some reason, there was very little face-to-face debate with the other candidates in those days and unfortunately, I didn't have any personal debate with Gwynfor. Another feature of the election-eering in the last week or so was a large cavalcade throughout the constit-uency. About 50 cars drove under the Labour flag for about 6 hours one day, promoting me and our message.

When I campaigned in Llangadog, the village where Gwynfor lived, I always received a very warm welcome. It appeared as if I had a great deal of support there. Plaid supporters had understandably been very active there and there were many, many Plaid posters throughout the village. But it became apparent early on that I had a great deal of support there too. One day, I received a phone call from the *Western Mail*'s David Hew-itt. He told me:

> *The poster count on the roads and hedges doesn't look good for you, Gwy-noro.*

My reply was:

> *According to the hedges, Gwynfor has won, but according to the houses, I have!*

As Polling day drew ever closer, Gwynfor's words at the start of the cam-paign were becoming increasingly true: *Let's not kid ourselves—this will be a tough scrap.*

Thursday 18 June 1970

There were two big changes to voting on that election day. Polling stations would be open until 10 o'clock, not nine, for the first time. And also for the first time, 18-year-olds were given the vote. So, more people could vote, and they had longer in which to do so. I had sent a birthday greeting to everyone in the constituency when they reached that 18-year-old milestone.

They announced the result at 3 am, to a packed Guildhall Square in Carmarthen town centre. The vast majority of them were Plaid supporters. This was the result:

Lloyd Havard Davies (Conservative) 4,975
Gwynfor Evans (Plaid Cymru) 14,812
Gwynoro Jones (Labour) 18,719
Huw Thomas (Liberal) 10,707

It was impossible to hear Huw Thomas' result. Plaid supporters were obviously and vocally angry. The *South Wales Echo* reported the response:

The hundreds of youngsters who had jammed the square could not believe it. Some of them cried like babies, others shook their fists and jeered the man who had ousted Gwynfor. It had been a feverish election vigil in Carmarthen—perhaps the most tense and highly charged wait polling has produced the length and breadth of the country. Flags and flagons were waved. Fighting broke out in the crowd and fruits started flying. A lot of youngsters were screaming 'if you're not Plaid you must be English'.

Tensions were running so high; the police were concerned about how I could leave the building safely. The *Echo* reporter felt the same tensions.

Just after midnight, I got a tip from a policeman that things were likely to boil over when I took cover in an outside broadcast scanner van directly outside the Shire Hall. The scanner van was under pressure and like being under siege. The crowd refused to let Gwynoro Jones be heard as he spoke from the balcony of the 210-year-old Shire Hall, which houses the assize courts and where some of the most famous murder trials of the last two centuries were heard. But this time it was the crowd outside who were hollering murder.

I wasn't allowed to address the crowd, in the usual way the successful candidate was expected to, because of the way the crowd was behaving.

But the time came, of course, when we had to leave the Guildhall. The police were still unsure how and when we should leave. They suggested that I put on a policeman's uniform as a disguise. I rejected that suggestion. Eventually, at 5 am, we were led out through the narrow corridors at the back of the building and out through the rear entrance and into a police car.

The confrontation that night is a clear picture, an image, of the relationship between Plaid and Labour, as we have discussed in this book. It can be traced back for decades but was captured on the square in Carmarthen in a few hours. The whole situation saddened me, there's no doubt. It wasn't just the short-term fear, in the face of such an angry crowd. It was also a deeper sadness that the democratic process had been abused in such a way. The vitriol extinguished any graciousness in defeat in that constituency and it also endorsed an early headline of mine in the Carmarthen papers, that Gwynfor and I were poles apart and the animosity between our parties was palpable.

That said, I had the comfort of victory to lean back on. It had been a good night for me at least. My seat was the only one Labour regained. It hadn't been a good night for Labour as the party lost 60 seats throughout the UK.

15.

The MP for Carmarthen

Friday. The morning after the night before. It was of course a day of reaction and analysis. They summed my reaction up in a *Carmarthen Times* article:

> *This has been a victory for organisation and a readiness to meet the people on the doorstep. But, of far more importance, the people of Carmarthen wanted to show they want to go back into the mainstream of politics. They have grown tired of pessimistic talk.*

Plaid Cymru's response in the same paper was:

> *We are very sorry. It is sad that Carmarthen people have taken a step back.*

Side by side with the party responses, the editor gave his analysis. He began by saying that Plaid supporters expected a sweeping victory, but that their candidate wasn't so optimistic. He repeated Gwynfor's comments at the start of the campaign, that it would be a tough battle. But he then added Gwynfor's next sentence in that original speech, which didn't get much attention at all throughout the campaign.

> *'Let us be under no illusions,' he said in his adoption speech. 'It will be a hard fight.' And he added: 'We have a tremendous amount of leeway to make up.'*

He then considers what *'leeway to make up'* meant. Were Plaid concerned that the 1966 majority was so small? Did they think that they had lost ground since 1966? Had the support for Gwynfor dwindled since then? The editor complimented Gwynfor for his untiring work as an MP and then said:

> *But the trail he was blazing did not contain sufficient fire to please some of his supporters.*

On the Saturday after the result, the *Western Mail* had their own analysis. One article, written by their Welsh Affairs Correspondent, Geraint Talfan Davies, offers three points to sum up the election for Labour in Wales.

- *1970 was the lowest Labour poll in Wales since 1945*
- *Despite a swing of 4.5 percent from Labour to the Tories in Wales, the Conservatives' percentage share of the poll was lower than in any election since 1950.*
- *Plaid Cymru have overtaken the Liberals in Wales and recorded their highest poll ever, despite losing Mr. Gwynfor Evans's seat at Carmarthen.*

Plaid Cymru was the only party that had increased its vote. That gives a broader context to Gwynfor's loss in Carmarthenshire. Such a statistic also casts some doubt on a comment Gwynfor made after he lost Carmarthen. He said that the media were against his party:

> *... the election had been rigged against Plaid Cymru by television and deliberately so...*

These words were carried by more than one newspaper. They carry little weight in the light of Plaid being the only party to increase its vote. Another example of some wild comment by him. But another comment of his is more on point and is a fair reflection on the election results for his party.

> *Plaid Cymru is now well established in most constituencies in Wales as the only challenge to the Labour Party.*

In the same edition of the *Western Mail*, there was an article on four of Wales' new MPs, Michael Roberts, John Stradling Thomas, Wyn Roberts and me. Interesting to note that Wyn Roberts came from a television background and I from the marketing world—an early sign of how politics was changing.

My victory was described as '*... quite an achievement...*', echoing Trevor Fishlock's comment that me beating Gwynfor would be like '*... toppling a king...*'. The response of Gwynfor's supporters, as shown by those gathered on the square in Carmarthen, was more like me having dethroned one of God's own.

Maiden speech

On arriving at Westminster, the Monday after the election, four of us asked to swear the oath in Welsh; Denzil Davies, Caerwyn Roderick and Tom Ellis and myself. The story was that Gwynfor claimed to be the first to do so four years previously. But we looked in vain through the Parliamentary records for any reference to that. If he had done so, the four of us would have been granted permission to do so in 1970, as there was a precedent. But we weren't.

The new MP arrives at Westminster.

My maiden speech was less than a month after arriving at Westminster, setting a pattern I continued with throughout my parliamentary career. I made regular speeches and submitted dozens of written questions monthly—over my period as MP, I asked over 800 of them. Research for this book shows me

I made more speeches in Parliament in my first year than Gwynfor did in his whole four years as MP. Most of the questions he asked were written as he was rarely in the House. I made so much use of written questions because I had seen that they were an effective weapon in Gwynfor's politicising. But they weren't my principal weapon.

Taliesin

The reaction to the result in Carmarthen rumbled on for months afterwards. In October, in the periodical, *Taliesin*, one particularly bitter article was published. It contained some criticism of me, but it fired the main shots at the people of Carmarthen for choosing me and rejecting Gwynfor.

> *It makes us thankful that D. J., J. E., J. R., T. I. Ellis and Trefor Morgan to name only five, did not live to see the name of this constituency degraded not merely to dust but to depths of a wasteland... We now know the real quality and value of the constituency which we were foolish enough to believe had awakened'*
> *A renowned village like Llanddowror; it is completely dead culturally; St Clears—which pretends to be a village in Hampshire; Carmarthen itself—a town which hates to hear a word of Welsh except on market day, and a place—like every old garrison town—which dotes on all sorts of bumph and royal ballyhoo. Llandeilo is exactly the same.*

Naturally, I responded to these comments and used one speech in particular to do so. Carmarthenshire, I stated, was one of the most Welsh counties in Wales, adding that when I was canvassing, I spoke Welsh 70% of the time on the streets and on the doorsteps. All the local press picked up on this speech. This was in the *Carmarthen Times* on 9 October 1970:

> *I am astounded at the attitude shown. The bitterness expressed because the Nationalist candidate lost the election stems from the belief such people hold of their own importance. They think that they alone are mindful*

of the problems of Wales. It is indeed time that they were told that there is no monopoly of working for Wales.

The quote then turns to capital letters, as if I was raising my voice to say the words:

THERE ARE THOUSANDS OF PEOPLE WHO VOTE FOR THE LABOUR, LIBERAL AND CONSERVATIVE PARTIES WHO ALSO LOVE WALES, IT'S CULTURE AND TRADITIONS.

Once again, it was an opportunity to attack the fact that comments made by some nationalists regularly contained nothing more than rhetoric. Facts were prominent in their absence. My response continued:

Our people might not read the propaganda the Nationalists desire them to read, nor perhaps idolise the people they do. But that is not to say that the people of our constituency are not lovers of Wales and the language.

In the *Taliesin* article, there was one particularly personal comment about me:

… they wanted no Welshman, but one who was as materialistic, as rootless, and as mistaken as they themselves.

It's obvious that whoever wrote this article believed that there was only one type of Welshman and that I wasn't one of that type. I had to respond to this too:

Suffice to say that I need no lecture from anyone on how to be a Welshman. And not on how to work for the constituency of my birth.

Another newspaper picked up a different point:

As a Member of Parliament for this constituency, and one born and bred there, I feel it is my duty to tell these people not to be so arrogant in their

*assertions. The quality of the people in our constituency has not deterio-
rated just because the Nationalists have lost the election. Our constituency
has a fine history, and it epitomises the culture, tradition and history of
our nation. The bitterness of the article turns sour when it questions the
Welshness of the constituency.*

To this day, when my own political standpoint might well have changed,
I still cannot understand the insulting and arrogant attitude amongst
many Nationalists who give the impression that they are the true Welsh
people. Incredible. Without doubt, this is still a stumbling block for
Plaid Cymru.

The nuts and bolts

Ever since I developed an interest in the politics of Wales from around
1960, I had often read of Plaid Cymru's claim that not only was a London Government bad for Wales and had done nothing for Wales, but, in
particular, Labour had done nothing to further the economic interests of
Wales. In those years, the argument that Wales was too small a country
to survive economically was a very strong one, stronger than it has been
in more recent years.

I was an economist by background, a research obsessive, and knew a
great deal about the economic history of Wales since 1945 and particularly the performances of the Tories from 1951 to 64 and how Labour
was trying to turn things round in their way. Added this mix, it was
always in Plaid Cymru's interest if there were economic problems and job
losses in Wales.

Plaid officials often commented on how adverse economic factors
were good for them. For example, Dr Gareth Morgan Jones, assistant
general secretary of Plaid, in the *Western Mail* in January 1968 (and that
was a difficult time in Wales) openly commented:

*We do not mind the Labour Government making a mess of things. It will
mean great electoral benefit for us.*

The Welsh MPs of 1971 – in the same room at least!

As the years went on, I kept up the research, using parliamentary written questions to gather further and better particulars, and in 1973, I published a 25-page booklet called 'The Record Put Straight'. Jim Griffiths wrote the preface to it.

It was a review of the 13 years of Tory rule till 1964, then six years of Labour government and the first two years of the Ted Heath government 1970-72. A fair spread of years.

Of course, the 1964-70 Wilson government made mistakes, and they did not find solutions to many of Wales' problems. It also had to contend with a poor economic inheritance and an adverse balance of trade of £800m in 1964 that actually defined the following six years, leading to devaluation and much industrial strife.

So, what was the inheritance in Wales after 13 years of Tory rule? Throughout the 1950s, the coal mining, agricultural, slate, transport and communication industries were in decline. Manpower in those industries fell by 82,000 over the 13 years. In the coal industry, employment fell by 40,000.

There were very limited attempts made to retrain those who had lost their jobs. Even by 1964, only 200 people were receiving retraining and expenditure under the Local Employment Acts on industrial development in Wales was a mere £1m in 1963/64. After six years of Labour in power, 12,000 a year received training.

Clear evidence is available that in those years there was hardly an adequate road construction programme to speak of. So, when Labour came to power, road schemes had to be planned and programmed more or less from scratch, which took a few years to come into fruition, culminating in the Welsh Office's 'Wales: The Way Ahead'. From 1964 to 1970, 86 miles of motorway and trunk roads were completed or planned at a cost of £57m. Then, in the road scheme's preparation pool for South Wales, there were 53 miles of motorway and major roads planned at a cost of £45m, and for North and mid-Wales, a planned programme of 34 miles and £28m expenditure. And after thirteen years of Tory rule, 800 miles of the railway network had been taken away.

Analysis of identifiable public expenditure in Wales on the major services showed that some £325.8m was spent in Wales in 1963/64 but that had risen to £842.7 million by 1969/70. Expenditure on education and health doubled and increased significantly on housing, hospitals and roads.

There were no investment grants or assistance to the coal industry in 1963/4 but in 1969/70 it totalled almost £50 million. It continued to be a period of employment changes. Jobs in mining and quarrying fell by 40.6k, construction 10k, agriculture 6.3k and transport and communications 12.5k. But 20,000 jobs were created in the professional and scientific sector, and in engineering and electrical skills, 17,000 jobs were made.

Space does not allow me to refer in detail to the 60 advance factory programmes, industrial building approvals, or dispersal of government offices to Wales. Moving the Royal Mint, DVLA, and Inland Revenue created 11,000 jobs in Wales. 195 new manufacturing firms set up and there was an extensive derelict land clearance scheme.

One could go on, but I think the point is made.

These were also the days of setting up the Mid-Wales Industrial Development Board and the Wales Tourist Board. In addition, they passed the Welsh Language Act in 1967 based on the Hughes-Parry report. One effect was to increase the number of bilingual government forms from 40 to 240. Some 90 forms used by the Courts were bilingual, and most of the forms connected with agriculture were available in Welsh.

Then there was a significant increase in funding for the supply of Welsh-language books generally and for use in schools. There were also grants to the Urdd and the Welsh Arts Council.

As I write all this, I can hear Gwynfor's words 'Labour has done nothing for Wales'.

Ted Heath unexpectedly won the 1970 General Election and one of his first acts was to dismantle Labour's regional development policy and investment grants system. The result was that industrial inquiries from companies declined sharply. The CBI carried out a survey that showed 21% of large firms and 34% of smaller firms abandoned or postponed expansion projects. At the time Heath won the election, there were almost 31,000 jobs in the pipeline in Wales. But by May 1972, this figure had declined to 18,000. Also, in those two years, 34,800 people were made redundant in Wales affecting 250 establishments. Public expenditure was reduced and unemployment increased from 3.4% in 1970 to almost 6% in 1972.

There was so much else. And yet Plaid Cymru and Gwynfor remained silent on such issues.

16.

Devolution and Labour in Westminster

I had been directly involved with the devolution debate through the Crowther Committee on Devolution initially, and then the Kilbrandon Commission when Crowther died. Now, I was an MP and could continue with my involvement with Kilbrandon and so many other devolution issues through Parliament.

I soon saw that reporting back to the Welsh Executive Committee and the Welsh Parliamentary MPs' group was a very fiery process. Every meeting was extremely heated. This is when I started to disagree strongly with George Thomas on many devolution-related issues. It's also where I saw the strong opposition from many Valleys' Labour MPs to the whole idea of giving Wales more powers. Their opposition could be quite bitter. In his introduction to the book he co-authored with Dennis Balsom, *The Road to the National Assembly for Wales*, Barry Jones notes another effect the opponents of devolution had within the Labour Party in Wales:

> *Welsh Labour's leadership was more concerned with placating anti-devolutionists within the party than with developing a policy to enthuse the Welsh electorate.*[122]

On many an occasion, Gwynfor said that that Kilbrandon's Constitutional Committee had been set up purely because he had won in 1966.

---

122. James Barry Jones; Denis Balsom (eds.): *The Road to the National Assembly for Wales*. Cardiff: University of Wales Press, 2000, p. 2.

Such a claim is simply factually incorrect. It also ignores another central influencing factor—Scotland. There was strong support from many Labour leaders in Scotland for increased devolution, and there was considerable pressure from their ranks to set up a Constitutional Commission.

Support with Westminster Labour for devolution included some prominent members of Harold Wilson's Cabinet until the 1970 election. These included Cledwyn Hughes, Goronwy Roberts, John Morris and significantly, Elystan Morgan, who was Jim Callaghan's deputy in the Home Office. They were responsible for constitutional matters. Callaghan had many conversations with Elystan about increased powers for Wales, and he would have received very positive and clear answers from the staunchly pro-devolution Ceredigion MP.

The Kilbrandon Committee took four years to prepare its report. It saw the light of day on 31 October 1973. The thirteen commissioners proposed three possibilities for Wales: statutory assembly, executive assembly, or consultative assembly. Without doubt, this was the most detailed and thorough enquiry into the governance of Britain that had ever been held. It's quite likely that this is still true.

When Harold Wilson announced in April 1969 that he wished to commission such a report, Plaid Cymru's response was to call it a 'charade' and a 'denial of the natural aspirations of the people of Wales'. When it had been published, they hailed it as an important step forward and that the months following its publication would be the most crucial in Wales' two-thousand-year history. That didn't surprise me. I was used to Gwynfor's statements of doom and then taking the praise for any good that might follow.

The impetus for any devolutionary measures had come from the Labour Party. Jim Griffiths had called for it when he was Secretary of State; it became official party policy in 1966 and three cabinet members, John Morris, Cledwyn Hughes and Elystan Morgan were instrumental in setting up the Constitutional enquiry.

The Prime Minister must publish a Green Paper immediately and this must contain a commitment to establish a Welsh Government with legislative powers before the end of the present Parliament.

But once again, it must be emphasised that there was unanimity within Labour on this issue. Having been involved in the drafting of the Kilbrandon Report, I knew that the proposals we put forward were far stronger than those actually published. In the book *The Welsh Veto*, Barry Jones comments on this:

> *The Executive of the Labour Party in Wales set up a study group to help prepare its evidence to the Kilbrandon Commission. By April 1969, the group had produced a draft proposal of a quasi-federal nature, suggesting a Welsh senate of 72 seats, with certain legislative powers, particularly in domestic and welfare matters. The proposals produced a storm of controversy.*[123]

I was the chair of that group, as the Research and Public Relations Officer and Barry, along with others such as Wyn Thomas, J. Gilbert Evans and Paul Flynn, produced this document which caused an almighty row in the Welsh Labour parliamentary group of MPs. I had to attend meetings at Westminster and there were many meetings of the Welsh executive on this issue. In the end, the quasi-federal features were dropped as were the legislative powers and instead there was to be a greater emphasis given to controlling and coordinating the nominated bodies in Wales and taking over administrative powers of the Welsh Office and Secretary of State. Initially, the group wanted a full legislative assembly. What was proposed, however, was an elected Council with administrative powers only. They had added a lot of water to the milk.

In November 1973, in an article and a speech, I discussed one particular point in the report. At the time, it was still receiving a great deal of attention. I addressed increasing powers in the regions of England as well as Scotland and Wales. Figures had shown that there was more of a call for increased devolved powers in nine regions in England than there was for the same measures in Wales and Scotland. For example, 60% wanted devolution in Yorkshire and 58% in Wales.

---

123. David Foulkes; J. Barry Jones; R. A. Wilford (eds.): *The Welsh Veto: The Wales Act 1978 and the Referendum*. Cardiff: University of Wales Press, 1983, p. 23.

The following month, I wrote an article saying that once the debate on the exact difference between legislative or administrative powers became long and drawn out, then those who opposed devolution would use that arguing process and the variety of arguments it would generate as an excuse to do nothing. I in no way considered the implications of those comments—the debacle of the 1979 Referendum.

Such comments on my part drew the same diametrically opposed responses—to my fellow Labour MP's, I was a nationalist; to Plaid Cymru, I was anti-Welsh. All that concerned me was that I was now in a place and a position to do as much as I could to argue for Welsh devolution.

Five Welsh Secretaries of State together.

A government more local

At this time, a group of us pro-devolutionists got together to gather some renewed momentum for an Elected Council for Wales. To gauge the mood, I suggested we put together an early day motion on the Commons' paper that MPs would be free to support. The aim was to get the majority of Welsh MPs to sign it. So, I acted like a whip, collecting names. We were getting very close to the required 16 MPs. As expected, there were heated debates inside the Welsh Labour group over the issue.

Frustrated by the anti-devolutionist's arguments, I leaked the names of those who were in favour of such a motion and those against. All hell broke loose. They called an emergency meeting with a full turn out. In fact, even Jim Callaghan and Michael Foot turned up, something they rarely did. Some sort of inquisition took place to find out the source of the leak. They knew full well who the culprit was, of course, but they couldn't prove it. I had been in the press world far too long and I had many friends in those circles in Wales.

My approach in these meetings was, what's the fuss about? Most people could name at least 10 of the 16 MPs who were for and against an elected council, anyway. So I survived any sanction.

I knew there was one key figure that would bring home the final 4 or 5 waverers and that was Michael Foot. Foot had been to my parents' home more than once when I was a candidate, and although we were on opposite sides on one or two policy areas, I was a great admirer of his and he knew it. So after a couple of sessions with Michael, he agreed to sign—that then brought in Fred Evans, Donald Coleman, Arthur Probert and Neil McBride into the Yes camp. So I went to George with the list. He read the tea leaves and then he also signed.

George moved an amendment to the Local Government Bill 1972 calling for an Elected Council for Wales—and I wonder why many did not like me at all within the party in Wales?

After the General Election, John Morris was Secretary of State and a Government Consultation Paper was published in June 1974—'Devolution within the United Kingdom'. It covered devolution of Scotland, Wales and the eight English regions. It also contained options for legislative devolution for Scotland and Wales; Elected Assemblies for Scotland, Wales and English regions, executive devolution to the aforementioned and also advisory councils. Again, this caused controversy and angry exchanges within the group of MPs and in the wider Labour movement in Wales. So much so that a special conference of Labour Party Wales was called for and held at Llandrindod. The Policy for an Elected Council was re-affirmed. No MP spoke against. Those of us who spoke for the consultation paper were Alec Jones, Caerwyn Roderick, Ioan Evans, Will Edwards, Denzil Davies and me.

In September 1974, another Government White Paper was published called *'Democracy and Devolution for Scotland and Wales'*. This went into greater detail about the various options mentioned in the June consultation paper. But this time, on page 8, in the section 'Government's Decisions' it states:

> *For Scotland and Wales, the Government now proposes the creation of directly elected assemblies.*

The policy was in the manifesto for October 1974 election, but this time it was in the UK manifesto as well. Sadly, for me personally, there ended my parliamentary days fighting the cause that had started eight years earlier.

Gwynfor's colours

There's another point to consider. Gwynfor rarely attacked the Conservative party. I can only think of a few occasions when he did so, and it's interesting to note that it was only after the two Dafydds became MPs that he became more critical of the Tories. Labour was his only target. If, as we've established more than once, he criticised Labour for doing nothing for Wales, he never said the same about the Tories. I looked a little more into this. What had the Tories done in Wales?

> *During the 13 years of Tory rule from 1951 to 1964, seventy percent of railway stations and halts in Wales were closed, a total of 800 miles of rail line. In 1951, there were 730 stations and halts in Wales. In 1964, only 215 remained open.*

I then compared this with only five miles of rail track closed by Labour between 1964 and 1970. But Plaid Cymru's leader accused Labour of decimating Welsh railways. The same was true of road expenditure.

When Labour came to power, there were plans to spend £17 million on Welsh roads. By 1970, expenditure on Welsh roads was up to £50 million. But the Tories were never questioned on these issues or any other. And Gwynfor was Mr Dual Carriageway, of course!

Elystan Morgan experienced the same contemptuous attitude towards Labour in his dealings with Gwynfor Evans. When Elystan was deliberating about leaving Plaid to join Labour, Gwynfor's riposte was:

Rwyt ti'n gwybod beth rwyt ti'n gwneud ond dwyt ti? Rwy ti'n ymuno â phlaid Bessie Braddock!

You know what you're doing, don't you? You're joining Bessie Braddock's party!

Bessie Braddock was a Liverpool Labour MP, a real working-class character, typifying her area. She was called Battling Bessie because of her unwavering commitment, but they never gave her any ministerial responsibility throughout her years as MP. A genuine woman of the people, in one opinion poll, they chose her as the second most popular woman in Britain, next to the Queen. But Gwynfor's comment didn't come from a position of admiration for her. Elystan Morgan was and is clear that the spirit behind the comment was one of belittling, that Elystan was joining the party of someone like her. His words showed an inability to identify with Bessie. He was in a different world to her.

In his autobiography, Elystan, Elystan Morgan comments on how he perceived Gwynfor's attitude:

Ystyriai fod Llafur yn Blaid ddi-Dduw, ac yn fudiad o bobl na fyddai am eu cymeradwyo. Ni chredaf fod Gwynfor erioed wedi deall teithi meddwl y llafurwr Cymreig nac wedi eu uniaethu eu hun ag ef—dim mwy nag y gwnaeth Saunders Lewis... Cysyniad rhyddfrydwr breintiedig oedd cysyniad Gwynfor.[124]

---

124. Elystan Morgan; Huw L. Williams: *Elystan: Atgofion Oes*. Tal-y-bont, Ceredigion: Y Lolfa, 2012, p. 164.

He considered Labour to be a no-God party and an organisation that he would not want to recommend. I don't think that Gwynfor ever understood the thought patterns of the Welsh Labour person—no more than Saunders Lewis did… Gwynfor's concept was that of a privileged Liberal.

Politically, I can well understand the tactic of attacking Labour constituencies that Plaid wanted to do well in. I can also understand the need to attack Labour's record when things weren't going well for the party and therefore the country. Coalmines were closing, unemployment was rising, and Wales was being ignored by Westminster.

But this wasn't the entire picture. It's still surprising that the Tories, the Unionist party, received no attention from Gwynfor. He was quiet during Ted Heath's time as Prime Minister, and on the Tory record between 1951 and 1964. When we faced power cuts and three-day working weeks, Gwynfor never said that Wales was 'in a state of ruin' as he said when Labour was in power. There was no comment on the fact that two ministers in the Welsh Office were from constituencies in England. In his autobiography, Elystan Morgan recalls conversations he had with Gwynfor about the Conservative party:

Rwy'n cofio iddo ddweud wrtha'i fwy nag unwaith, 'Rwy'n ffeindio bod y Toriaid yn hynod o ffeind,'. Dywedais hyn wrth Jim Griffiths un diwrnod a'i ymateb oedd: 'Elystan bach, maen nhw'n trio cael Gwynfor i wneud y gwaith budr maen nhw wedi methu ei wneud o gwbl yng Nghymru, sef dinistrio'r Blaid Lafur.[125]

I remember him saying to me more than once, 'I find the Tories to be really nice people'. I told Jim Griffiths this one day and his response was 'My dear Elystan, they have been trying to get Gwynfor to do the dirty work that they have completely failed to do in Wales, which is to destroy the Labour Party.

Gwynfor's remarks, quoted above, are in stark contrast to his oft-repeated remark that Labour was morally bankrupt. This takes his attacks on

---

125. Ibid., p. 163.

Labour much further than just being politically expedient. My reflection on seeing this was that Gwynfor, in all essence, was an old-fashioned Victorian right-wing Liberal at best, and at worst, a secret Tory. In his last year as MP, there were 106 voting sessions in Parliament. Gwynfor only voted in 20 of them, and 16 times he voted with the Tories.

17.

Rome and Some Ministers

The battle for Welsh identity and the Welsh language took a different turn in 1971, at least as far as I was concerned. These were the days of increased militancy in the campaign for further recognition of the language in public life. It was a time of protest and imprisonment. But in that year, I proposed that the Treaty of Rome, the cornerstone of the European Common Market proposals, should be available in the Welsh language. What the Treaty proposed would obviously affect Wales and have a considerable impact on Welsh farmers. A high percentage of the population and a higher percentage of farmers spoke Welsh.

This issue captured the imagination of newspaper letter-writers and to my surprise, there were many who supported my call. A majority of these opposed the militant campaigning of Cymdeithas yr Iaith, but supported the principle of bilingual documentation and legislation. Here's one letter from someone supporting a copy of the *Treaty of Rome* in Welsh, in Swansea's *Evening Post*:

> *The tragedy these days is that any reference to parity of language is unfairly tainted with a degree of suspicion and disrepute. This is because sign-daubing and the almost ritualistic burning this week of English-only licenses takes away much of the credibility from those who possess an honourable cause.*

That same year, in March, at public meetings in Llangadog and Brynaman, I called for a permanent Commission for the Welsh language. My argument was that establishing such a body would ensure a practical way of implementing the principle of equality for the language, as laid out by the Welsh Language Act of 1967. I called on Welsh people in every party to tone down the passion a little and to stop playing politics with the language. The newspapers again reported on my speech and quoted from it:

I am becoming increasingly convinced that one essential need is for the issue to be brought from the realms of party politics. The language, its survival and encouragement are greater than any political gain for any person or party. Everyone should now work for the loosening of the tension that surrounds the concern over the future of our national language, and when I say this, it means that those who want to progress at a quicker rate than hitherto must display a degree of patience and understanding, whilst those in authority, be they in local or central government, must acquire a greater sense of understanding and urgency than hitherto.

I suggested that such a Commission should advise every level of government on how to ensure equality for the Welsh language.

I had a specific opportunity to apply the principles of my argument ironically enough in the imprisoning of two prominent Cymdeithas yr Iaith members, Dafydd Iwan and Meinir, Gwynfor Evans' daughter. They drew my attention to the fact that while they were in prison, they were not allowed to speak Welsh with their visitors. The argument was that the prison officers wouldn't be able to understand them, which could be a threat to security. This was also highlighted by the imprisonment of four women in Pucklechurch and one student in Cardiff. I asked to speak to the Governor of Cardiff Prison, having gathered that at least one prison officer there spoke Welsh. They refused my request. I strongly objected to any legislation that prevented people from speaking their mother tongue.

I also supported the introduction of bilingual road signs, as had the Labour Party since 1971. In that year, the Labour Party in Wales, in its evidence to the Bowen Committee, accepted the principle of road signs throughout the whole of Wales. The party considered it reasonable that 'main signs' should be made bilingual over three years and a five-year target should be set to complete the rest. I regularly lobbied the department in the Welsh Office responsible for looking into this matter, urging them not to take too long to publish their findings. I was concerned about the cost of introducing bilingual signs. Yes, I was, and I suggested that they should phase the signs in over time in order to ease the financial burden. My issue all along with the road signs campaign was the law-breaking tactics used by many who advocated them. I was not alone, as Martin Johnes shows in this example:

> *A Cardiganshire survey suggested that only 19% of Welsh speakers and 7% of non-welsh speakers thought that pulling down signs was sometimes justified as a form of protest.*[126]

Through all these individual issues, all from 1971, one line quoted in a newspaper report on one of them sums up my underlying attitude to any issue to do with Welsh in public life:

> *But above all, there is a need to stop this talk of "them" and "us" in relation to the language.*

But of course, this was Wales, and it was impossible to avoid the 'them' and 'us' as I was about to discover from an unexpected source.

Pulpit power

A storm brewed between me and a group of Nonconformist ministers from Wales. A large number of ministers, specifically from Undeb yr Annibynnwyr (the Union of Independents), made a stand in favour of those who used law-breaking means to protest on the languages' behalf. They addressed the protesting that happened in the name of calling for bilingual road signs and the establishment of a Welsh TV channel.

A letter signed by 40 chapel ministers in 1971 was sent to the press, thus generating an argument that went on for years. I still have one letter that was a part of this debate, dated June 1974! The tone of the debate

---

126. Martin Johnes: *Wales since 1939.* Manchester: Manchester University Press, 2013, p. 229.

hadn't mellowed over three years either. This letter, criticising the ministers, wasn't exactly subtly headed:

Next claim will be that Jesus Christ died for Plaid Cymru

'Political' Ministers accused of emptying chapels

CHRISTIANS OR HYPOCRITES ?

MP urges membership showdown

IN a blistering attack Carmarthen M.P. Mr. Gwynoro Jones last week accused ministers of religion of using the pulpit to further the cause of the Welsh Language Society. Mr. Jones, speaking to the Carmel and Milo Labour Party, added that the trend of ministers to "further their cherished dreams" was dividing chapels and driving people away.

"If these ministers are true to their calling," he said, "it

pastures to concentrate on in their sermons.
"One of the worst features of the debate on breaking

by the Welsh Language Society and its leaders.

"Where were the leaders of the Nationalist Party at

I was strongly against the ministers making such a stand, based on my upbringing in the Christian faith and my understanding of it. For me, they had crossed the line between faith and politics. In addition, if they propagated their argument from their pulpits, they were flying in the face of the Nonconformist tradition they were part of, which emphasised that the pulpit shouldn't be used for politicising. I was clear enough in my condemnation of them:

One is tempted to say that the sooner some of them leave our chapels, the healthier the situation will be. It is high time they realised that there are people of all political persuasions inside their chapels and their calling should transcend all party-political talk. They have done far more harm to the religious cause this week than anything else for many a year.

Equally disturbing is the call of these ministers to break the law on television licences and yet how many of them are quite prepared to take fat cheques for appearing on television themselves?

The ministers were equally forthright in their condemnation of my reply. They released a press release calling on Harold Wilson to discipline one of his MPs for threatening and trying to divide leaders and members of the Christian Church. Twenty-four ministers signed this press release. The *Carmarthen Times*, on 13 October 1972, listed the names of the ministers and an outline of their arguments. I added some further comments:

... there are names connected with the statement who are active supporters of, and other active workers for, Plaid Cymru. Indeed, I have seen some of them campaigning in elections held in Wales during the last few years. So I am far from impressed by their assured impartiality.

Plaid Cymru would also respond, of course. According to their organiser in Dyfed, Peter Hughes Griffiths, I hadn't behaved with the dignity expected of an MP. According to Gwynfor Evans, Christianity encompassed every area of life and subsequently, a minister of religion had the right to enter the world of politics. He ended his comments by referring to me:

... the sooner one capable of such effrontery leaves politics, the healthier the situation will be.

Gwynfor contributed further to the debate, in a letter to the *Carmarthen Times* in 1973:

The Welsh language is the vehicle of the great Welsh Christian tradition. To uphold this Christian tradition is the duty of all Christians in Wales, to ensure that they transmit the values embodied in it to future generations is an especial responsibility of the Church.

The symbolic action of the ministers was a courageous act of leadership in this at a time of acute crisis in Wales. The relevance of the language to Welsh Christianity is illuminated by the fact that 75% of Welsh-speaking people are members of a Christian Church; of monoglot English-speaking persons, the proportion is about 15%.

Scant use of facts and statistics once more. 15% sounds a low figure to me, considering how many would have been going to English-speaking nonconformist, Evangelical and Church in Wales places of worship.

A letter in October 1972, from someone in Lampeter, sums up very well the attitude of those who opposed Gwynfor and the ministers:

If ministers of religion want to preach politics, let them share platforms with political speakers of any party, not attempt to use the cloth or a place of worship as a means of undue persuasion. If they consider it their duty and right to do so, then chapel members have an equal right and duty to express resentment. True Christianity has no barriers, least of all language, and the sooner some of these ministers realise it the better for all concerned. Mr Gwynoro Jones is right. We cannot praise the Lord and attack the television service in the same breath and with the same conviction.

The *South Wales Guardian* was involved too. A headline of theirs in October 1972 read 'The Union of Welsh "Inconsistents"'. It refers to the campaign to refuse to pay the TV licence until they established an Independent Broadcasting Authority in Wales. Many ministers joined this campaign.

This suggests that such Christians would view the Welsh programmes transmitted at present without paying. Is this the Christianity that the ministers referred to preach every Sunday?

I suggest that the Christian way to protest is for all who feel the need for the Authority referred to disconnect their television sets when the current licence expires and put them away until the said Authority is set up for Wales.

This would ensure that all (especially the so-called Christians) would not be viewing programmes free of charge, which would be un-Christian.

The flagship daily Welsh news magazine programme, *Heddiw*, made by the BBC, invited me to appear on the programme to discuss the issue. Gwynfor was to be the other guest. I declined the invitation. Plaid heavily criticised me for refusing to take part, and they accused me of being a coward. If they had only bothered to ask the actual reason I said no, they would have heard a different story. A week before this invitation from the BBC, I had taken part in HTV's current affairs programme, *Yr Wythnos*. This was a half-hour programme and there were two ministers of religion on the programme with me. It was a good, thorough half-hour discussion. I, therefore, saw no point in taking part in a three- or four-minute item on the BBC on the same issue.

The fact that Gwynfor would be the other contributor on *Heddiw* was also a lesser consideration. I asked if I could debate the issue with a minister of religion, not Gwynfor. They said no. I asked what the justification was of asking someone who wasn't a minister of religion. The BBC's reply was that he was the Treasurer of the Union of Welsh Independents! As if they would invite the Treasurer of the Welsh Rugby Union to speak on a rugby issue to do with players! Or even more relevant, asking the treasurer of the Welsh Labour Party to contribute instead of me!

Gwynfor again voiced his objection to my refusal to debate on the BBC in the local press. A letter was sent to the *Carmarthen Times* defending me. It was written by a Roger Thomas, who would play a far more prominent role in my story in years to come. He said:

Of the three dozen ministers involved in activity which had aroused the criticism of Mr Jones, not one had been favoured by being invited to defend their actions. This was at least how the bright boys of the BBC read the situation...

Mr Jones' refusal to appear was fully justified, and I admire this as an example of the political acumen he is fast acquiring.

Mr Evans' appearing on this programme was meant to further his own political cause. That he has people of influence, highly sympathetic to his cause, in the current affairs' presentation of Welsh Language television, has never been more clearly highlighted.

This one episode shows clearly how strong and deep the feelings were, and how firmly rooted the identity of Wales was and is in the Christian heritage. It also shows that many of Plaid's big battles weren't run by politicians.

Statistics and disillusionment

While these battles were continuing between me and Plaid, the fight with my fellow Welsh Labour MPs hadn't gone away. Many felt that the Welsh language was receiving far too much attention. For men like Neil Kinnock, Alan Williams of Swansea West, Leo Abse, Roy Hughes and others, far too much emphasis was placed on the ability to speak Welsh. Specifically, the ability to speak Welsh gave an advantage to many candidates for many top public appointments in Wales. After having heard this argument for quite some time, I decided to find out how many Welsh speakers the government departments employed. I asked a question in the House on it.

Gradually, the answers came back. For example, the Welsh Office employed 130, which was 13.5% of its staff. 316 Welsh speakers worked in the Ministry of Employment, 18.5% of the total. No huge bias towards Welsh speakers in those two departments. That was the case throughout. The only exception was the Ministry of Agriculture. They employed 600 Welsh speakers, 45% of their staff. Those figures didn't silence Kinnock and his like, of course. The language wasn't important to them, whatever the statistics were.

This clear water between some of my fellow Welsh Labour MPs and myself, on the issue of my mother country, was a constant cause of disillusionment for me, and it was there soon after I entered Westminster. As the years moved on, other areas of policy put some more clear water between me and them. But that's another story.

18.

The Three-Vote Win

As 1973 drew to a close, the Conservative government introduced an emergency Budget. It was clearly a move that heralded an imminent General Election. The economic situation of Britain at the time was far from good. In the *Carmarthen Times*, 21 December, I argued that it was up to the government to sort out such difficulties, not split the country further by heading towards a General Election.

> *The country faces its gravest economic crisis since 1931… ordinary people, farmers, miners and the rest, have seen costs rise at an unprecedented rate and are looking for an amelioration and to bridge the divisions that exist. There are sinister elements on the extreme left and right of politics which are ready to undermine our parliamentary system if given the opportunity.*

In a letter, I urged Prime Minister Ted Heath not to play politics with the disputes the mining industry faced.

> *I urge you to cease looking at the dispute in terms of political advantage. It will be to your eternal discredit if you were to engineer a possible election victory at the expense of doing untold damage to mining and the coal industry, which will cause havoc with the economy.*

At this exact time, Gwynfor published a book, *Wales Can Win*. Many comments in it angered me, for example:

German invaders could not have caused more than a fraction of the havoc to Welsh national life that the British system had been wreaking for generations.[127]

M.P. slams publication and asks Plaid chief

Would Hitler have given freedom?

"German invaders could not have caused more than a fraction of the havoc to Welsh national life that the British system had been wreaking for generations."

This extract from a publication "Wales Can Win" by Plaid Cymru president, Mr. Gwynfor Evans, was referred to this week by Carmarthen M.P. Mr. Gwynoro Jones, when he addressed the Carmarthen Borough Labour Party.

Said Mr. Jones: "It really does take someone with a bitter hatred of Britishness to state that."

"But according to him these wars were waged 'not to defend anything of great value to the Welsh people'.

"Not of great value? What about family life? What about freedom of expression? And what about religious freedom?

"But far worse in my view was Mr. Evans's apparent acceptance that those who fought in the 1939-45 war were defending England and not Wales people who did make the supreme sacrifice in the war were 'murderers.' "

Mr. Jones was referring to Britain.

"Was the choice that difficult Mr. Evans? What would the fate of Wales have been if Hitler had been allowed to proceed unchallenged?"

Said Mr. Jones: "The worrying point is that these are the views of the reputed moderates in their nationalist party.

"What, one wonders, are the views of the reckless fringe found in every nationalist movement throughout history?"

SURVIVAL

He made similar comments when Russia invaded Czechoslovakia, saying that the oppression that Wales suffered at the hands of the English was much worse. This is what he said in relation to the Second World War.

At a time when the vast majority of their fellow countrymen had been brainwashed by Britishness... to ask them to kill their fellow human beings for England in these circumstances was, they felt, to become murderers.[128]

---

127. Evans, Gwynfor: *Wales Can Win*. Llandybie, C. Davies, 1973, p. 65.
128. Ibid., p. 67.

I attacked such comments in the local press:

> *Gwynfor cannot accept that in both World Wars, a great deal was at stake for the people of Wales, but according to him, these wars were waged 'not to defend anything of great value to Wales'.*

Nothing of any value? What about family life, freedom of expression, religious freedom? I then turned my attention to the comment associating soldiers from Wales with murderers:

> *Murderers, he called the Welsh soldiers. Well, those tens of thousands of Welsh people fought to ensure our security today… to guarantee a Welsh way of life could exist and guaranteed its survival so that politicians like Gwynfor Evans and Gwynoro Jones can discuss important issues facing Wales today without fear of persecution or imprisonment.*

It's not only the comments themselves that deserve condemnation, but their timing as well. These were dire economic times. Coal mining was facing a serious disaster, one which would have a severe impact in Wales, of course. But here was Gwynfor publishing a book on issues that didn't exactly address the need of the hour or the needs of the majority of his people.

To the Polling Booths once more

It wasn't long before the miners went out on strike. Two days later, Ted Heath called a General Election to be held on 28 February. The Prime Minister's tactic was obvious. He blamed the miners for the economic condition of the UK. They were the ones on strike. There were power cuts every day, with candles having to be used at home in the evenings. And the working week was now three days, not five. The miners weren't only blamed for this, but also for deliberately plotting to overthrow the government by their actions. Conwy MP Wyn Roberts was vociferous against the miners, regularly appearing on the media accusing them of wanting to destroy the government.

I had hundreds of coal miners in my constituency, in Cynheidre, Cwmgwili, Betws and Abernant collieries. I decided to visit them at their place of work. While underground at Cwmgwili, some of Wyn Roberts' comments came to mind:

> *I thought that if he had been with me, he would be much more careful about what he says. These people to whom he was referring are ordinary people who have lived ordinary lives in the ordinary valleys of Carmarthenshire and elsewhere, who have nothing of the sort in mind and want only to make a decent living and give of their best for their country as they have done for decades past.*

The miners' stance wasn't the cause of the economic situation of the time, of course. Britain's debt had increased considerably since 1970, prices were rising quickly, and the pounds' value had fallen.

From the 1972 miners' strike onwards, Plaid Cymru had failed to identify with these workers, who, after all, are so central to the development of Wales. There was a by-election in Merthyr in 1972, following the death of their long-standing and influential MP, S. O. Davies. Plaid chose Emrys Roberts. Many in the party, however, including Gwynfor, weren't happy with this choice. But Emrys Roberts did very well in that election, coming second, less than four thousand votes behind Labour's

Ted Rowlands. Plaid were fourth in 1970 and Emrys Roberts had nearly quadrupled the votes for his party in two years.

In his biography of Gwynfor Evans, this is how Rhys Evans sums up this achievement:

As it happened Emrys Roberts achieved an excellent result taking 37% of the vote, coming close to ousting Labour in April. He was helped by Labour divisions over Europe, but Gwynfor chose to ignore this factor. He saw the Merthyr result as a turning point and, like others in his party, misread the signs. Merthyr turned out to be the high watermark of Plaid Cymru popular support, not a promise of better things to come.[129]

He then refers to the effect this had on Plaid Cymru:

After 1972, Plaid Cymru lost its appeal in the valleys—not least because of energetic young Labour leaders like Elystan Morgan and Gwynoro Jones. But Gwynfor himself did much to hasten the decline by failing to maintain Plaid Cymru support in the valleys between 1967 and 1972, and after Merthyr, played Plaid Cymru did virtually nothing to nurture the South.[130]

Gwynfor's focus, and therefore his party's, was on Carmarthen, Meirionnydd and Caernarfon. They were the only areas important to him. He didn't bother with other areas where the Welsh language wasn't so strong. In any discussions on the Common Market and the Miners' Strike, Gwynfor had very little to say. He had his own agenda. Such a stance benefited Cymdeithas yr Iaith more than anyone else.

Canvassing once more

The various issues relating to the devolution debate, which have already been highlighted as they apply to my interaction with Plaid and my fel-

129.Rhys Evans: *Gwynfor Evans: Portrait of a Patriot*. Tal-y-bont, Ceredigion: Y Lolfa, 2008, p. 325.
130.Ibid.

low Welsh Labour MPs, all came to a head when the campaigning for the General Election started. I was regarded with some suspicion by the Welsh MPs in my party because of my stance on devolution. I was Parliamentary Secretary to Roy Jenkins and seen as one of the 70 or so Labour MPs who sided with him in a political stance that would, in years to come, lead to the formation of a new political party, the SDP.

Plaid Cymru, by the beginning of 1974, were far more organised in Carmarthen than they had ever been. That was, without doubt, down to the skills of party organiser Peter Hughes Griffiths. He put a definite strategy in place and introduced better campaign literature. By election day, Plaid had distributed a leaflet, Gwynfor and You, to every household. They had a full-page advert in the local press six days before polling.

The story for Labour was completely different. I had the same team as in 1970, but four years later the energy levels weren't the same! That was true of me as well, partly because of my changing attitude to my party and partly because of the effect of the opposition I'd had from some fellow MPs within my party. As far as Labour in Wales was concerned, this is what John Gilbert Evans says in *Labour and Devolution in Wales*:

> *In the general election in February 1974, Labour's Welsh manifesto promised an elected council to be "an effective democratic force in the life of Wales", but there was no mention of devolution in the National manifesto.*[131]

The Plaid Labour tensions came to the fore unexpectedly a few days before the General Election. That year's National Eisteddfod was to be held in Carmarthen, by coincidence. I was invited to be one of the Presidents for the Day. Plaid Cymru were furious! In the party's publication, *Y Ddraig Goch*, Peter Hughes Griffiths wrote an article under the title *'Pam Gwynoro?'* (*'Why Gwynoro?'*) He questions the wisdom of Eisteddfod officials in inviting someone so young.

---

131. John Gilbert Evans: *Labour and Devolution in Wales*. Tal-y-bont, Ceredigion: Y Lolfa, 2019, p. 21.

Usually, he said, those asked to fulfil such a role have made a lifetime contribution to their field. I was only 30. As part of the same argument, he said that the Eisteddfod had nothing to do with politics or sport. But he seemed to ignore the fact that there was a precedent to inviting MPs when the Eisteddfod was in their constituency—Jim Griffiths in 1962, Ivor Davies in 1964, John Morris in 1966. Gwynfor was invited to be President for the Day in 1970 before the General Election but had lost his seat by the time the Eisteddfod was held. Each one of these was within 12 years of the Carmarthen Eisteddfod.

Peter Hughes Griffiths questioned if I had ever competed in an Eisteddfod or if I had ever been a member of the Urdd (The Welsh League of Youth). I wasn't aware that such selection criteria were applied to everyone. Then he got to what I saw as the crux of Plaid's opposition to my invite—I had opposed the stance taken by the ministers of religion and I had nothing good to say about Cymdeithas yr Iaith! And there's me thinking that the Eisteddfod shouldn't have anything to do with politics! He then said that I made very little use of my Welsh and that he had not seen anything during the campaign written in Welsh by me. That was untrue and bad timing. I've already outlined various stands I made for the language. And the week his article was published, I had a Welsh language article in the Carmarthen papers. It wasn't the first. Again, scant disregard for facts!

Naturally, those Carmarthen papers got hold of the story. In a *Carmarthen Times* editorial on 1 February 1974, the editor responded to some individual points made by Peter Hughes Griffiths and offered his own interpretation:

INCONSISTENCY NOTE: Later, Mr Hughes Griffiths listed eleven men who would have made a 'worthier' choice. Among them are: Dafydd Iwan (hardly middle-age) Tom Ellis, Labour MP (nothing to do with politics?) Barry John (nothing to do with rugby?)

He responds to the accusation made by Peter Hughes Griffiths, that he, as editor, was 'ultra-Tory':

INCONSISTENCY NOTE: If the charge of ultra-Tory was correct, then why is 'endless space' being allowed to Labour—or any other party for that matter?

He sums up his argument:

... to attempt to publicly discredit the MP when his only 'crime' is to accept an invitation from the National Eisteddfod Committee to become a day president when the event is held in Carmarthen is not only untimely but thoroughly unworthy.

My invitation stood, thank goodness, and I took my place as day president on the Friday of the August Eisteddfod. But before that, there would be an election to fight!

Four Welsh MP's inducted into the Gorsedd of Bards, 1965

A night of mounting tension

I arrived at the count at about midnight. The betting people still made me favourite to win, but as I walked in, I was told that it looked as if I was ahead by about 800 votes. I had an inkling then that it would be close. The candidates were told that the result put me 10 votes in front. Gwynfor naturally asked for a recount. The result of the second count put me ahead by four votes. Gwynfor called for another recount. This time Gwynfor was ahead by four votes! It was my turn to ask for a recount. By now, it was 6 o'clock in the morning. It's hard to describe the excitement and the tension in that room. It was decided that it wouldn't be fair to hold another recount immediately, as the counting team had started their work eight hours previously. It was decided to give them a break and to hold the next recount at 4 pm. That did nothing but intensify the tension inside the building and amongst the crowd outside.

While this was all going on, outside Carmarthen, Labour had suffered significant loses—Elystan Morgan to Geraint Howells, for example, and Goronwy Roberts and Will Edwards to Dafydd Elis Thomas and Dafydd Wigley. Throughout Britain, the situation between Harold Wilson and Ted Heath was very tight. Such a scenario meant that there was a great deal more attention on Carmarthen that Friday afternoon than there might have been otherwise.

By 7.30 that Friday evening, the count put Gwynfor ahead by one vote! I asked for another recount. But before that went ahead, the candidates were told that however close the new count would be, there would not be another. There would be no sixth count. There was also to be a change in the way the votes were counted. The candidates' votes would be counted one at a time, starting with the one who had the least amount of votes in the previous count. That increased the tension even more!

The result was announced. Bill Newton-Dunn, Conservatives, 6,037. David Owen Jones, Liberals, 9,698. In second place, me, with 17,161 votes. I had lost. Before Gwynfor's votes could be announced, one of those counting the votes raised his hand. He said that there were only 46 votes in a bundle that should hold 50. Gwynfor defeating me by one vote turned out to be a victory for me by three votes! Once again, Carmarthen

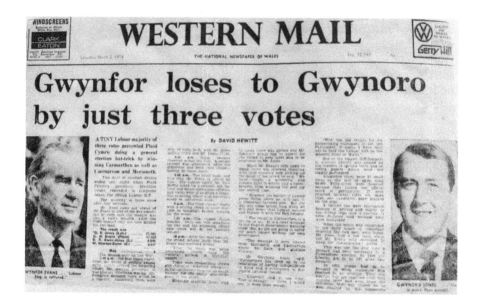

had given Wales another dramatic electoral episode. I was back as MP in this tempestuous constituency.

When I walked onto the balcony to address the crowd outside, I had a fiery reception! There was no way in the world that I could make any kind of speech. The jeers aimed at me were ferocious and personal. To his credit, Gwynfor asked the crowd to be quiet so I could make my speech. I said a few words and then went back inside. This time, at least I could walk back to my car and go home.

But all was not as it appeared. When I got home, there was a police car parked outside. Without me knowing, they had been keeping an eye on the house for a while. Within an hour of announcing the result, the threatening phone calls had started. There were four in total. Each caller had said that they knew where I lived and that they would come for me. The police had been monitoring my calls, and they promised to do so for a further three days after that. There would be a police car outside the house on the following two weekends. These threats were deeply worrying, especially as we had two children under five. I wondered then, as now, if this was one consequence of the refusal to condemn violent protests.

Reaction and response

The analysis went on for days after, as you would imagine. Many expected me to win comfortably. How, therefore, did it end up being so, so close? How did Plaid nearly take the seat back? The *Carmarthen Journal* offered this interpretation:

Mr. Gwynoro Jones . . . won election with three-vote majority.

THREATENING CALLS TO LABOUR MP

By DAVID ROBERTS

THREATENING TELEPHONE calls have been made to Mr. Gwynoro Jones, the Labour MP for Carmarthen, who returns to Westminster with the smallest majority in the country.

A police watch which had been kept at his home at Carmarthen, where he lives with Mr. ... porters and helpers.

> *This is a most difficult question to answer, but it might be that the people in the Carmarthen constituency, like in Scotland and elsewhere, are disillusioned with the big parties and were registering their protest.*

This was the *Carmarthen Times'* analysis:

> *Disillusioned with the two major parties because of their agricultural policies, local farmers (arguing that the Liberal candidate was young and untried) were openly saying that they were switching their allegiance to Plaid Cymru—as they did in the by-election in 1966.*

This hurt me quite a bit. I had worked tirelessly for the farmers, through both the NFU and the FUW.

Also, some stories about events at the count started to circulate. At one point, we were told that 97 ballot papers hadn't been received because they didn't have the official pin marks in them. Both my agent and Gwynfor's went through these 97 papers one by one, holding them up to the light to see if they could find a pin mark. Some were accepted as a result of this. It's all part of an election count night. But Gwynfor had to make some point out of it. In his book, *For the Sake of Wales*, he says:

Poor old Gwynoro was on tenterhooks at the count... going over to the returning officer to inspect the slips that had been spoiled. He would hold one up against the light and examine it closely.

Yes, I did so. But for one reason only. My agent Ivor Morris, who had been with me since 1967, had worked tirelessly all night. He was in his seventies by then, so I took over from him and started to look at the papers. Gwynfor had to use that as a way of further belittling me. Using the word 'poor' is completely uncalled for in a reasoned argument.

As much as I admire Rhys Evans' biography of Gwynfor, Portrait of a Patriot, I must correct one story in it that refers to the evening of the count. It is said that Gwynfor was under considerable pressure to call for a sixth count:

Gwynfor came under immense pressure to demand a sixth count, but wiser counsel prevailed. Wynne Samuel advised Gwynfor to accept the result, because it was better to lose by three votes than win by the same margin.[132]

But I have already stated that we were told that there would be no sixth count before the fifth took place. The interpretation in the quote plays with the idea of Gwynfor giving his permission to lose, as opposed to just having lost.

---

132. Rhys Evans: *Gwynfor Evans: Portrait of a Patriot.* Tal-y-bont, Ceredigion: Y Lolfa, 2008, p. 334.

19.

George, Roger, Tony

I might well have secured my majority, but on a UK level, there was no clear majority for any party. We were heading for a hung parliament. In such a situation, there was always going to be a lot of negotiating. Heath tried to hang on to power, specifically through negotiations with Jeremy Thorpe, the Liberal leader, but he failed to carry his party with him. Heath had to then resign. Harold Wilson was asked to form a Government, albeit a minority one. So I was once again an MP, but this time with a Labour government in power. Because of this politically fragile situation, there was talk of a second General Election that same year almost as soon as we took our places.

Gwynfor was right in his response to that prediction, saying that if there was going to be a second election, then Plaid Cymru would be in a stronger position than I would be. I agreed with him on that. Throughout the summer of '74, Gwynfor was active in trying to attract the support of the Liberal and Conservative supporters, which was the natural thing for him to do. However, there was an element of dishonesty in such an approach because Plaid were moving more to the left, as was the Labour Party. As far as I was concerned, no one needed to remind me how fragile a majority of three was!

In that February election, Labour's vote across the UK was down and even the Labour MPs who had been returned, their vote was down by between two and five thousand. In that respect, Carmarthen had done well in losing only 1,600 votes. Overall, in Wales, the Liberals came third, replacing Plaid Cymru. The Liberal vote increased from 6% to 16% while Plaid's dropped to 10%.

Glass houses and Europe

Now that he was Prime Minister once more, Harold Wilson had an opportunity to do what Tom Ellis, Caerwyn Roderick and Brynmor John and I had been urging him to do for quite some time—to replace George Thomas as Welsh Secretary. We had lobbied Harold Wilson twice on this issue and suggested that John Morris should replace George. Harold listened in courteous silence on each occasion but made few comments.

For more than a year before the election, George Thomas had caused considerable damage to the Labour Party in Wales. Through his regular column in the *Liverpool Daily Post*, he took every opportunity to disparage the Welsh language, the Eisteddfod and the culture and identity of Wales. I have no doubt that such a militant stance cost Labour votes in February '74, and further fuelled the accusation of Labour being anti-Welsh. We argued that his stance was divisive and harmful and that he had to go.

Harold Wilson could see the problems that were being caused by George. He had seen Elystan Morgan, Goronwy Roberts and Will Edwards lose their seats and me hanging on by 3 votes. He could see that the damage was being done. He could also see that we didn't have it in for George but that, electorally, he was turning the Welsh-speaking areas against the Labour party. So he appointed John Morris as Welsh Secretary in March 1974. Needless to say, George was extremely unhappy. I felt the full force of his vitriol not long after. Cledwyn Hughes told me the first week we were back after the Election, that there was talk of me being appointed as Junior Minister, either in Agriculture or Northern Ireland. Neither happened, and I was later told by the Agriculture Minister, Fred Peart, that George had poisoned my name to Harold Wilson.

George's response to this period is noted in his book, *Mr Speaker*:

I knew that I had annoyed some Welsh Labour MPs by my strong resistance to Welsh nationalism. In retrospect, I think I was unwise to disregard their feelings the way I did. When Harold told me the names of a small group of Welsh MPs who had gone to him to protest about my views, I was even more outspoken.[133]

It is easy in retrospect to see how my views on devolution were an embarrassment to people like Cledwyn Hughes, Elystan Morgan, John Morris and others who lived in a world of their own cocooned by nationalist aspirations.[134]

But we didn't only tell Harold Wilson about his 'resistance to Welsh nationalism'. His attacks on the language and Welsh culture—especially the Eisteddfod—were also mentioned. I had discussions with George himself on these issues too. I often reminded George that the people who are prominent in Eisteddfod circles and who attend year in, year out were Labour voters and working-class people at that.

Harold Wilson, despite his silence, did listen and got rid of George, making John Morris Welsh Secretary of State. George himself describes the occasion in his book:

'George,' said Harold, 'you've been a good friend to me'. I replied that we had been good friends to each other and what is more we had been loyal to each other.

And then he blurted out—and that is the only way to put it, 'How would you like to be Deputy Speaker?' I nearly fell out of my shoes. 'What, Deputy Speaker and not Secretary of State for Wales?'[135]

The telling point was this despite being Harold's ear, nose and throat for years (we used to call him George ENT) he was the only former Minister from 1970 not to go back into the Cabinet.

George was not a nice man at all, totally different to the god-fearing, Christian image he always portrayed. He was one of the most devious,

---

133. George Thomas: *Mr Speaker: The Memoirs of Viscount Tonypandy*. London: Century Publishing Co. Ltd., 1985, p. 127.
134. Ibid., p. 129.
135. Ibid., p. 127.

nasty, rumour-spreading gossipers in the House. He took great delight in hearing of people's misfortunes and talking about them.

Here he is, again in his book, five years after being dropped as Secretary of State and two years after being made Speaker:

> *When the referendum they forced on Wales… This did not prevent me from telephoning Cledwyn Hughes, a leading protagonist of devolution ever since his entry to Parliament, and expressing my delight at the resulting four-to-one rejection of a Welsh National Assembly.*[136]

This sums up George—make an enemy of him and he did not forget it.

Europe and a bottle of champagne

Speaking at the European Council.

136. Ibid., p. 129.

I was appointed as one of Parliament's representatives to the Council of Europe. I went to my first session there in May '74. I decided to make my first-ever speech there in Welsh. Later to be Labour leader, John Smith had planted the seed in my mind the day before. As I rose to my feet to make the speech, John whispered, 'Do you want your standing ovation now or later?' As I spoke, I could hear the translators saying, 'I think Mr Jones is speaking in Welsh'. This is how I began:

Rydw i'n ddiolchgar i chi, Mr Llywydd, am ganiatàu i fi ddweud ychydig eiriau yn fy mam-iaith er mwyn pwysleisio bod dirprwyaeth Y Deyrnas Gyfunol yma yn cynnwys cynrychiolwyr tair cenedl... Efallai bydd y Cyngor am ystyried fy mod i wedi siarad mwy o Gymraeg yng Nghyngor Ewrop nag yr ydw i yn Senedd Prydain Fawr.

I'm grateful to you, Mr Chair, for allowing me to say a few words in my mother tongue so that I can emphasise that the United Kingdom delegation includes three nations... Maybe the Council would like to consider that I have spoken more Welsh in the European Council than I have in Great Britain's parliament.

In the press conference afterwards, John Smith said, '*... I think that it's a great thing he's done.*' Back home, however, the reaction was different. The *Western Mail*'s political correspondent, David Cornock, said:

That's not what some of his colleagues in Westminster are thinking.

And he was right. Once again, I felt the strong opposition of some fellow Labour MPs. Network news picked up on my speech. When I phoned home to say what I'd done, my then-wife Laura said that she already knew; she'd seen the fuss over it on TV. Some Labour officials in my constituency had seen it too and had phoned my wife to ask why on earth I had done such a thing! Once again, I had to argue that making such a stand for the language didn't mean that I was a closet Plaid Cymru member!

As well as John Smith, I had one other, rather amusing, positive response to my Welsh speech. On the plane home, the pilot came in to

Gwynoro speaks in Welsh in Europe and translators are speechless!

MR. GWYNORO JONES, M.P. for Carmarthen, became the first delegate to speak Welsh at the Assembly of the Council of Europe and confound the simultaneous translation facilities.

Mr. Jones, speaking about the importance of energy resources, opened his remarks in Welsh. Other delegates waited in vain for a translation through their headphones.

"It is clear that we have to concentrate on what we should do in terms of co-ordination and the pooling of resources." Mr. Jones warned that European oil would not last forever. He said: "I speak as member of a delegation from country which is now in unique position, with the bonanza on its doorstep. It h

see us passengers and asked if there was a Mr Jones present. I put my hand up, and he gave me a bottle of champagne, saying:

I come from Llanelli and I've been flying this route for over 20 years. When I heard what you did in the Council, you made me feel so proud!

Some people appreciated what I had done, at least!

Benn and Roger

Very early in the Parliament of '74, I was increasingly in confrontation with the Left within the Labour Party. This came to a head during a very public disagreement with Tony Benn. He was, without doubt, a much-respected figure within the party, and he still is. He had then just advocated

286

a broad-ranging programme for nationalisation, including nationalising large areas of land in the UK for development. This gave other parties a golden opportunity to spread the message that Labour was after your land! This was, of course, particularly relevant for me in my constituency and in my battles with Gwynfor and Plaid.

My response to Benn was to say that such plans were irrelevant in the current political and economic climate. A significant section of the party feared that Benn's influence was increasing and that Harold Wilson was finding it increasingly difficult to reign him in. I spoke on two meetings of the Labour Parliamentary Committee, saying that Benn's stance was harming the party electorally. In discussions with Cledwyn Hughes, I released a statement which included this sentence:

The captain of the ship in the middle of a storm does not attend a meeting called by his first mate to discuss the future direction of the voyage.

Everyone knew immediately that Wilson was the captain and Benn the first mate. Robert Kee interviewed me on ITN *Lunchtime News* about this. On my return to the Commons after the broadcast, Harold Wilson's Parliamentary Private Secretary was waiting for me. He asked me, 'You weren't having a go at Harold, were you?' 'No, of course not,' was my reply. My path within the party was clearly set.

Naturally, Gwynfor took hold of some of Benn's comments, using them to spread fears that Labour, as a party, intended to put large areas of Welsh land into public ownership, and that farmland and gardens would be taken under such a scheme. Understandably, this raised great fears in Carmarthenshire.

As far as I was concerned, I was called for the second time in a short period to a meeting of the Constituency party to explain myself. I had avoided being censured following my speech in Welsh in Brussels. Thankfully, I also avoided being censured for publicly standing against Benn as well. The chair of the Constituency party, local GP Roger Thomas, was quoted in the local press, following the meeting with me:

Alan Evans Photography

Dafydd Wigley   Dafydd Elis Thomas

I suspect that the left-wing element in the party could be upset by what was said, but that perhaps is inevitable.

Consciously or not, this occasion was the beginning of Roger Thomas being far more active in writing to the local press and the *Western Mail*. Looking back, it's clear that he had considered the next step in his own career. In one of these articles, he compares the politics of the two Dafydds of Plaid Cymru with Gwynfor's:

> *On television the other night, Dafydd Wigley reminded us he and his fellow member had in the past three months supported the Labour Government no fewer than on fifteen occasions with only three times against… Mr Evans, when he was our MP in 1966-1970, found himself able to support the Labour Government on few and far between occasions… the two present members are so far left that they make Mr Evans appear to be the apotheosis of reactionary attitudes.*

Roger's profile was to increase significantly from now on.

20.

The Heat Turns Up

There's no doubt that the main topic of political debate from the summer to the autumn of 1974 was devolution. The call for legislation on an Assembly for Wales was gathering pace and intensity. Gwynfor called for a full Assembly within three years. Even though I agreed with the principle of what he was saying, there was no way in the world that what he called for would happen in three years. But the Government was taking steps towards such legislation.

Two White Papers were published in the summer; *Devolution within the United Kingdom: A Democracy* and *Devolution Proposals for Scotland and Wales*. Another was planned for November. It's not possible to accuse Labour of doing nothing for Wales on the basis of that summer's activity alone. That didn't stop Gwynfor, of course. In one article, he wrote:

> *Every Labour voice which favours devolution and self-government has been silenced.*

Where did he get his facts from? Who published the two White Papers? His call for an Assembly within three years was indicative of previous Plaid calls for action within unrealistic timetables. This is what the chair of Plaid's Constitutional Committee said in 1969:

> *... that Plaid would have more MPs after the General Election, and the inauguration of a Welsh State by 1973 was possible.*

Further, the *Guardian* on 23 September 1968, reports on a speech made by Gwynfor in his party's conference:

A prediction that Wales would be a one-party state for up to three years after independence came from the President. 'Plaid Cymru will hold the reins of power for one, two, three years after self-government. By then, we have no doubt that other parties would have emerged, and we could contest elections.'

Such comments clearly damaged Plaid's political credibility. Anyone who understood the system would know that the timescales they proposed were not workable and were very naïve.

Kilbrandon continues

Following the publication of the report, the Welsh group of Labour MPs reaffirmed support for party policy of establishing an Elected Council for Wales. Emrys Jones, the party organiser, then organised a series of area conferences to discuss the report.

Wilson Cabinet 1974

Then in June 1974, the Labour Party in Wales held a special conference on the Kilbrandon report. In my speech at that conference, I argued strongly that we needed to move far more quickly towards devolution, by establishing an Assembly with wide-ranging powers for Wales, and parity with any powers given to Scotland. I quoted Lloyd George:

A generation that goes back on ground already gained doubles the march for its children.

No prizes for guessing who he thought was responsible for any ground gained in the devolution debate that year. Gwynfor was vociferous enough in speeches and articles, saying that any ground gained resulted from his victory in 1966. That's what triggered the Kilbrandon report and any subsequent step forward.

Gwynfor claimed as much in his party's conference in the last week of October 1973. There was a full report, including many quotes from the speech, in the *Carmarthen Times*, 2 November, the day after publishing Kilbrandon. He is unequivocal in what he says:

There would have been no Constitutional Commission but for Plaid Cymru. The process began with the Carmarthen by-election in 1966. It illustrates the truth that the way to get things done by government in Wales is through an independent national party.

There's that word naïve again! Such a sweeping statement ignores two central factors. First, the key role played by Labour MPs in preparing the report for the Commission, on the back of many years of campaigning within the party for a variety of devolutionary measures. Cledwyn Hughes argued for such measures in the 1950s, years before Gwynfor's success.

In 1965, a year before Gwynfor was elected, the Executive Committee of the Welsh Labour Council called for an elected council for Wales; a small step, but an important one on the road to reforming the British constitution. In 1968, the Labour party established a Constitutional Commission, based on discussions held for years before that, when Gwynfor was a County Councillor. In 1972, before the publishing of Kilbrandon, even George Thomas supported the adaption to the Local Government Bill that called for the establishment of an Elected Council for Wales by 1976. The measure was supported by 16 Labour MPs—Fred Evans, George Thomas, Donald Coleman, Brynmor John, John Morris, Cledwyn Hughes, Michael Foot, Denzil Davies, Tom Ellis, Caerwyn Roderick, Elystan Morgan, Goronwy Roberts, Wil Edwards, Neil McBride, Arthur Probert and me. Perhaps the proposals on the table weren't advocating a full Welsh Assembly, but a large proportion of the 26 of us supported such a development.

The second factor that Gwynfor's claims rides rough-shod over is quite simply, Scotland! Claiming that it was the one constituency of Carmarthen that opened the devolution doors ignores the work and campaigning done in Scotland for years before that. The SNP were obviously a force in Scotland, but so also were many Scottish Labour MPs. In fact. Their pressure was actually stronger than those of us within Labour in Wales.

There's another example of Gwynfor overemphasising his own importance, claiming that his victory had changed everything throughout Britain.

Pushing the door open

On other matters, my disillusionment with the Labour Party was increasing. Decision-making processes, administrative structures, the union block vote and so on caused me many a political headache. It all came to a head on 27 June 1974. I wrote an open letter to the Executive Committee of the constituency Labour Party in Carmarthen:

I cannot any longer conceal my acute concern about some developments in the Labour Party, which will not, in my view, enhance the prospects of the Labour Party and also affect the long-term unity of the Labour Movement. I happen to believe strongly in the principles of social democracy. Some doctrines which are propagated on the extreme left of the Labour party are neither cherished nor supported by the majority of those who vote Labour.

I had nailed my colours to the mast. Again, there were further calls for me to be censured in some way, with some saying that they should remove the Whip from me. The reaction this time came not only from the Labour Party. It was a far broader response. In Gwynfor's biography, Rhys Evans sums up my situation:

Since around 1972, Gwynoro Jones had angered some stalwarts because of his support for Europe and his hesitant response to the NUM's pay claims. Even more unpalatable to his opponents, however, was his alignment with Labour's right wing, a faction containing men like Bill Rodgers and Roy Jenkins who would seven years later breakaway to form the SD P. By the summer of 1974, Labour's left wanted Gwynoro Jones's head on a plate and some of his less loyal supporters began to distance themselves from him. This happened to such an extent that Neil Kinnock, the member for Bedwellty and a prominent figure on the left, could claim with confidence that Gwynoro was: 'a myopic old fool who, by denying the elementary conviction of party has probably committed electoral hara kiri—so we won't have to worry about him'.[137]

Llywydd y Dydd

In the midst of such political storms, it was a refreshing respite to visit the National Eisteddfod in Carmarthen in August 1974. The time had come for me to be President for the Day, on the Friday of the festivities. I felt this to be a great honour, one which I was really proud to do. As a result, I worked on my speech for some weeks beforehand. When it was finished, I committed it to memory, aiming to deliver it without notes. No doubt this was a discipline instilled in me during my Sunday School days. When the day came, the media, no doubt because of the fuss created earlier that year when I was given the invitation to be at the Eistedd-

---

137.Rhys Evans: *Gwynfor Evans: Portrait of a Patriot*. Tal-y-bont, Ceredigion: Y Lolfa, 2008, p. 338.

fod, thought I would have a rather hostile welcome when I arrived. This is how the *Western Mail* looked forward to the event:

> *With the festival motoring along in low key up until now, this is the after-noon everyone has been waiting for, and at 3 pm, we were all packed into the pavilion to hear what he was going to say. The big question will be, 'What will happen?' when the Labour MP for Carmarthen by three votes in the last election, steps up to the mike. Are the lads from Cymdeithas yr Iaith Gymraeg going to keep quiet, or is it all going to hit the fan?*

Personally, I didn't expect a hostile reception. And it didn't happen. In my speech, I shared my pride in my square mile and my culture. I noted the contribution made to Wales by some prominent people from the county.

> *Rydym yn barod ddigon i frolio heddiw beth a wnawn dros y Gymraeg, ond gyfeillion beth am ymdrechion y cewri ddwy ganrif yn ôl? Llwyddodd y rhain i gyhoeddi cyfrolau yn y Gymraeg wrth y miloedd heb gymorth cyngor, cymorthdal llywodraeth na chyfleusterau modern i'w masnachu.*

> *We are more than ready these days to brag about what we have done for the Welsh language, but friends, what of the efforts of the giants two cen-turies ago? They succeeded to publish volumes in Welsh by the thousands without any support from a council, government subsidies or modern means of marketing.*

I then referred to the media, which was by then an ever-increasing pres-ence in our lives:

> *Yn sicr mae ein defnydd o'r cyfryngau yma yn ddiffigiol—ac yn arben-nig y teledu. Felly pan ddaw Sianel Deledu Gymraeg, ac nid ydym am gymeryd na fel ateb, 'rwyf yn ffyddiog y gwelwn hi y tu fewn i dwy neu dair blynedd, cofiwn wneud y defnydd gorau ohoni. Mwy o raglenni Cymraeg bid siwr ond pa fath o raglenni? Mae angen codi'r safonnau yn y fan yna.*

Our use of these media is deficient—especially the television. Therefore, when a Welsh language TV station happens, and we won't take no for an answer, I'm confident we shall see it happen within two or three years, let's remember to make the best use of it. More Welsh language programmes without doubt, but what sort of programmes? We need to raise the standards.

The speech was warmly received. When I arrived home, I gathered that it had been broadcast live as my grandmother, who was housebound, had seen it. When I walked in through the door, she started to cry as it was the first time she had heard me deliver a speech. The full text of the speech was published in local papers. My own reflections centred on wondering whether the speech had any impact on my electoral hopes. I decided that it wasn't possible to know if it had or hadn't, but at least I didn't think that I had done my chances any harm.

The door closes

Some weeks later, on 18 September, Harold Wilson announced that there would be a General Election on 10 October. The last person I spoke to when I left Westminster to return home was Plaid MP Dafydd Elis Thomas. He told me, 'You know you're going to lose, don't you?' 'Yes, I do.' I replied with certainty. He continued, 'The Liberals and the Tories will tactically vote for Gwynfor, against Labour. Remember, I'm sorry that's how it will be.' He left me with the distinct impression that there was not a lot of love between him and Gwynfor.

His remarks reminded me of comments made by the chair of the Labour Party in Wales, Ray Powell, who would soon be MP for Ogmore:

Look Gwynoro, you might as well know that there are many of us in the Labour Party who are deeply unhappy with your stance on various party policies and will be hoping that Gwynfor will win this election because it's best to cope with the enemy from the outside than the enemy inside the party.

I'm sure that those two comments sum up my predicament in 1974 better than any others—and from completely different points on the political spectrum!

The campaigning in autumn 1974 was as intense as 1970 and in complete contrast to February 1974. But this time I didn't feel so confident myself. The warmth of 1970 was not there. This was a battle between two candidates, no more, no less. Both Gwynfor and I spoke at many meetings throughout the constituency. In my case, I spoke at 53 meetings. The main topics of discussion were devolution, the problems of the coal industry and Labour's nationalisation programme. And of course, agriculture.

The Saturday after announcing the election, there was a large NFU protest in Carmarthen town centre and then two public meetings in Pontargothi and Llanybydder. I spoke at both meetings, as did Fred Peart, the Agriculture Minister. They were stormy meetings. As I drove from both occasions, I knew that I had lost the farmers' vote.

Things weren't all plain sailing for Gwynfor either. Plaid were still divided, with many members criticising Gwynfor's leadership style. His myopic, anti-Labour stance was commented on by Emyr Price in his biography of Cledwyn Hughes:

Onid polisi tymor byr, polisi a fydd yn y pendraw yn wrth-gynhyrchiol ac aflwyddianus yw dibynnu ar gefnogaeth amheus, carfannau cymdeithasol esoterig, gwrth-Lafur ac mewn rhai achosion, adweithiol, yn hytrach nag apelio at drwch y bobologaeth—y bobl gyffredin weithgar.[138]

The policy of depending on the dubious support of esoteric social groups, anti-Labour, and in some cases, reactionary, is a short-term policy, a policy that will prove counter-productive and unsuccessful, instead of appealing to the majority of the population—the active, common people.

Rhys Evans sets such a specific comment in its broader context:

---

138. Emyr Price: *Yr Arglwydd Cledwyn o Benrhos.* Caernarfon: Cyhoeddiadau Mei, 1990, p. 208.

Gwynfor's basic problem was that his cherished idea of a national move-
ment was more suited to the 'fifties and 'sixties—when Plaid Cymru was
seeking a foothold on the political ladder. That had now been achieved,
and it needed more than the limited cultural agenda of a 'national move-
ment' if Plaid was to break out of its western stronghold.[139]

On the big day, the vote-counting was moved from the usual Guildhall to
St Peter's Church Hall in the town. I have no idea why. The space available for the public was severely restricted, and it was not long before the
tensions between the opposing supporters were at fever pitch.

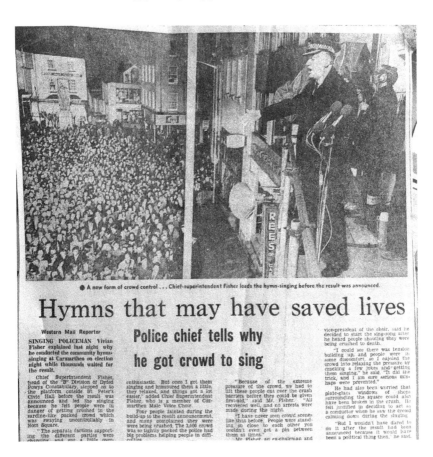

● A new form of crowd control . . . Chief-superintendent Fisher leads the hymn-singing before the result was announced.

Hymns that may have saved lives

Western Mail Reporter

SINGING POLICEMAN Vivian Fisher explained last night why he conducted the community hymn-singing at Carmarthen on election night while thousands waited for the result.

Chief Superintendent Fisher, head of the "B" Division of Dyfed Powys Constabulary, stepped on to the platform outside St Peter's Civic Hall before the result was announced and led the singing because he felt people were in danger of getting crushed in the sardine-like packed crowd which was swaying uncontrollably in Nott Square.

"The separate factions support-ing the different parties were changing and got a little over-

Police chief tells why
he got crowd to sing

enthusiastic. But once I got them singing and humoured them a little, they relaxed, and things got a lot easier," added Chief Superintendent Fisher, who is a member of Car-marthen Male Voice Choir.

Four people fainted during the build-up to the result announcement, and many complained they were being crushed. The 3,600 crowd was so tightly packed the police had big problems helping people in diffi-culties.

"Because of the extreme pressure of the crowd, we had to lift these people out over the crash barriers before they could be given first-aid," said Mr. Fisher. "All recovered well, and no arrests were made during the night.

"I have never seen crowd scenes like that before. People were stand-ing so close to each other you couldn't even get a pin between them at times."

Mr Fisher, an ex-chairman and vice-president of the choir, said he decided to start the sing-song after he heard people shouting they were being crushed to death.

"I could see there was tension building up, and people were in some discomfort, so I cajoled the crowd into relaxing the pressure by cracking a few jokes and getting them singing," he said. "It did the trick, and I am sure serious mis-haps were prevented."

He had also been worried that plate-glass windows of shops surrounding the square could also have been broken in the crush. He felt justified in deciding to act as a conductor when he saw the crowd calming down during the singing.

"But I wouldn't have dared to do it after the result had been announced because it would have been a political thing then," he said.

---

139. Rhys Evans: *Gwynfor Evans: Portrait of a Patriot.* Tal-y-bont, Ceredigion: Y Lolfa, 2008, p. 343.

Thankfully, Chief Superintendent Viv Fisher was on top of things. He stopped the emotions boiling over by leading the three thousand plus crowd in hymn-singing! Excess emotion was suitably diverted! A masterstroke on his part.

The result itself was no surprise to anyone. The predictions were that Gwynfor would win and that the Liberal and Tory vote would collapse. That's what happened. Gwynfor's vote increased by 6,000. The Liberals lost 4,300, and the Tories lost 3,000. My vote increased by 2,500 and it was a 1,000 higher than in 1970. I could take some comfort from that, at least.

Gwynfor, understandably, was elated, predicting a full Welsh Parliament in no time. Nothing had changed!

My parliamentary career was over. It was the end of a fascinating and challenging period of political activity for me. I now had big decisions to make about my personal work situation, but also, more significantly, decisions to make in terms of the narrative of this book, my place in

the political battles for establishing devolution for Wales and how that would now be carried out. This, of course, was a far broader issue than just my personal involvement in it. That would carry on regardless of what I happened to be doing or wherever I happened to be. The battle for Wales, for Welsh identity, for Welsh accountability, was about to enter a protracted five-year confrontation that would set the Welsh against each other, whichever party they belonged to. 1979 was on the horizon, and that's where the next section of the book takes us.

PART THREE:

The Road to Referendum
1974–1979

21.

Power Cuts and a New Broom

1974 had been a volatile year, and not only because it was the year of two General Elections for the first time since 1910 and the first hung parliament since 1929, and for good measure, it was the year that New Year's Day was officially made a Bank Holiday. But it also heralded the beginning of a three-day working week in the UK, with homes and industry having to significantly reduce their use of electricity. They could only use electricity on three consecutive days each week. Television stations could not broadcast after 10.30 pm, and most pubs were shut. Prime Minister Edward Heath took such action against the backdrop of the 1973-74 oil crisis when the Arab oil-producing companies introduced an embargo on the oil they sold, having a world-wide effect on petrol prices and the knock-on effect of that. The coal miners of the UK had begun their industrial action, predominantly over pay disputes, but with an element of unfinished business following the success of the 1972 strike and the relative erosion of miners' wages since then. Heath believed that the only way to deal with this crisis in energy was to control the use of it. The three-day week ended on 7 March.

It was also the year of a State of Emergency in Northern Ireland and a succession of bombings by the IRA on the mainland, including the M62 coach bombing, the Guildford Pub bombings, the Birmingham bombings and a bomb attack on the Houses of Parliament. There were then significant issues and serious tensions in industry, foreign affairs, employment, terrorism and constitutional issues with Northern Ireland. And of course, the woes of '72 were still a real living memory.

The British public lived with a shorter working week, power cuts, petrol price increases and, in many parts, a fear of bombing attacks. On their part, politicians could be easily forgiven for not having enough parliamentary time to deal any further with devolution issues amongst a catalogue of such big issues all happening within the same year. Such circumstances distracted the attention of many from any devolution discussions that they might have otherwise been involved in. But devolution didn't disappear without a trace.

In particular, between the two General Elections of 1974, one appointment was made by Harold Wilson that had a significant impact on the devolution debate: that was the aforementioned appointment of John Morris as Secretary of State for Wales, and equally significant, the removal of George Thomas from that position. The arrival and the departure reflected the division between opposing factions within the Labour Party over Wales. The House of Commons Research Paper on *Wales and Devolution* (19 May 1997) says:

> *It is important to look at the attitude of the Labour Party to Welsh devolution in the 1970s, since the political dominance of Labour in Wales meant that the history of the devolution debate was largely an internal Labour Party debate.*

This was certainly true in 1974.

A blank sheet of paper

Before he was appointed Secretary of State for Wales, John Morris had not been involved at the forefront of Welsh political life to any great degree. By his own admission, there was no point doing so while George Thomas was in the position he was in, championing his own particular agenda. Like most others, John Morris believed that George would be re-instated as Secretary of State for Wales under the Labour Government formed in February 1974, as he had been the Shadow Secretary of State from 1970 to 1974, and Secretary of State before that.

When he was given the news of his appointment, John Morris was told by Harold Wilson, hours after they had announced the election results, that his new responsibility was to bring devolution to Wales. He was not told how he should do so, an understanding that suited John Morris:

It suited me fine, a blank sheet of paper; I could carry out the Prime Minister's instructions with the freedom I interpreted I had. I decided to announce that we were going ahead with devolution and it was to be my main priority. I did so and restated our commitments to the establishment of an elected body for Wales with executive and administrative responsibilities and raised the possibility of it being the foundation for a legislative body in advance of consultation with colleagues. I was mapping out the ground, following my instructions from the Prime Minister to bring forward my own proposals.[140]

It particularly pleased Morris that he could include Scotland and Wales in the same discussions about devolved power. He believed that each country might well need different solutions, but to argue their cases

---

140. John Morris: *Fifty Years in Politics and the Law*. Cardiff: University of Wales Press, 2013, p. 102.

together, he believed, was a strengthening of the overall argument for devolution. When the Queen's Speech to form the new government was drafted, it did not initially include references to Scotland or Wales. The pragmatic politician in John Morris knew that whatever the principles he firmly believed in, there was also another factor to consider—a minority government couldn't ignore Scotland or Wales completely. He advocated this point to the drafters of the Speech in the Cabinet Office, and amendments involving both nations were then included in the Queen's Speech.

In taking up his new role, John Morris was more than mindful of Jim Griffiths' legacy. That began, not with policy, but with bricks and mortar. As significant a step as appointing Jim Griffiths as the first-ever Secretary of State was, Whitehall was not likely to give the new Welsh Office any differential treatment. Amongst civil servants, the perception was that the Welsh Office would be just another department run by them from London, but that some officials would be in Cardiff. Jim Griffiths didn't see it that way and refused to accept an office within the Ministry of Housing and Local Government. He demanded a separate office, a stance John Morris said was fundamentally important.

Jim's action went completely across the grain of the wishes and intentions of the Whitehall establishment, but they signified in a crucial way that the Welsh Office was to be a separate department of state, with its own executive powers. I am absolutely confident that if Jim had not had the prestige of a former deputy leader of the Party and had not been an experienced and successful Cabinet minister, the magic moment would have been lost.[141]

Jim Griffiths had responsibility for the activities of six of the governments' departments within Wales, further extended, little by little, under the three Welsh Secrateries after him. John Morris wanted to go much further.

... I decided on a campaign to win more powers for the Welsh Office across the board. I was continuing the work of decentralisation, but on

---

141. Ibid., p. 109.

a much bigger scale and with a greater aim than merely acquiring addi-tional responsibilities for myself.[142]

He then gives a personal reflection on this:

It is curious that the importance of this has not been recognised by com-mentators. Without the building bricks of executive powers over as many functions as possible, there would have been no experience of managing them for a Welsh Assembly of the future to exercise.[143]

He was certainly looking ahead.

Within the Welsh Labour Party, John Morris received general sup-port in his aims. There was a feeling that the narrowest of victories for the party in February was more important to work on than standing in the way of Morris' devolution aims. But this doesn't apply equally to Morris' fellow Labour MPs, of course, as history has taught us. The late Duncan Tanner, writing in *The Labour Party in Wales, 1900-2000,* sounded an ominous note when he summed up the party's victory in 1974 and the path it followed for the ensuing years:

The unexpected victory of Labour in 1974 brought the Kilbrandon Report on to the political agenda and devolution was to dog the govern-ment until its downfall in 1979.[144]

John Morris immediately set about arranging consultations with a broad range of individuals and organisations, as he recalls:

I carried out extensive consultations in the summer of 1974 with every major organisation representing the people of Wales, including the politi-cal parties, employers and unions and local government.[145]

---

142. Ibid.
143. Ibid.
144. Deian Hopkin; Duncan Tanner; Chris Williams (eds.): *The Labour Party in Wales 1900-2000.* Cardiff: University of Wales Press, 2000, p. 256.
145. John Morris, ibid., p. 114.

By September 1974;

It does not follow that Scotland and Wales must be treated exactly like each other What is important is that the needs and aspirations of the Scottish and Welsh people are properly met.[146]

So, there was a great deal of devolutionary activity between the two General Elections of 1974. This is how the previously mentioned House of Commons' Research Paper summed up these months.

The minority Labour Government of February 1974 published a Green Paper in June 1974, and a White Paper in September of that year announcing directly elected assemblies for Scotland and Wales, with legislative powers for the Scottish Assembly and executive powers only for the Welsh Assembly. The Assemblies would be financed through a block grant allocated by the Treasury, and there was to be no reduction in the number of Scottish or Welsh MPs, and no abolition of the Offices of Secretary of State for Wales and Scotland. These broad themes were to be maintained as Labour's devolution policy for Wales was eventually enacted in the Wales Act 1978, despite significant Parliamentary reverses.

The Second General Election

The results of the October General Election Labour gained 18 seats overall, and the Conservatives lost 20. It needed 318 seats for a Parliamentary majority; Labour had 319. Unlike in February, they had a majority this time, but they were still not in a very strong position. In the context of devolution, the significant development was the return of Gwynfor Evans to Westminster. There he joined the two Dafydds, Wigley and Elis Thomas, who had been there since February. The three could now press on with their campaign for the Wales they wanted to see.

---

146. Ibid., p. 109.

Three Plaid MPs, October 1974

There was understandably much euphoria surrounding Gwynfor's return as an MP. There was renewed hope and optimism, a new belief that Wales would have the Assembly they craved for. But, as Rhys Evans stated:

... euphoria had blinded some within Plaid Cymru to minor cracks that would, within five years, become deep chasms.[147]

This centred predominantly on the relationship between the party's three MPs. The two Dafydds had worked well together between February and October. Now Gwynfor was back, this highlighted allegiances differently. Dafydd Elis tended more to the left, and Wigley to the centre. If there were differences of opinion between Gwynfor and the other two, Wigley

---

147.Rhys Evans: *Gwynfor Evans: Portrait of a Patriot.* Tal-y-bont, Ceredigion: Y Lolfa, 2008, p. 343.

sided with Gwynfor. Thus began a rift between Gwynfor and Dafydd Elis that would be the chasm Rhys Evans referred to.

Gwynfor sought to form a Westminster group of Celtic nationalists and entered into discussion with SNP MPs. Between them, Plaid and the SNP had 14 MPs, a sizeable enough group in a Parliament where the government only have a majority of 42. Such a nationalist presence caused many to sit up and take notice, and to be wary of the influence they might have in Westminster. But the formation of any type of coalition between the nationalists came to nothing, even though that was something that Gwynfor set about to achieve on his first day back in London. Interestingly, in the light of some previous comments made by Gwynfor about the influence of Plaid Cymru on the broader devolution debate, a formal coalition between Plaid and the SNP broke down because of the disorganised nature of the SNP Parliamentary group, and as Rhys Evans points out, a definite perception amongst SNP activists:

> *A tendency among some caused a further complication in the SNP to consider their Plaid Cymru counterparts as more conciliatory nationalists than they were—after all, SNP's official policy was Scottish independence.*[148]

This again highlights two points. First, Gwynfor's tendency to claim that any victory won on the devolution trail was down to Plaid Cymru, whereas the SNP viewed Plaid as 'conciliatory'. And then, it emphasises the point that Plaid were not campaigning for independence, nor had they since they were formed. Their call was for Dominion Status for Wales, while their Scottish counterparts were calling for full independence.

In practical terms, from October 1974 until the 1979 referendum, the two parties only worked together when they had to. Plaid had its own battle to fight back in Wales, on the back of their poor performance in the General Election. Yes, they had three MPs, but they had suffered heavy losses in other places and once again, their appeal in the Valleys came to the surface. Celebrations in the West of Wales, rejoicing on the

---

148. Ibid.

three victories, again glossed over more strategic, long-term issues. Some sounded the alarm bells, but they were lone voices. Emyr Price was one, as early as December 1974, in the party's publication, *Y Ddraig Goch:*

> *Even in the seats that were won, apart from Merioneth, where Plaid has identified itself with the Labour movement, especially in Blaenau Ffestiniog, it made very little impression on the Labour vote. It is not a short-term policy, a policy that will be counterproductive and futile to rely on uncertain support, esoteric, anti-Labour social groups, and reactionary ones sometimes, rather than appeal to the population at large— ordinary working people.*

But buoyed by John Morris' comments that Labour would deliver an Assembly within the term of that Parliament, and the Party's announcement of a Devolution Bill, Gwynfor saw no reason to be anything but optimistic. However, not only did the Party's three MPs begin to disagree, the Party itself was also in organisational and strategic trouble. In a 'mess' and 'chaos' were two words used to describe how the Party was being run.

It was on this footing, then, that Plaid left 1974, to play their part in the four years or so of devolution battles that were to follow, leading up to the Referendum.

Ancient kingdoms and new counties

John Morris' appointment might well have been a surprise, including to the man himself, but there was one significant change implemented in 1974 that had been on the cards for a few years. They had introduced the Local Government Act in 1972 but it came into effect on 1 April 1974. It was an Act that was to have a big impact on Local Authority in England and Wales, but specifically so in Wales and in the context of devolution. In a nutshell, it created a more streamlined local government in Wales, consisting of counties and county boroughs.

Eight new counties were created: Gwynedd, Clwyd, Powys, Dyfed, West Glamorgan, South Glamorgan, Mid Glamorgan and Gwent. South

James Callaghan and John Morris

Glamorgan was the only local authority the Conservatives controlled in the early years, doing so from 1977 to 1981. The other counties were all named after ancient Welsh kingdoms, a significant point in terms of establishing a Welsh identity. The Act also established Monmouth as being officially a part of Wales—a matter of some discussion one way or the other since the 16th century. Wales and Monmouth was the phrase of common usage. Within these new counties, new districts were created, 37 in all. For many, however, this additional layer of local government in Wales was enough to satisfy any devolutionary desires. With the new County system, there was no need for more devolved powers.

All these changes were of relevance in the broader, ongoing debate about devolution. The power base within the nation had been redefined.

The forces contributing to the debate had been reorganised. There were different issues at stake, different priorities.

On a broader scale, this Local Government reorganisation was the second biggest change in constitutional terms that decade. It followed close on the heels of the Act that had taken the UK into Europe, a couple of years previously. These were two major changes in the nature of the UK and each of its constituent parts.

Looking at all this in its totality, 1974 was, without doubt, a momentous year!

22.

Tactics, Rugby and TV

Trouble lay in store for John Morris. After the October election, there was increasing opposition to the idea of an elected Welsh Assembly by Labour MPs and constituency parties. Early in 1975, a very significant move along the path of devolution came from within one of the newly created authorities. The Caerffili Constituency Labour Party forwarded a motion calling for a referendum on Devolution for Wales. This was a new move. It was a new tactic based, so its proponents argued, on bringing the principle of democracy to devolution. If there's to be such a radical constitutional change, then the people need to decide, was the cry.

The Secretary of the Caerffilii Constituency Labour Party, Robert Blundell wrote what has been described as an extremely formal letter to Labour Party Wales organiser, Emrys Jones. He stated that he understood the need to have rushed the 1974 White Paper through, as there was another General Election looming. But he added:

> ... *In the light of subsequent events, it has resulted in many party members wondering if the views of rank-and-file members are to be completely ignored. Since the white paper appeared, the process of finalising the detailed arrangements for a Welsh Assembly seem to proceed rapidly whilst consultations between the Welsh Regional Council of Labour executive committee and C. L. P.'s remain almost non-existent.*

By the time Blundell put pen to paper, his local party declared they opposed devolution. Other local parties began to support them. Rhondda did. But in their case, while joining the call for a referendum, they re-asserted their support for devolution.

Blundell went further than writing to Emrys Jones. He distributed a pamphlet to all 36 Welsh constituency Labour Parties, arguing that a referendum was the ultimate sign of a modern democracy that Wales should embrace. Many responded favourably and sympathetically to his pamphlet. The pattern that was emerging was one of the Labour Leadership and the TUC backing devolution, but strong elements of their grass-roots voicing opposition, backed by a few MPs. The Welsh Labour Executive and the TUC felt the need to publish a pamphlet of their own, opposing Blundell's. This is quoted in *The Welsh Veto: The Wales Act 1978 and The Referendum*, edited by Foulkes, Jones, Wilford.

> *Those who advocate a referendum must accept the full implications of this change and must be aware that any radical changes proposed by a Labour government would have to overcome this new hurdle before being carried out. In effect, Clause 4 of the party constitution would have to be rewritten—'to secure for the workers by hand or brain the full fruits of their industry etc., subject to referendum'.*[149]

The Referendum tactic

The call for a referendum came despite the fact that devolution had been accepted as a Labour Party policy in its manifesto in 1974 and that the 1975 annual conference had voted by 4-1 in favour of an Assembly. That was the main argument against a referendum from those within Labour who championed devolution. The referendum was in fact a means to hinder, slow down, stall, a debate that had been gaining momentum within Labour. The debate on consequences of referendum became heated and often boiled over. The Labour Party's argument that a referendum would be divisive and polarise people turned out to be the case, but not in the way it was meant originally. Those fears related to the consequences of the referendum. But the debate about having a referendum or not proved

---

149. David Foulkes; J. Barry Jones; R. A. Wilford (eds.): *The Welsh Veto: The Wales Act 1978 and the Referendum*. Cardiff: University of Wales Press, 1983, p. 27.

to be extremely divisive in itself, before they even got to the referendum and its subsequent result.

In contrast to the strong endorsement given to devolution in the 1975 conference, the debates on the same issue in the following year invoked real confrontation, as Barry Jones states in his chapter in *The Welsh Veto*:

> *The Labour Party Welsh Conference in May 1976 was characterised by a series of acrimonious debates which revealed an ominous gulf between the leadership and substantial sections of rank-and-file activists... By the end of 1976, the momentum for a referendum had built up to such a pitch that a general conviction emerged which presumed that progress towards devolution could only be assured if a referendum were conceded.*[150]

For more than a century, referenda rarely occurred, although Wales had experienced some over Sunday licensing. However, one was scheduled for June 1975 on Britain's membership of the EEC, and this generated more interest in such a device.

Leading anti-devolutionist and future party leader Neil Kinnock initially opposed the idea of a referendum, showing loyalty to the manifesto pledge, even if he disagreed with it. The split in Labour's divided opinion on the issue became a wide chasm when the first Labour MP broke rank publicly. That was Leo Abse, who backed the call for a referendum. Swansea East MP Donald Anderson soon followed him. Two Welsh MPs going public was now bad news for Labour. In Donald Anderson's case, he aired his views in the *Western Mail*, on the 3 and 4 September 1975. This is from 4 September article:

> *All Welsh MPs accept the need for increased Democratic control on the numerous ad hoc all-Wales' bodies in fields like health and water. Many become more critical as the argument progresses from that simple proposition to the case for executive and eventually legislative devolution.*

Leo Abse wrote to Emrys Jones later that month:

---

150. Ibid.

*For my part, I shall be looking with care at any Bill that may be pub-
lished and would certainly be exceedingly hostile to any suggestion which,
even in the long run, could lead to a situation where Wales should have a
Stormont, which could only lead not simply to what some may regard as
the comparatively unimportant matter of a reduction in the number of
Welsh MPs but would lead to a situation where the Labour Government
could never get a majority in the House of Commons.*

George Thomas gave his full support to Abse's stance but said that he could
not do so publicly because he was Deputy Speaker. Others did publicly
back Abse and Anderson, Newport MP Roy Hughes for one, while Neil
Kinnock subsequently joined them. This conversation between Kinnock
and George Thomas is quoted in Gieschen, who took the quote from a
printed conversation between the two men in *The House Magazine*:

*It was simply that, provided with the proposals in the initial White Paper,
I actually looked at them through the eyes of somebody from the valleys,
who feels very deeply Welsh. I thought at that stage that they couldn't add
up in terms of advantage for people of my area, whom I happened to represent... but the fact remains that there is still something unresolved about
accountability and democracy... But that was the wrong way to approach
them. The same requests exist through the rest of the country, too.*[151]

Gieschen says that Abse told him personally that he could 'blackmail and
bluff' the government to call for a referendum. Gieschen then elaborates:

*In his book, Margaret, daughter of Beatrice, he describes how he man-
aged to get enough signatures to a reasoned amendment to the second
reading of the Scotland and Wales Bill. He maintained that his friend-
ship with George Thomas, by then the Speaker of the House, ensured
that against usual parliamentary practice his amendment was called as
it was entirely in the speaker's discretion. In the words of Leo Abse, 'On*

151.Hubert Gieschen: *The Labour Party in Wales and the 1979 Referendum*. Frankfurt:
Haag and Herschen, 1999, p. 25.

| Neil Kinnock | George Thomas | Leo Abse |

the eve of the Second Reading, the government cracked and announced a referendum'.[152]

The referendum debate now overshadowed devolution itself. So much so that the executive of the Labour Party in Wales and the Wales TUC produced their own pamphlet rebutting the referendum proposal.

Abse's approach was a political one, but he was also effective in using emotive slogans in his campaign. He claimed that a Welsh Assembly would 'increase bribery and corruption'. It would be dominated from Cardiff by a Welsh-speaking bureaucratic elite. His attacks on the Welsh language were always nasty and forthright.

Not surprisingly, John Morris remembers the occasion of the calls for a referendum being accepted.

Michael Foot rang me up one night during the first Bill and told me to get the legislation through in reasonable time—we did not have the majority for a guillotine—we would have to concede a referendum. So we did, but it was a black day for our cause, and the Tories cackled their triumph. They were the beneficiaries of our caving in. Our general standing in Wales was shattered.[153]

---

152. Ibid., p. 26.
153. John Morris: *Fifty Years in Politics and the Law*. Cardiff: University of Wales Press, 2013, p. 123.

Morris' words are emotive and show the impact that having to accept a referendum had on him, and on his party in Wales.

Conceding a referendum eventually proved to be a major error, bearing in mind the decades-old divisive nature of devolution within the Welsh Labour Party. The vociferous and leading anti-devolutionist Neil Kinnock claimed in the *South Wales Echo* 18 December 1977 that the referendum:

> *had been wrung out of those whose enthusiasm for devolution was only exceeded by their determination not to allow the people of Wales to make a real decision through the ballot box on their future.*

Barry Jones, in *The Welsh Veto*, says:

> *The Government were faced with an unprecedented problem of trying to get through legislation, which it can be argued, it had been forced to introduce for reasons of political expediency; which was strongly opposed by a substantial number of its own backbenchers; but which nevertheless had become a symbol of its ability to survive... transferring the final decision to the electorate meant that the immediate aim was no longer the establishment of the Welsh Assembly but merely the passing of a Bill through parliament. Thus, the Government no longer had to take final responsibility for the success or failure of Welsh devolution because its fate had been transferred to the electorate to decide'.*[154]

The view from Number 10

The Labour Prime Minister James Callaghan was not greatly motivated by the devolution issue. That really set the seal on the way devolution's argument would unfold until 1979. Callaghan only spoke at one Yes campaign meeting, in Swansea. For the policy to be pushed through and implemented, it needed the backing of the man at the top. If he believed

---

154. David Foulkes; J. Barry Jones; R. A. Wilford (eds.), ibid., p. 47.

in it, then it was far, far, more likely to happen. We need no better example of that than Tony Blair's solid belief in devolution in the run-up to the 1997 referendum.

Callaghan himself had clear views, not only on devolution itself, but on the way the devolution campaign played its part in his broader political role as leader of his party and as the Prime Minister too. In his book *Time and Chance* he says this:

> *The attempt at Devolution was important for its own sake, but I am bound to admit that it had other incidental advantages. So I did not complain unduly about the technical manoeuvres of the opponents or their procedural ambushes... for they helped to distract parliamentary attention from a morbid preoccupation with the state of the economy.*[155]

The referendum debate raged on. By the end of 1976, Wales' national daily, *The Western Mail*, who strongly supported devolution, then came out in favour of a referendum. But that wasn't the main development in that year. That came from a London MP, George Cunningham. He put forward an amendment to the Scotland and Wales Bills, suggesting a 40% threshold that a Yes vote would have to cross in order to succeed. This was considered towards the end of the committee stage. It was accepted, putting a further obstacle in the devolutionists' way. The anti-devolutionists, in securing a referendum and with the acceptance of this amendment, had put a significant spoke in the wheels of Welsh devolution.

Devolution was a Labour manifesto policy. They had fought a referendum on that issue for and won. But how did this fit into the bigger picture? Not only in Wales, but the rest of the UK as well? This is summarised in *The Welsh Veto*:

> *It took place against the unique parliamentary and political background the worst economic crisis since the 1930s come the expediency of the Lib-lab pact a succession of damaging government defeats on what had previously been considered 'resignation' issues; and a Government,*

---

155. James Callaghan: *Time and Chance*. London: Politico's Publishing, 2006, p. 509.

which, having lost its slim majority, was obliged to make a series of deals with both minor parties and individual MP's. It was not, therefore, the ideal launch-pad from which the government might mount an effective and enthusiastic referendum campaign. Instead, as the weeks passed into months and the months into years, the impression grew that the exercise, particularly the Welsh dimension, was a massive irrelevance.[156]

When Labour first proposed Devolution for Wales, and included it in their manifesto, they never really contemplated the prospect of a referendum. The decision to organise one had a profound influence on the conduct of the campaign for a Welsh Assembly, as we shall see later.

Rugby and TV

Before we look at how this 'massive irrelevance' actually dominated Welsh politics, there are two other not so overtly political issues to look at. They might not be political, but they played their part in the debate.

The role of rugby in Welsh life has been long documented. But its influence on devolution came to the surface in the 1970s, a decade that was a golden era for the Welsh rugby team on the pitch. The record speaks for itself—six Five Nations Championships between 1969 and 1979, three Grand Slams and six Triple Crowns.

These successes shaped a sense of Welsh pride, of what a small country like Wales could achieve. Off the pitch, we were a small nation, not even recognised as such by so many. On the pitch, we existed. The *Times* even acknowledged that the game gave the Welsh a way of expressing a certain type of nationalism. The Welsh came together to see their country play, either at Cardiff—in the stadium and without—or through the increasingly popular TV coverage.

Martin Johnes deals at length with this relationship between rugby and a sense of Welsh identity Wales Since 1939.

---

156. David Foulkes; J. Barry Jones; R. A. Wilford (eds.), ibid., p. 28.

Rugby, an important part of male popular culture in South Wales since the late 19ᵗʰ century, was now embracing a much broader social and geographical spectrum. It was becoming a genuinely national game. Regular victories created a sense of confidence and even arrogance among Welsh fans, something that offended many English people within the sport.[157]

This emerging way of expressing identity spilled over into the political spectrum. Kenneth O. Morgan argues that the Welsh felt that such a showing of nationalism was enough for the Welsh. That's why the overwhelming success of the rugby team, and the impact that had on the fans, translated to underwhelming support for devolution. Martin Johnes says:

Quite simply, the successes on the rugby field in the 1970s did much to overcome the old insecurities that beset an English-speaking Welsh identity and to bring together the strands that had emerged in the 1950s and 1960s over renewed Sense of Welshness. However, those insecurities never quite disappeared and the dismantling of much of the traditional industrial base of Wales on the debacle of the 1979 referendum on devolution injected new life into old worries. By the 1980s, talk of the death of Wales had resurfaced.[158]

The other cultural arena that spilled over into politics was broadcasting, and television in particular. A call for a Welsh language television channel had been prominent since the early Seventies. The Conservative Government set up the Crawford Enquiry to study broadcasting in Wales, Scotland, Northern Ireland and rural England. The Enquiry's finding recommended that there should be a fourth TV channel in Wales, dedicated primarily to the Welsh language.

An active campaigner in Westminster corridors for such a new channel was John Morris. Throughout the summer of 1974, he lobbied Home Secretary Roy Jenkins regularly, writing to him and meeting him face to face. He did so for the next two or three years. But the proposed fourth

157. Martin Johnes: *Wales since 1939*. Manchester: Manchester University Press, 2013, p. 282.
158. Ibid., p. 285.

channel wasn't unquestioningly welcomed by Welsh speakers either, or by some people prominent in Welsh public life. There was an involved debate whether putting all Welsh programmes on one channel was, in fact, the best move.

John Morris had his doubts initially, but he then gave his full support to a new Welsh language fourth channel. This is from one of the letters he wrote to Roy Jenkins in the Spring of 1976. Morris quotes it in his own book:

I am very concerned about reports I am getting about the vitality of the Welsh language. Despite considerable expenditure on bilingual education and manful efforts by voluntary bodies such as Urdd Gobaith Cymru, the signs are that the language is inexorably continuing to lose ground to English, even in the Welsh-speaking areas. A decision to delay the fourth service indefinitely would, I am sure, be seen as a tacit acceptance on our part of the continuation of the process which can only end in the extinction of the language.[159]

Morris saw broadcasting as one central strand of his push for devolution and a clear sign that his own personal push for an Assembly in Wales went beyond the stricter confines of the political realm.

159.John Morris: *Fifty Years in Politics and the Law*. Cardiff: University of Wales Press, 2013, p 163.

23.

Yes, No, Maybe

Campaigning in Wales got underway as soon as 1977 was in, with the formation of the Wales for the Assembly Campaign (WAC) led by Elystan Morgan.

The WAC campaign comprised the Executive of the Welsh Labour Party and the majority of the party's MPs; the Welsh Liberal party; Plaid Cymru; Wales, TUC and the Conservative Party. It was a broad-based alliance which set out to emphasise a non-partisan approach to the devolution debate. Michael Foot, the Ebbw Vale MP who was at the time also the Deputy Leader of the Labour Party, was named as a patron of the group, along with Wales TUC Secretary, George Wright. For R. A. Wilford, one editor of *The Welsh Veto: The Wales Act 1978 and the Referendum*, these appointments were one example of failing to maintain that initial non-partisan aspiration. In his chapter, *The Character of the Lobbies: Some Theoretical Considerations*, he says:

> *Although officially an umbrella, non-partisan lobby, its supporters found it virtually impossible to avoid the temptation to score party-political points over its opponents.*[160]

It only took a few months for this inability to maintain a bi-partisan stance on the same issue to spill over into the public campaign itself. The Labour Party in Wales, the Wales TUC and the Co-op Party set up their own Yes Campaign in order to put clear water between them and Plaid.

---

160. David Foulkes; J. Barry Jones; R. A. Wilford (eds.): *The Welsh Veto: The Wales Act 1978 and the Referendum*. Cardiff: University of Wales Press, 1983, p. 109.

In many instances, Labour local constituency members were reluctant to share platforms with Plaid members, even though they were fighting for the same thing. In Ceredigion, for example, many of the members and officers, including John Marek, future MP and Assembly Member, joined the No Campaign, and in a vote, prevented the party from contributing to the Yes campaign. Some were reluctant to be seen working with other parties, Plaid and Liberal, but there was a very strong anti-devolution element in the party too. The fear of being tarred as Nationalists was real, just as Gwynoro Jones experienced in the late Sixties when he suggested a separate Welsh Labour Party.

The WAC slogan was Vote Yes For Wales on March 1, with a clear emphasis on a sense of nationhood. The Labour Party/Wales TUC slogan was different, with a wider dimension—Vote Yes; For Democracy, For Wales, For Britain. One was about Wales, but the other was about Wales, the rest of the UK and participatory democracy.

The WAC all-party Yes campaign tried to promote this broad front by recruiting well-known Welsh men and women from sport and popular culture, such as Harry Secombe and Barry John. These people weren't immediately associated with any political party and much was made of that by the Yes lobby.

But it's from the world of sport that Wilford gives an example of his points-scoring comment above, and it takes us back to the role of rugby discussed earlier. The WAC allied their cause to the role of rugby in Wales quite clearly. As well as recruiting names from the game to support them, they distributed leaflets at international games—the Wales-Ireland game in February 1979, for example. That leaflet was called The Other Big Match: Wales v Rest. The 'Rest' of that leaflet were named as 'Mrs Thatcher and hard-line Tories, Leo Abse's group of MPs and the National Front'. Wilford argues that this 'guilt by association' exposed the partisan nature of the campaign.

National Library of Wales

The No Campaign comprised of The Conservative Party in Wales; seven of the eight County Councils; the National Federation of the Self-Employed; NALGO and The Country Landowners Association.

But as with the Yes campaign, the No campaign was also split in two. On the one hand, there was the predominantly Conservative Party No group. Their prime reason for saying no was that devolution would endanger the unity of the UK.

But there was also the predominantly Labour-led No Campaign. The leading lights of this group, The Labour No Assembly Campaign, were the so-called 'gang of six', the Welsh Labour MPs who went against their Party's pro-devolution manifesto: Leo Abse, Donald Anderson, Ifor Davies, Fred Evans, Ioan Evans and Neil Kinnock. Their main objection to this issue was the economic cost of devolution.

Just as the pro-devolution Labour members wanted to distance themselves from being tarred as Nationalists and being too close to Plaid Cymru, so the No Labour MPs wanted clear water between themselves and the Tory Party. But the No division was not as damaging as the Yes division, as Jones and Wilford say in *The Welsh Veto*:

> *But far from being a weakness, the organisational distinctiveness of the two campaigns proved to be a tactical and functional advantage.*[161]

The two-pronged No attack gave the No campaign a broader base, appealing to those who held the unity of the UK dear, and appealing to those concerned about the cost of this new form of governance.

A significant change happened in November 1977. Instead of one Bill to cover both Wales and Scotland, two separate Bills were decided upon, leading to the Wales Act and the Scotland Act of 1978. As previously mentioned, John Morris was an advocate of one Act for both countries, believing it strengthened the devolution argument and specifically as it applied to the respective countries. This change did also have the effect of reducing some opposition—some who originally opposed the

---

161. Ibid., p. 118.

joint Bill because they believed that the Welsh didn't really want devolution anyway, changed their minds.

The official referendum campaign lasted only three weeks, between 8 February 1979 and polling day on 1 March, but more on that later. The pre-campaign lasted a lot longer. But it wasn't a campaign marked by stirring passion. In an interview with Hubert Gieschen in 1997, Lord Cledwyn summed it up in this way; 'The whole thing lacked spirit at the time'.

Disunity

The reasons for this lack of drive on such a historical issue are not unfamiliar to the narrative of this book. Neither Plaid nor Labour could stand in complete internal unity on the devolution issue, albeit for different reasons. Labour's divisions have been looked at. It might be more surprising that Plaid could not show a strong united front on a Bill calling for more autonomy for Wales. Wasn't this after all their raison d'être? Wilford outlines their stance:

> ... Plaid Cymru regarded the provisions of the Act with real ambivalence. One faction perceived the Act as totally inadequate, as it did little, if anything, to weaken the Power of Parliament at Westminster over the future of Wales. The other larger faction, whilst critical of the provisions of the Act, adopted a pragmatic position, regarding it as a step in the right direction, a means of achieving, in the long run, the end of an independent and sovereign Welsh state.[162]

Even through these crucial days, there was still talk of internal divisions and the need for Gwynfor to relinquish the Presidency of the party. He agreed to stand down but said that should happen after the referendum results were announced. This was hardly the unflinching unity that the party needed to fight a robust campaign. In fact, Gwynfor had also

---

162. Ibid., p. 110.

secretly told his brother he was not intending to stand in a General Election again as he was 'utterly exhausted'.

But he continued to lobby passionately for a Yes vote, of course. He knew that Callaghan needed the support of Plaid. This was an opportunity to secure some gains for the party and for Wales. As Rhys Evans says:

Plaid Cymru's terms were blatantly pragmatic: in exchange for concessions for Wales, they promised they would not try to bring down the government.[163]

This promise reiterated what Gwynfor had told John Morris personally, earlier in 1978. Plaid's conference of that year inevitably discussed devolution, but maybe not in the way expected. A motion was put forward calling for Plaid to boycott the Wales for an Assembly campaign. It was defeated, but only by 62 votes to 47. *The Western Mail's* description of that last Plaid Annual Conference before the devolution vote was clear enough:

If there was one thing that characterised Plaid Cymru's Annual Conference, it was a feeling of discomfort.

Gwynfor was understandably undeterred. He backed the referendum wholeheartedly, calling it '... the most considerable improvement in Welsh government that Westminster has ever agreed to'.

This conviction needed to be implemented at the grassroots level. One strategic option was proposed by Carmarthen constituency, which has been the subject of the second section of this book, and was the battleground between the two leading figures in the Plaid-Labour fight. In 1979, this constituency, too, played into the broader devolution debate. It was predominantly pro-devolution. But the underlying suspicions of any close association with Plaid were still real. The feelings that led to some within his own party calling Gwynoro Jones a nationalist had not gone away.

---

163. Rhys Evans: *Gwynfor Evans: Portrait of a Patriot.* Tal-y-bont, Ceredigion: Y Lolfa, 2008, p. 374.

Emlyn Hooson

Plaid's West Wales organiser, Peter Hughes Griffiths, in February 1977, suggested that an umbrella body of pro-devolutionists be set up to cover the whole of Dyfed, the three counties of Carmarthenshire, Pembrokeshire and Ceredigion. That could be, he argued, a first step towards a geographically broader group. It would comprise Labour, Plaid and Liberal members, and other interested individuals and organisations. Gieschen outlines the response to this proposal:

The local Labour Party was not interested at all. They did not seem to have given it much consideration as it took Victor Thomas, the Honourable Secretary of the Carmarthen Labour Party, three months to pass a copy of the Plaid approach to Emrys Jones at the Labour Party in Wales. There was, however, complete agreement on how to deal with Plaid Cymru as the reply from Emrys Jones dated 13 May 1977 shows: 'I am glad that you have turned down the request. The Labour Party could not in any way co-operate with Plaid Cymru on any campaign of any sort'.[164]

---

164. Hubert Gieschen: *The Labour Party in Wales and the 1979 Referendum*. Frankfurt: Haag and Herschen, 1999, p. 34.

The Liberal presence in the Devolution for Wales debate had been silent for more than a generation. Not that many Liberals didn't have a view on the issue since the days of Lloyd George, but any voice they had was inevitably a small voice in the wilderness because of the broader political structure. When the debate raged again in the 1970s, they did have a vociferous champion in the form of Emlyn Hooson. In his biography, *Essays and Reminiscences*, editor Derec Llwyd Morgan, summarises Hoosons' stance:

On very many public occasions, Emlyn also emphasised the false move achieved by the Conservative government of 1970-1974 in prejudicing the debate on devolution by their doctrinal determination to rush through the 'reform' of local government—their so-called reform of health services and the reorganisation of water supplies. It would have been wiser to deal with all those matters as part of a wider and comprehensive devolution plan. The government had rushed on blindly, as if the Kilbrandon/Crowther Commission had never existed.[165]

Hooson was an active contributor to the devolution debate in Westminster. In one such debate, on the Scottish and Welsh Bills, 15 January 1976, he outlined his five key elements. Derec Llwyd Morgan adds some comments of his own:

First... that transfer of existing powers from such Welsh institutions as the Welsh Office to a Welsh Assembly... was not devolution from Westminster to Wales.

Second, that the model proposed for the Assembly was essentially that of a local government council as opposed to a parliamentary model, in that decisions would be made by committees. In his opinion, that would be a massively retrograde step.

Third, and fundamentally, that the Assembly would have no real legislative powers and would thus lack the status of a parliament.

165.Derec Llwyd Morgan (ed.): *Emlyn Hooson: Essays and Reminiscences*. Llandysul: Gomer, 2014, p. 140.

Fourth, he submitted that such changes could only operate successfully within the structure of a Bill of Rights.

Fifth and last, he returned to his favourite plea for proportional representation, reminding everyone that this was the sole recommendation in regard to which the Crowther/Kilbrandon Commission had achieved unanimity.[166]

During that debate, and on other occasions, Hooson would argue that each of the states of the USA had legislative powers, as did the states in the Länder Parliaments of Germany. On addressing the fact that there was no such provision for the Welsh Assembly, he told the House:

Wales is not having any legislative powers. It is an absolute sham.

A dip in support

Labour's difference of emphasis, or opinion, was more than the obvious Gang of Six Welsh MPs against the rest. Amongst those who wanted devolution, there were differences in why they wanted it. John Morris' earlier quote about Welsh television and Welsh culture showed that it was more than political for him. Many would stand with him on that. Others, however, saw the Wales Act as a means of beginning the process of extending participatory democracy throughout the UK. It was about governance, not so much any strain of nationalism.

The Liberals predominantly saw it in the same way.

Within the three parties, as well as within the Yes campaign itself, there was not a united front. Wilford summarises the situation:

Thus, there were real differences in motivation and purposiveness evident within the pro-Assembly lobby, differences that were to have a marked effect upon the nature of its formal campaign.[167]

---

166. Ibid., p. 141.
167. David Foulkes; J. Barry Jones; R. A. Wilford (eds.), ibid., p. 110.

It is perhaps surprising to read so many words such as 'ambivalent', 'lack of spirit' and 'lack of motivation' in the campaigning for a Yes vote. What made that task more difficult was the fact that a referendum had been called for. This changed the situation for the pro-devolutionists. It determined the nature of the campaign for them. They now had a big selling job to do. They had to convince people of the virtues and benefits of the Wales Act. They had to promote its principles and summarise its main points in a way that would appeal to and convince the voters.

This was evidently being picked up by the electorate, as the increasing number of opinion polls during '78, '79 show. On 5 May 1978, a BBC poll showed that both sides were really close—40.8% said they would vote Yes and 40.8% said they would vote No. In the autumn of 1978, a poll in the *Western Mail* showed the Yes support had dropped to 38%. A BBC poll in the same month showed 27% support for Yes and 41% support for No. By the beginning of the official campaign, in early February, Yes support was up to 33%.

But what accounted for this drop in the public support as the Yes campaign neared polling day? Some reasons have already been looked at. There had been increasing calls for a General Election to be called in the autumn of 1978, which looked very likely. But surprisingly, Callaghan decided against calling an election, despite the urgings of many in his party. Considering the UK's experience in the ensuing "winter of discontent", this decision proved to be a strategic error.

That decision also had a direct impact on the referendum campaign. At one time it had been expected that the referendum was going to be in September 1978. That wasn't going to happen if there was a General Election as well, so it was postponed. This lost considerable momentum for the campaign, as the September figures above indicate.

The battle continues

The parliamentary debate on the proposed devolution for Scotland and Wales was long and drawn out. The man leading the debates in the Commons, Michael Foot, was reluctant to introduce the guillotine in order to curtail the debate. As a result, after the equivalent of over four days' debate, they had discussed only three and a half clauses of the Bill. On the first day of committee, they put 350 amendments forward. Barry Jones, in his chapter in *The Welsh Veto:*

Numerous and significant amendments were tabled by both pro-and anti-devolution sides, but in addition, there were many other amendments which served, as intended, to discredit the Government's proposals and take up valuable time before the guillotine precluded further debate. The large number of amendments tabled was partly a result of widespread unease about the legislation on all sides of the House. There were many ready to defend the principle of the Bill but few (and probably none who were not on the Government payroll) who were willing or able to defend its details.[168]

There were amendments from Plaid Cymru and other pro-devolutionists to strengthen the Bill, whilst other amendments were aimed at reducing the powers of the Assembly and those nearly all from Conservative MPs.

This catalogue of amendments also had the effect of leading to many cross-party and intra-party alliances. The most crucial one was between the Welsh Labour anti-devolution MPs and Tory opposition MPs, and even at times, the Tory front bench. So the Callaghan government was increasingly dependent on Plaid Cymru and the Liberals primarily to get its legislation through.

The Callaghan government, and the Yes campaign generally, but specifically, WAC, suffered significant blows in the run-up to the beginning of the official campaigning at the start of 1979. The referendum issue, the separation of Wales and Scotland, the amendments and the 40% threshold needed to secure the passing of the Act were all significant hurdles, all made worse by the nature of the campaign trying to champion devolution in Wales.

168.Ibid., p. 35.

24.

The Road to No

The three weeks between 8 February and 1 March 1979 were weeks of frantic travel for politicians of all persuasion, from one end of Wales to the other. There was a great deal to achieve in a very short space of time, especially for the advocates of devolution for Wales. And of course, it was historical. Wales had an opportunity to vote on its own future for the first time.

The focus of the campaign, however, was far from being on the historical bigger picture. Other more immediate issues dominated the arguments, for and against.

The Labour Party, as the Party in government and the party that had introduced the devolution legislation in the first place, went into the campaigning period in a very weak position. From a series of by-election defeats, by 1976 they had lost the slim majority of October 1974. In order to continue to govern, Labour entered a pact with the Liberal Party in 1977.

Former Liberal leader, David Steel says of this period, in his book, *A House Divided*:

> *Without support from at least one other party, no new devolution proposals were likely to get through…. our talks on devolution were virtually the runner of the Lib-Lab pact itself.*[169]

The year after that, during what was the coldest winter in the UK for 16 years, Britain experienced a wave of industrial disputes and the resultant economic hardship, collectively labelled "The Winter of Discontent".

---

169. David Steel: *A House Divided*. London: Weidenfield and Nicholson, 1980, p. 93.

Roads could not be cleared of snow, thus isolating many communities. Lorry drivers were on strike, affecting the supply and distribution of goods, with food and fuel in short supply. Refuse collectors joined the strike later, causing problems with disposal of waste and piles of rubbish in residential streets.

There were many, many strikes in both the private and public sector through the winter of 1978-1979 as workers demanded pay rises over and above what the Government recommended, bringing the Government into conflict with their usual allies, the unions. Leader of the Opposition, Margaret Thatcher led the Tory attack on the way the Labour government was handling the crisis.

As far as the devolution debate was concerned, this discontent meant that most people in the UK were experiencing economic and day-to-day hardship during severe weather. When 1978 turned to 1979, a month before the official Referendum Campaign would start, this was still the living reality for most people in Wales. This situation also meant that there was, subsequently, a growing discontent towards both the Labour

Party and the trade unions. Labour's devolution campaign wasn't only weakened by those within its ranks who opposed devolution. Barry Jones in *The Welsh Veto*:

> *WAC's strategy based upon a popular labour Government and the personal prestige of Jim Callaghan was destroyed by a bitter winter of industrial discontent. The ace in the 'Yes' coalition pack had been trumped, not by their opponents but by the industrial action of the trade unions. Thus the pro-devolutionists entered the final stage of the campaign under attack.*[170]

The official campaign period did nothing to quell the bitterness between the rival factions in the Labour Party. George Wright, Secretary of the Wales TUC, mentioned the anti-devolutionist MPs in the *Western Mail* on 21 February 1979:

> *By their disloyalty, they are not reneging on their own commitments and that of their manifesto, but they are dividing the Labour Movement in Wales, indulging in personal attacks on fellow party members and acting in such a way that they could bring down a Labour government.*

Foresight indeed, as that is what precisely happened. However, he didn't see the irony that he himself was part of a group that was dividing the Yes campaign into two as well, as pro-devolution Labour stood their ground with their own Yes campaign.

Neil Kinnock in a Commons debate, on the other hand, defended his anti-devolution stance:

> *We do not need an Assembly to prove our nationality or our pride. This is a matter of hearts and minds, not bricks, committees and bureaucrats.*

In a public debate at the King's Hall, Aberystwyth, with 800 present, Elystan Morgan said this to Kinnock:

---

170. David Foulkes; J. Barry Jones; R. A. Wilford (eds.): *The Welsh Veto: The Wales Act 1978 and the Referendum*. Cardiff: University of Wales Press, 1983, p. 32.

Please don't think for a moment that you can trample the life of a Nation in the mud of your own miserable self-interest.

The appeal to an awareness of Welsh nationhood as a basis for devolution received strong support from a very surprising direction within the Labour camp, some weeks before the vote. Speaking at a WAC rally in Newton, the then Foreign Secretary David Owen said that devolution:

... Is not a mere mechanical legalistic or constitutional issue: it represents a great political cause lying at the core of Democratic politics. It has its roots in the Noble objective of self-government. In Wales, it stems from the final military consequence of the overthrow of Prince Llywellyn, the last in 1282.

Labour and Plaid together

Gwynfor Evans was, outwardly at least, his usual confident, upbeat self in the early months of 1979. Rhys Evans notes, however, that '... any evidence to support his confidence was in short supply', adding:

Indeed the only reasonable conclusion is that Gwynfor had decided that it was by his faith and missionary zeal alone that he could sustain his party, and himself, during this referendum.[171]

Such zeal was not in short supply. It was stretched by one particular aspect of the campaigning that grew out of the partisanship that was a feature of the Yes campaign, referred to earlier. As was mentioned earlier, on the one hand, there was that reluctance on the part of some Labour MPs and members to share platforms with Plaid MPs and members. When it came to campaigning, however, Plaid played a very prominent role. Labour was experiencing great difficulty in finding grassroots members to speak at meetings and to pound the streets canvassing. There were many examples of constituency

---

171. Rhys Evans: *Gwynfor Evans: Portrait of a Patriot.* Tal-y-bont, Ceredigion: Y Lolfa, 2008, p. 378.

party officials being unable to suggest one of their own to speak at local campaign meetings. Gieschen quotes an example from West Flint.

> *This is shown in a letter from Meirion Hughes, the local constituency organiser, to a request from Emrys Jones for public speakers in favour of the proposed Welsh Assembly where he made the point that apart from himself, hardly anyone was willing to actively campaign for the Assembly.*[172]

Such reports were coming in from various parts of Wales. The Yes campaign work had to be done. So who was doing it? Labour had their active champions of devolution in Cledwyn Hughes, Michael Foot, Elystan Morgan and John Morris. But Plaid were in no doubt who was doing the hard work out of the public eye, as Rhys Evans notes:

> *... it fell to Plaid to do all the campaigning, although Gwynfor could not afford to publicly acknowledge that reality. He confessed to Carwyn James that the campaign was being run 'in fact by Plaid, although Labour does not realise it'. 'We', he added, 'have prepared every leaflet and arranged which speakers go where and organized all the meetings'.*[173]

Rhys Evans concludes that as it became more and more apparent that this was the situation throughout an increasing number of constituencies across Wales, that it was left to Plaid Cymru 'to revive a dying campaign.'

But within the ranks of the broader Nationalist cause, there was open opposition to the forthcoming Referendum from individuals and organisations. Jennie Eirian Davies, Editor of Welsh language weekly, *Y Faner*, criticised the Yes campaign for being 'terribly ambivalent' in its attitude towards the Welsh language in their campaigning. Cymdeithas yr Iaith Gymraeg decided that it would not join the campaign for devolution. Their stance can best be summed up by a quote from a letter written by one of the Society's leading members, Angharad Tomos. Writing to Welsh weekly, *Y Cymro*, she said that she would be carrying on her Welsh TV

---

172. Hubert Gieschen: *The Labour Party in Wales and the 1979 Referendum*. Frankfurt: Haag and Herschen, 1999, p. 34.
173. Rhys Evans, ibid., p. 379.

channel protesting as opposed to joining the devolution campaign. They preferred the broadcasting campaign, she said, 'rather than work for a strong vote in favour of a Labour conspiracy to tame Welsh nationalists.'

The successful co-operation between opposing political ideologies on this one uniting issue can be shown clearly by the two local authorities who were at the forefront of the No campaign—Tory-led South Glamorgan County Council and Labour-led Gwent Council. They had no issues with being bedfellows across the political divide.

A sore thumb

While the Yes campaign spent a great deal of time outlining the details of the Wales Act, thus concentrating the public's attention on so much parliamentary detail, the No campaign focused on issues that were closer to home for those who would be voting. They focused on the Welsh language, on costs, on threats to our town halls and on the way an Assembly would divide Wales itself. There was also the emotive slippery slope argument.

Such issues were relatable, part of living day-to-day experience for Welsh people in one way or another. The argument that the people of Wales would be hit in the pocket if an Assembly was introduced was a particularly potent one, especially considering that the Winter of Discontent was still biting. Times were hard and making the people of Wales think that they would be worse off if there was an Assembly was a timely and effective tactic. Compared to other areas of the UK, Wales did very well in terms of the per capita money it received. It received £167 more than every other region in the UK. This financial difference would lead to regional division, the No Campaign guide said:

With the creation of the Scottish and Welsh Assemblies, the whole issue will take on a different aspect; the demand for resources would be framed in nationalistic and sectional terms, and the debate over resource allocation, now held in Cabinet, would be exposed to the rigours of competitive clamouring from all the regions of Britain. Rather than partnership, competition would become the theme.

In less formal language, on the same issue, the Labour No leaflet said that Wales would 'stick out like a sore thumb'.

On the detail of the allocation of the block Rate Support Grant to Wales from Westminster, Jones and Wilford in *The Welsh Veto* say that this highlighted two issues at once:

> *First, that the role of the local authorities in negotiating the RSG would be diminished by the assembly; and second, that since there was no compulsion upon it to deliver the RSG, the local authorities would have either to increase rates to make up the deficit or alternatively to cut those services they provide to the public. This latter scenario was, of course, straightforward scaremongering. If such an event were to happen, it would be tantamount to an act of political suicide by the assembly men.*[174]

The NAC campaign guide was clear enough on this issue:

> *'... if the assembly were to hold back completely on RSG, rates in Wales would have to rise... if all government grants were 'consumed' by the Assembly then rates would have to be more than three times higher than their present level to recoup the loss.*

In addition to the money in the pocket, the language people spoke in Wales was also a central pillar of the No campaign. We've heard already how Leo Abse approached the prospect of an Assembly dominated by those who spoke Welsh. Two more quotes of his are mentioned by Gieschen:

> *The overwhelming majority of young men and women from areas like Gwent and Cardiff would be disqualified from participating in the administration of their own land.*

His next quote is quite astounding:

> *Four out of five Welsh men are monoglots endowed with the talent to use*

---

174. David Foulkes; J. Barry Jones; R. A. Wilford (eds.), ibid., p. 121.

English with the fluency and concrete imagery denied to mere tongue-tied Anglo-Saxons.

Whether the Welsh spoke better English than the English was not the real issue. It was the prospect that non-Welsh speakers might not get jobs at the new Assembly that was the real concern. Eight days before voting day, Abse continued with this attack in an article in the *South Wales Echo*:

> *The English-speaking majority would be condemned to be strangers in their own land. The nationalists, by insisting on Welsh being spoken in the Assembly, will ensure the creation of a Welsh-speaking bureaucratic elite who will attempt to impose a false homogeneity upon Wales. There is no magic superiority of one language over the others, though Nazi and German academics practised that dangerous doctrine.*

It was also more than that. There were language implications for those that would not be directly linked with the new Assembly as Barry Jones and R. A. Wilford argue in their chapter in *The Welsh Veto*:

> *They were also seeking to evoke the fear among English-speaking Welsh-men that if the different proposals were accepted, not only would linguistic criteria increasingly come to be applied in the employment market, but also that bilingual education would become the norm.*[175]

Further to this linguistic divide within the small nation of Wales, the No campaign argued that there would be a geographical one as well. The new Assembly would no doubt be in Cardiff, thus giving increasing power to that city, and by default, it's hinterland. The rest of Wales, particularly the North, would suffer as a result. Jones and Wilford quote a letter that sums this up succinctly:

175.Ibid., p. 126.

People in South Wales are very charming, but as a crowd, they are loud and coarse. We do not want to be governed by Cardiff. The assembly will be permanently dominated by Labour. It will be a dictatorship.

The *Liverpool Daily Post* editorial of 1 March 1979 was harsh;

Wales deserves better than this half-baked folly, a pretentious little super council housed in a Cardiff backwater, trifling endlessly with minor government issues and failing to achieve anything of primary importance.

   The role of the media is worth noting, or more accurately, it's spread. Even in 1979, London-based papers accounted for over 40% of newspapers read in Wales, and a good proportion of the TV viewing was tuned in to English rather than Welsh transmitters.

Geographical concerns sat side by side with obvious party political concerns for Mrs Gwen Mostyn Lewis, chair of the Clwyd No campaign, in her letter to the *Western Mail*. Conwy MP Wyn Roberts expressed similar concerns in his letter to the same newspaper:

The assembly would establish a more complex and cumbersome machinery of government... tailor-made for the Labour Party caucus in South Wales.

Further, the No campaign argued that an Assembly would be a threat to the county hall and its place in local Welsh government. A new body would interfere, or take over, areas dealt with up to then by local government. There was a threat, then, to these relatively newly formed County Councils in Wales. This threat was taken seriously. Dyfed County Council reversed its pro-devolution stance. Mid-Glamorgan's leader urged the people in his area to vote against devolution. The argument that affected such actions was that the Assembly would not bring a decision meeting closer to the people. In addition, the anti-devolutionists said that the number of Welsh MPs would be cut, thus reducing Welsh influence in Westminster.

The slippery slope

But perhaps one of the most effective emotions the No campaign drew on, certainly, the most effective slogan, was that an Assembly for Wales would be just the start of the 'slippery slope' towards separating Wales from the rest of the UK. It would hasten the break-up of the United Kingdom. This turned out to be the main thrust of the campaign as polling day drew ever closer. Fear is a potent political tool.

Pembrokeshire MP and Shadow Welsh Secretary, Nicholas Edwards focused on this issue in a speech in Conwy on 21 February:

> *How is the British government going to control the economy of Britain in the future faced by a rebellious assembly in Wales that challenges its efforts to act in the interests of the British people? It is appalling that on top of all the other problems that face the government in managing the economy and controlling inflation; we had to see an Assembly claiming all the authority of a nationhood, standing up and challenging its rights to do so.*

The Assembly would be inherently rebellious, constantly challenging Westminster, at the expense of the rest of Britain. Those not of the same political persuasion as Edwards, but who stood with him against devolution, also saw that an Assembly would be separatist, as Jones and Wilford note:

> *The prospect of separatism which they perceived to be implicit in the Assembly proposals was, they argued, against the interests of the working class and would serve to divide the Labour movement in Britain. Neil Kinnock, MP for Bedwellty, was prominent in arguing this, maintaining that the Assembly debate represented a distraction from the main objectives of the British Labour movement since it would tend to excite regional loyalties that would only serve to weaken the unity of the working class.*[176]

The proposed Assembly for Wales then stood at the apex of two slippery slopes.

---

176. Ibid., p. 131.

The fight-back

The response from the Yes campaign to these issues was actually not much of a fight-back. In his only speech during the pro-devolution campaign, Jim Callaghan did address the scaremongering that the No campaign had used extensively. In Swansea, 21 February 1979, at an unusually well-attended pro-devolution meeting, referring to the scaremongers he said, quoted in the *Guardian* the day after:

> *They paint a picture of a Welsh Assembly totally dominated by Welsh speakers actively practising discrimination against non-Welsh speakers. I believe the Assembly by its very composition will put a stop to any such tendency—it is inconceivable that a body representing all parts of Wales should or could discriminate against the vast majority of the electorate of Wales.*

Callaghan included this in his speech as opinion polls at the time had indicated that the language issue as promulgated by the No campaign was gaining ground and making people cross from Yes to No. The Prime Minister felt sufficiently challenged by this to refer to it in his speech.

The WAC Yes campaign launched their manifesto on 7 February, outlining the main benefits of an Assembly for Wales:

i. better job opportunities through democratic control of the Welsh Development Agency on the supervision of an economic plan for Wales
ii. better housing through the Assembly's power to win more cash from central government
iii. better health services through the Assembly's ability to decide what hospitals are wanted and where
iv. better education for the Assembly's power to cut class sizes.

That manifesto made little impact amongst the public. The fight-back to that lack of interest was the release of a statement by the Yes campaign, attacking the anti-devolutionists for statements that were either misleading or untrue. This has been seen as another ineffective strategy by the Yes campaign, as Jones and Wilford summarise:

> *The evidence suggests that this desire to expose the falsehoods and confront the anti-Assembly coalition distracted the pro-assembly campaign from its only effective cohesive value, the objective of devolution.*[177]

So, in addition to the initial focusing on the mechanics of the Wales Act, they were now concentrating on attacking the perceived inaccurate claims of the opposition. The actual potential positive virtues of the proposed devolution were disappearing more and more into the background.

A resounding no

As the historic day approached when the Welsh people would vote on constitutional change for their country, it was increasingly clear that history wouldn't be made. The Yes campaign, in its various guises, had run out of steam. It limped its way to polling day.

Gwynfor Evans' zeal kept going almost until the end. He admitted in an article in the *Liverpool Daily Post* on 28 February and published on polling day, that 'not enough work had been done on the doorstep and that his dream of a devolved Wales had been shattered'.

John Morris was also aware of imminent defeat before people went to the polls:

> *I knew, of course, from all the intelligence I had, that we were marching to defeat. After a lunch given to me by some executives of HTV close to the referendum polling day—it felt like the Last Supper—I made it quite plain that I would have one go, and one alone, in delivering a satisfactory devolution scheme for Wales. It would be for others to carry the baton thereafter. It would need new leadership and possibly a more flexible one.*[178]

177. Ibid., p. 122.
178. John Morris: *Fifty Years in Politics and the Law.* Cardiff: University of Wales Press, 2013, p. 123.

No one, however, predicted the scale of the defeat when it eventually came. The count took place the day after the voting. The figures are clear enough. Yes—243,048 votes. No—956,330 votes, on a 58.3% turnout. The breakdown of that turnout was 11.8% Yes voters, 46.5% No voters.

All percentages reflect how the argument and the campaigning had gone for the year before voting. Jones and Wilford state:

> *The initiative had passed from the Yes campaign at an early stage; the decision not to persevere with promoting the aspirational objectives of devolution but to adopt a more limited pragmatic and normative approach had trivialised what should have been the resolution of a great constitutional issue and played into the hands of the Assembly's opponents whose act-centred tactic was directed towards exciting a conservative reaction in effect an implicit endorsement of the status quo.*

The two men who could be seen as being at the very forefront of the Devolution for Wales campaign, John Morris and Gwynfor Evans, had suffered bitter blows. From two different parties, they had argued passionately and consistently for the Wales they wanted to see. There were differences of interpretation and application, of course, but their underlying principle was as one. John Morris' response had to be instant and on camera:

> *I had to go on television; I believe it was the Nine O'clock News, on the night we lost the referendum to make the most of a bad job. There was no ammunition to do what so many politicians try to do and justify a bad election result, and most of us do it so badly. There was no possibility or minimising our defeat, or the scale of it. I merely said, 'if you see an elephant on your doorstep, you know it's there'. The election was a horrendous defeat; a knock-out blow. It was the best I could do, and it was my way of explaining the catastrophe on the main TV news, which I did from the few words I had hastily put together. I had put so much into the whole project that our defeat left me utterly dejected.[179]*

179.Ibid., p. 124.

Gwynfor Evans felt equally crushing emotions. Rhys Evans sums up the effect the defeat had on Plaid's leader:

> *Gwynfor experienced many highs and lows in his career, but this was the nadir. For him and his generation of nationalists, the referendum was more than a ballot on the administration of Wales; the referendum was a vote on the spiritual and existential question of whether Wales existed. After decades of posing the question, Gwynfor had now received an une-quivocal answer. He was devastated, not knowing which 'made him feel more sick… Welsh toadyism or Labour deceit and corruption'. His only consolation was what he saw as the heroism of those who had campaigned for devolution.*[180]

The effect that the defeat had on the parties of both men has been well-documented and analysed over the years since. We deal with this in the Appendix to this book. For the UK, it heralded the end of a Labour government. Margaret Thatcher would be Prime Minister before the year was out. She was not put in power solely because of devolution. But that issue was a Labour one, and one they had lost. The London-based broadsheet newspapers barely thought the event worth reporting, but from opposite political ends, the *Guardian* and the *Telegraph* thought that this was the end of the whole devolution debate as far as Wales was concerned. The *Telegraph* qualified its initial statement, however:

> *Of course it does not mean that the nationalists have been exorcised— nationalism in Scotland and Wales is essentially a heart-cry against the excessive power of the modern state. If that power is not sharply and swiftly diminished, then the fortunes of SNP and Plaid Cymru will soon revive, and there may be no stopping short of the full disintegration of the United Kingdom.*

The *Western Mail* saw the situation similarly.

---

180. Rhys Evans: *Gwynfor Evans: Portrait of a Patriot*. Tal-y-bont, Ceredigion: Y Lolfa, 2008, p. 382.

We have to accept that this concept of a Welsh Assembly is now dead and buried. However, devolution will not die with this particular Wales act. The rejection of the Assembly doesn't mean that the status quo has been fully endorsed.

David Melding MS, in his book *Will Britain Survive Beyond 2020?* wrote:

The rejection of devolution was overwhelming in Wales and it cannot be casually explained away in retrospect as a historical aberration. Even in Gwynedd, two-thirds of the electorate voted 'No'. One problem was the failure of devolutionists to engage the industrial communities of south Wales. Consequently, Labour supporters had little sense of ownership over their government's own policy.... Less often remarked upon is the standard and nature of the 1970s devolution debate, which at times descended to poisonous parody. It became difficult afterwards to understand what question had been settled. Critics had made a grotesque man of straw to characterise the dangers of devolution, and the illusion worked wonderfully.[181]

Historian Martin Johnes takes a broader view, turning to underlying emotions more than to political convictions.

The ties of the welfare state, the pool of trade unions that worked across the UK and the memories of the shared experiences of the Second World war we're still strong, but Britishness was a popular emotional sentiment too, just in the way Welshness was.[182]

Having looked back at 1979, he then returns to the theme of rugby to offer the way forward he thought faced the defeated devolutionists in March 1979:

---

181. David Melding: *Will Britain survive beyond 2020?* Cardiff: Institute of Welsh Affairs, 2009, p. 90.
182. Martin Johnes: *Wales since 1939.* Manchester: Manchester University Press, 2013, p. 299.

If Welsh separatism was to grow, then what would have to happen was a politicization of the emotional patriotism that was only too evident at a Welsh rugby international.[183]

1979 was indeed a historical year. Within weeks of the resounding devolution defeat, the Labour government was also defeated, the Conservatives returned to power with a convincing victory, and the UK had its first-ever female Prime Minister. But that's not quite the history that so many in Wales were hoping they would see that year. The fight for greater autonomy for Wales, for greater recognition as a nation which echoed back to the last decades of Victoria, through Lloyd George, T. I. Ellis, Jim Griffiths, S. O. Davies, Gwynfor Evans and so many more had received a crushing blow. The next decision was quite simply, where would this cause go next, if anywhere?

183.Ibid., p. 307.

PART FOUR:

The Years of Moving, Respite and Return
1979–2020

The fourth part of this book reverts to the approach taken in Part Two—Gwynoro Jones' involvement and response to the changes in the devolution narrative. We continue with the chronology from such a perspective. For him personally, it was a time of changing political parties, being active in the founding of a new one and then, for a few decades, disappearing from politics completely. But through all these changes, he maintained his solid conviction that Wales needed increased devolution. When he re-entered the political arena, an Assembly had been established in Wales. Lately, Yes Cymru and the call for Welsh independence has flourished. But there's no sense of resting on his oars for Gwynoro Jones and not all that's happened in the name of the devolution cause he's championed for so long is to his liking.

25.

A New Party

The chapters of this book have spanned over 140 years of the story of devolution and the nationhood of Wales. We have covered the twists and turns, the hopes and shattered dreams, bitter divisions between and within political parties and long periods of general disinterest amongst Welsh voters. These chapters have chronicled the range of issues that have divided the people of Wales over that period on devolution, nationhood, greater autonomy, culture and language.

Following the referendum rout, James Callaghan lost a vote of confidence in the Commons and was replaced by Michael Foot. Amongst all parties, the loss of '79 had the effect of practically placing any thoughts of any form of Elected Council for Wales way into the backwaters. Labour, Conservatives and even Plaid Cymru hardly raised the matter throughout the 1980s. In addition to the referendum effect, the Eighties was a decade of significant major events such as the Falklands War, the 1984/85 miners' strike and periods of economic turbulence, that might well have contributed to taking attention away from any changes to the system of governance in the UK's four nations. The result also had a profound influence on my own political career. It will be for others to debate the political history of the 1980-2020 period in the way we have done so in this book for the 1880-1980 period. This is the nationalism debate post-referendum as I have lived it.

The Me-First Decade

The Eighties was a decade of major significant events. The UK was being led by a female Prime Minister for the very first time. As soon as the decade started, the whole concept of British identity was brought sharply into focus by a Royal Wedding; not just any Royal Wedding, but the one of the heir to the throne. And as far as Wales was concerned, he was Charles, Prince of Wales and his wife would be the Princess of Wales. Here was an opportunity to celebrate both Welshness and Britishness together. The wedding played into the bigger picture of national identity, as Charles' Investiture had in 1969.

Later in that Royal Wedding year, the UK had its first Aids-related death, and that disease dominated the minds of people for many years after that. It brought our fear, prejudice and, of course, suffering for many. It took over the public consciousness very much like the pandemic did in 2020.

A year later, the war with Argentina over the Falkland Islands was underway, with generations at home experiencing 'war' for the first time. Again, this was an event that flagged up, literally, a sense of national British identity. Britain was at war. The area of Britain that the soldiers who suffered the most casualties came from was Mid Glamorgan, which also experienced the highest fatalities. Welsh soldiers were fighting in the British forces.

The wedding and the war were unifying factors that flew the British flag a matter of years after the Welsh people voted No to devolution. The Falkland war, in particular, gave Margaret Thatcher a huge boost in popularity which carried her through the decade. The virus concentrated the minds of everyone on a totally new enemy.

Far more divisive was the miners' strike of a few years later. This was a bitter, confrontational battle that would last a whole year. It set unions and government against each other and led to large-scale closure of coal mines and the end of a coal industry that had been particularly central to life in Wales. The defeat of the miners was a severe blow to Wales, and South Wales in particular. This was a blow against their sense of who and what they were.

Thatcher's least popular policy was referred to as the Poll Tax. Margaret Thatcher had outlined the whole idea of replacing the existing rateable system herself in 1974 when she was Shadow Environment Secretary. She implemented it throughout the UK, but not until 1989 in Scotland and 1990 in England and Wales. It proved to be a hugely unpopular scheme. Instead of the old rates system, Thatcher introduced a single flat-rate per-capita tax for all.

How *The Sun* saw it.

There was widespread popular protest against the tax. After it was introduced, the opinion polls clearly showed a lead for Labour over the Tory government. Thatcher's leadership of her party was challenged, and her three challengers promised to abolish the Poll Tax. Thatcher didn't receive the required number of votes in the second leadership ballot to move on to the next step, and she resigned on 22 November 1990. Kinnock had vowed to abolish the tax if he were in power. This one issue shifted the balance back to Labour for a while. It also drove some back to the devolution issue, claiming that such an injustice as they saw the Poll Tax being could be dealt with differently with a Welsh Assembly.

All change

My personal recollection of issues surrounding the 'matter of Wales' came with the Parliament for Wales campaign of the early mid-1950s. Even though I was in my early teens, I recall people in the locality discussing it. It was a major topic of conversation. I remember clearly the impact that the result of the Petition calling for a Parliament for Wales had. In the days before social media, with very little TV presence and only the *Western Mail* as a remotely national paper, that the petition drew 250,000 signatures is phenomenal. I remember the discussion and the buzz surrounding it on the streets of Cefneithin village, both while the petitioners went from door to door and after they announced the result. Rejoicing today in a petition with 20,000 seems rather hollow in comparison.

Following that, when I studied history for my A levels, there was controversy emerging over whether Wales should have a Secretary of State and a Welsh Office. I remember arguments in the locality over who was right, Jim Griffiths or Aneurin Bevan. The two, as we have discussed, were on opposing sides.

My personal involvement in the debate, indeed the battle, has been dealt with in Part Two of this book. These are my thoughts and recollections on the period after the overwhelming No vote in 1979. It was a time of disillusionment, and the disappointment of defeat hung heavy in the air.

I had believed for months before the referendum that it was a lost cause. There was little enthusiasm for it within my party, the Labour Party. Deep divisions that stretched back to the 1960s and accelerated during the 1970s, as chronicled in this book, had taken their toll. I blamed the defeat on the complete failure of the Labour Party in Wales and the lack of direction and leadership that came from the then Prime Minister, Jim Callaghan.

By 1979, I was already disillusioned with the Labour Party, but not just over its abysmal failure to campaign vigorously for the nationhood of Wales. I also opposed its anti-EEC stance and its lack of vision on the need for an overhaul of the way the UK was governed, especially its voting system. In those days I had also become an advocate for a Federal UK, so devolution, as envisaged in those days, did not begin to meet up with what I believed was essential. I still felt a huge allegiance to the Party. I put my name forward for the General Election of 1979 in Ogmore, but more significantly, I put my name forward in the European Elections, for the Mid and West Wales constituency. I received over 70 nominations from local constituencies, to Ann Clwyd's 6 nominations. I wasn't even put on the shortlist, however. Then finally, I put my name forward for the

Gower constituency after the MP Ifor Davies died—with the same result! So it was becoming obvious that it wasn't only me thinking of leaving the Labour Party, the Labour Party was thinking of leaving me too. They had no room for a Social Democrat.

'Shunted off' Euro short list — ex MP

FORMER CARMARTHEN MP, Mr. Gwynoro Jones, claimed today he was "shunted off" the short list of candidates for the European Assembly at a Labour Party selection conference in the town during the weekend because of the tactical voting procedure.

There was only one step I could take. I had to leave the Labour Party. In 1980, after being a member for 20 years, I left.

The travails of me leaving Labour have been well documented. It was never an easy decision. I owed a lot to the Labour Party in Wales, and especially in Carmarthen. I had forged close friendships that were hard to disengage from because I knew leaving would not only mean upsetting people but that I would become a pariah and yes, as so often told for years after, 'a traitor'.

During that leaving process, I was often asked why I did not join Plaid Cymru? It was an option that did not much cross my mind. That was for two reasons. As the second section of this book shows, a decade of bitter fighting between Labour and Plaid, between Gwynfor Evans and me, had coloured my thoughts against the party. But also, given the structure of the Welsh economy, I did not believe that an 'independent Wales' was a viable and serious proposition.

I have since realised that I had rather unexpected bedfellows in my uncertainty about Welsh independence. Oddly enough, it was only in the last few years that I realised Saunders Lewis and Gwynfor Evans were also not enamoured with independence either. One spoke of Dominion Status, claiming that

> *... independence for Wales was impracticable... because it's not worth having... we want not independence, but freedom and the meaning of freedom in this respect is responsibility.*

Gwynfor, on the other hand, argued for a confederation and a common market for Britain.

To this day I do not understand why Plaid Cymru allowed itself to be called 'separatists' because Gwynfor was not one. Having looked through the minutes of Plaid Cymru Executive meetings and conference decisions, some two years ago, they also show that the Party was not in favour of independence either. The word didn't appear in any of the minutes I looked at, which covered the 1960s and the 1970s.

Gwynoro Jones and Roy Jenkins

I was not the only one disillusioned with Labour as the Seventies drew to a close. There was a growing number of MPs who weren't happy with the direction in which the party was going. During that period, Roy Jenkins was President of the European Commission. We communicated regularly and met up in Brussels some three times. I was well aware of Roy's disillusionment with the Labour Party and of his intentions. Upon his return from his Brussels position in 1981, I knew he would endeavour to launch a new party. Plaid Cymru wasn't an option for me then, but this new party that was being formed was. I had many discussions with Roy Jenkins about this from 1979 onwards.

SDP for Wales

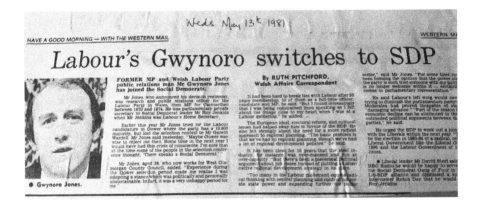

I was involved from the outset with establishing this new political party, the Social Democratic Party, in Wales. I saw them as a vehicle to move forward the debate over devolution and greater sovereignty in and for Wales. Central to the vision was also forming an alliance with the Welsh Liberal Party.

From the outset, along with Tom Ellis, who, in 1981, was still a Member of Parliament, and others, we were determined to ensure a strong Wales SDP. Both Tom and I had experienced the years of struggle to get Labour in Wales to establish a clear identity. We didn't want that same difficulty with the SDP.

A new political party in Wales had to set its stall out on so many central issues, of course, such as economy, education and health. The SDP did that. But they also saw devolution and constitutional reform from the outset as being one of those major issues. It was on the table from the first day.

SDP pledges PM and cabinet for Wales

WESTERN MAIL
8.9.82

WALES WOULD have its own prime minister under devolution proposals revealed by the SDP yesterday.

By DAVID HUGHES,
Political Correspondent

racy of Whitehall would be stripped of much of its power and size.
The scheme would scrap the

opportunity to participate sion-making" and says that mic and political life in this has been "enervated" by o tralisation.
The concentration of Whitehall overloads Gov departments, Ministers an creating inefficiency and

Our first SDP Consultative Assembly in Wales, in March 1983, debated a draft 60-page policy document that included a call for the establishment of a Welsh Assembly. *The Western Mail* was forecasting trouble ahead for the leadership in Wales on the issue '*SDP set for clash on Welsh Assembly*'. Some members of the committee believed that an assembly was a vote-loser—harking back to what happened in 1979 referendum—others at the grassroots level, especially from Cardiff, the Eastern Valleys and a few in West Glamorgan, did not want the matter debated at all.

Again, I and others were determined that the issue had to be debated and faced up to. Decentralisation and reform of government were at the heart of what the SDP was all about. It was on that basis that we were promoting the Welsh Assembly—as part of a constitutional package across the UK. Our plans involve democratizing the Lords, making the Commons itself more democratic with a far more powerful select committee structure as well as voting reform. It also involved decentralizing power from Whitehall, linked with the question of reorganizing local government and the future of the plethora of nominated bodies.

However, there were echoes of my Labour days within the SDP as well, as several people inside the new party, some in Wales but more especially in London, placed hurdles in the way of promoting decentralization. But the opposition wasn't as volatile as it was within the Labour ranks. David Owen, after becoming the SDP leader, would blow hot and cold over the issue.

There was one occasion when we publicly disagreed with each other on devolution, during one of his blowing cold periods, no doubt. This was at a meeting in Edinburgh in May 1984 when the 400-strong policy-making body, the Council for Social Democracy convened. The Welsh SDP delegation had a fight on its hands. A decentralisation motion was being discussed, but it made no reference to Wales, only Scotland. Every effort was made to prevent a debate on a motion based on the one passed more or less unanimously at our Cardiff conference earlier in March, which insisted that Wales be included in the debate. Fortunately, our vice-chair, Eric Owen, from Wrexham, had managed to get an amendment to the platform's decentralisation motion. Eric's amendment stated that the Council for Social Democracy

'affirms its commitment to the introduction of a Welsh Parliament.'

The meeting overwhelmingly accepted the amendment very much against the wishes of the platform. Tactics of that kind were employed by David Owen on a couple of other occasions, so the SDP Council for Wales had to forever be vigilant.

An example of this was when, in 1985, an SDP-Liberal Commission of the great and the good had published a report *'Towards a new Constitutional Settlement'* that would give a Parliament to Scotland but only an enlarged Select Committee—to be called the Commission for Government in Wales—to Wales. The Commission's report had concluded:

It is not clear that there is popular support for an elected parliament in Wales.

Liberals want Welsh Grand Council

By CLIVE BETTS, Welsh Affairs Correspondent

A PLAN for the formation of a Grand Council for Wales uniting MPs and councillors and with the power to quiz Welsh Office Ministers has been drawn up by the Welsh Liberal Party.

The 95-member Grand Council would meet in Cardiff three times a year. Its powers would be limited to giving advice, although the Secretary of State would be forced to appear before it.

The executive committee plan will be presented to the annual conference of the Welsh Liberal Party at Newtown next Friday and Saturday.

It could presage a clash with the Welsh SDP, whose assembly a fortnight ago called for elected parliaments or assemblies for Wales, Scotland and the English regions.

The Welsh Liberal plan, though, is designed to avoid any major structural changes to government. They do not think people want them.

The motion will be proposed at the conference by Mr John Griffiths, of Brecon.

He said yesterday, "This motion is similar to those adopted by us in the days before the great devolution debate. At the time, such ideas received a certain amount of general support from Wales.

"But then a lot of such feelings were channelled into Plaid Cymru and ideas of a council were pushed aside. Now that that party has suffered so much, attention is returning to other ways of making Wales influence felt."

Mr Griffiths said he saw no clash with the Welsh SDP, whose plans were long-term. A Grand Council could be set up quickly.

The Grand Council would consist of the 38 Welsh MPs, the four MEPs, the chairman of the eight county councils, the chairman of the eight education authorities, and the chairmen of the 38 district councils.

The three annual meetings would debate and question subjects under Welsh Office remit.

plus the relationship of Wales to the EEC.

The Welsh Office Ministers would have to answer questions at plenary sessions. Each subject dealt with by the Welsh Office would be covered at least once a year.

The motion is likely to be passed. It calls for the formation of working parties to draw up detailed schemes before the general election.

The only listed challenge to the motion comes from Cardiff Central and its parliamentary candidate, Mr Mike German. They want the Grand Council to have its own secretariat so that members are better briefed and more able to challenge the Welsh Office.

Cardiff Central would also substitute 30 members nominated by the Secretary of State for the 49 members from education authorities and district councils.

The conference opens on Friday evening with a public meeting at Theatr Hafren, Newtown, when the speakers will include Mr David Steel, leader of the Liberal Party, local Liberal MP Mr Alex Carlile, and Mr Gwynoro Jones, chairman of the SDP Council for Wales.

In this period, the Welsh Liberals put forward a policy plan which was reported in the *Western Mail*. The executive committee of the Welsh Liberals had agreed a policy plan to form a 95-member Grand Council for Wales to be made up of MPs and councillors. It was set to be debated at their annual conference in Newtown within a week or so. Needless to say, I thought little of that at the time and wondered where the idea had come from. It clashed with what the Welsh Council of the SDP consultative conference decided, a fortnight earlier, when they voted for an elected Welsh Assembly and it also went against the joint SDP/Welsh Liberals Wales Alliance conference in November 1985 where over 250 people voted 3:1 in favour of a Welsh Assembly.

The Grand Council would meet three times a year and its powers would be extremely limited; mainly to advise the Secretary of State for Wales, but he would be made to appear before it. Each subject dealt with by the Welsh Office would be covered at least once a year.

It would consist of 38 Welsh MPs, the four MEPs, chair of the eight County Councils, the education authorities and the 37 district councils.

The various battles going on inside the SDP and the Welsh Liberals with their Westminster leadership had received considerable media coverage over a three-year period, whilst Labour and Plaid Cymru had been extremely quiet on the devolution front. It was the SDP that kept the debate alive during the years after the failed '79 referendum. But in 1986, things changed.

In response to the incessant internal battles, the two Davids, Steel and Owen, agreed to reconvene the earlier commission on constitutional reform. I wrote to the chair of the Commission, Sir Henry Fisher, itemising the various decisions that had been taken at successive conferences in the UK, that clearly reflected the fact that the majority of the membership was strongly in support of decentralisation. I quote from the letter:

> *Frankly, the two leaders of the Alliance have made rather a hash of things in recent months on the question of decentralization. And it is important that there is no further confusion and fudging, especially on the proposals for Wales.*

Gwynoro Jones and Paddy Ashdown.

After almost ten years of struggle, the battle was won. In 1992, in a policy document called We the People, the Lib Dems agreed a Home Rule for Scotland and Wales with the creation of a Scottish Parliament and a Welsh Senedd. I was the vice-chair of the Policy Committee with Paddy Ashdown as chair.

Labour and Two assemblies

The early Eighties was a period of turmoil for the Labour Party, with concerns about a push more to the left politically, an anti-Europe faction, unilateral disarmament disagreements and objections to the block-vote controlling influence of the trade unions. But devolution raised its head eventually, even if it wasn't a major concern.

The party's manifesto in 1983, under Michael Foot, and in 1987, under the new leader, Neil Kinnock, didn't contain any devolution commitment. Kinnock, however, did address devolution. In 1984, not to be outdone by the SDP, he came up with his own version of devolution for Wales. His proposal was that Wales should have two assemblies:

> ... *one in the industrial urban English-speaking areas in the South and another for the rural, Welsh-speaking areas of the North.*

Another Kinnock gimmick

SIR,—Mr Kinnock, the Labour leader, now wants to divide Wales by his proposal to create two assemblies for the Principality.

As I recall, he argued during the 1979 Devolution referendum that even one assembly was too costly and expensive.

sponsibilities of the Welsh Office, and the undemocratic nominated bodies in Wales, should be transferred initially to a Welsh Assembly.

● The reorganisation of local government by creating single tier, all purpose authorities.

● The reform of the House

Council for Wales nises that it will possible to put the constitutional p into effect in the c a single Parliamen

However, the ca be argued openly stantly, since c tional change will the consent of the

In a published *Western Mail* letter on 26 March 1984, I said that his tactic was

> ... *divide and rule. This is the same tactic used in relation to local government, and Kinnock sees such a divisive force working to weaken the Welsh dimension.*

I also asked

... where did the people of the old counties of Carmarthenshire and Cere-digion fit into his plan, and then what about North-East Wales?

In mid-March '86 the pro-assembly wing of the Welsh Labour Party suc-ceeded in getting the executive to unanimously accept a working party report calling for an elected Welsh Assembly, at the same time as propos-ing a single-tier system of local authorities hence bringing to an end the eight counties and 37 districts.

Devolution is backed by Labour's Welsh chiefs

18/3/86

THE PRO-ASSEMBLY wing of the Welsh Labour Party won a surprising victory yesterday.

The party's Welsh executive accepted unanimously a working party's report calling for a Labour Government to set up an elected Welsh assembly at the same time as inaugurat-ing a single-tier system of local councils.
Observers last night were wondering whether the

By CLIVE BETTS, Welsh Affairs Correspondent

The working party's report says, "Membe strongly favour a policy to end the present confusir division of services between the two tiers of loc authorities.
"Establishing a single tier of local authoriti with a directly-elected regional body for Wales wi similar developments in the English regions, seems

The working party report was to be debated at the annual conference at Swansea in May. There was press speculation about how this happened and how serious was the commitment. This was because the document made it clear that

*'It would not be possible immediately on the return of a Labour Govern-
ment to carry out the assembly plans'.*

Then David Jenkins, general secretary of the Wales TUC, who was a member of the working group, commented publicly that while an assembly was
a policy objective, it did not figure highly in the Wales TUC's priorities.

In 1987 at the General Election, the party's manifesto for Wales
proposed a new economic planning council, with consultations on the
future of local government in Wales. The manifesto contained no reference to an elected Assembly. Neil Kinnock had his way. In the early

1990s, the Labour Party held a policy revue called, Meet the Challenge, Make the Change. The proposal was a legislative parliament for Scotland and administrative assemblies for Wales and England. Wales once more was not meriting the same level of devolution of power, a trend which continues to this day.

Plaid Cymru

Like Labour, Plaid also went into its shell after the No defeat of '79. Gwynfor Evans was very quiet. The Welsh 4th channel, S4C, had been established in November 1982 and its formation was seen as a major victory for the nationalists. Gwynfor Evans had said that he would fast to the death if Wales wasn't given a channel for Welsh language programmes. When S4C started, Gwynfor's willingness to starve to death for its formation was hailed as the act of a hero. He, no doubt, played a significant part in that campaign, but to emphasise him alone doesn't do justice to people like Conservative MP Wyn Roberts, Lord Cledwyn Hughes, Sir Goronwy Daniel and many other church and civic leaders' contributions in lobbying Thatcher and Willie Whitelaw constantly. Wyn Roberts, in particular, was instrumental in making Whitelaw change his mind on a Welsh fourth channel.

Like Labour, it too faced accusations of moving further left. In their case, however, it was more to do with one of their MPs, Dafydd Elis Thomas. He contributed articles to *Marxist Today* magazine. By now, however, he admits that his 'socialist' experiment was a mistake.

14   WESTERN MAIL, TUESDAY, APRIL 29, 1986

Voters say Yes to a Welsh assembly

VOTERS ARE at last beginning to support the founding of a Welsh Assembly.

For perhaps the first time in the decade that an assembly has been on the political agenda a reputable opinion poll has found that a majority of voters favour its establishment.

By CLIVE BETTS, Welsh Affairs Correspondent

their minds. That boosted the Yes fig to 52 per cent.

Fifty-seven per cent of the No v refused to budge, but a high proport (27 per cent) then said they did know. Generally, however, the la number who, in the run-up to referendum, gave "Don't know" as

April 1986 Opinion Poll shows majority public support for Welsh Assembly

The timing of Welsh Labour's call for a Welsh Assembly, on 6 March 1986, more or less coincided with a *Western Mail* article on March 7 under the heading '*Plaid back down on self-rule*'.

Plaid's plans were contained in a document titled '*A Welsh Senate— and Industrial Future for Wales*'. Out went the self-government demand in the 1983 General Election manifesto and in its place, they were now suggesting a 100-member Senate elected by proportional representation but with no law-making powers. The Senate would take over the responsibilities of the Welsh Office, WJEC, Broadcasting and funding of the Universities. However, to change laws would require the permission of Westminster.

All this was driven by a strategy of arriving at an accommodation with the Alliance parties in Wales and hopefully Welsh Labour.

Party President Dafydd Elis Thomas said

We hope that the other parties will look seriously at these proposals.

Exits and entrances

As the various parties were working out what their stance was on devolution for Wales, I again had my own political decisions to make. Having been chair of both the SDP in Wales for two terms and joint chair of the Alliance Committee for Wales throughout its existence, I began to take a view it was best to move on.

In Alliance with the Liberals at both the 1983 and 1987 General Elections, we had polled strongly, with 23% in '83 and 18% in '87. The first past the post voting system as ever proved a stumbling block to an electoral breakthrough. A standout example is in 1983 when, despite winning 23% of the vote, the SDP Liberal Alliance only captured 2 seats in Wales. On the other hand, however, the Conservatives, with 30% of the vote, captured 14 seats. Conversely, Plaid Cymru, with just 7.8% of the vote, also won 2 seats.

The SDP and the Liberals had merged in 1988 and my interest moved towards playing a more UK-wide role within the new party. I stood for the presidency of the party and became vice-chair of its Policy Committee with the leader Paddy Ashdown as chair. I worked closely with him until 1992.

At the 1992 General Election, I contested Hereford, having opted for that constituency as opposed to Bath. My thinking was that it would make more sense for me to stand in Hereford as it was a border constituency. I enjoyed the two years campaigning in the constituency and especially in the villages of the 'Golden Valley'. But it wasn't to be, although I came a close second to the Tory MP Colin Shepherd. I was three thousand votes behind him and seventeen thousand ahead of the Labour candidate.

After 1992, I had another major decision to make. I had been engaged in politics for the best part of thirty years and was about to take early retirement at 50 from my post as Assistant Education Officer with West Glamorgan County Council to start an education and training consultancy. Good friends of mine made it clear 'Gwynoro, to succeed it will have to be no more politics'. I was not perturbed by that thought because I had given politics my best shot—but did not always get it right!

We had two consultancies; EPPC in Wales and Severn Crossing in England. They merged into one company in 1999. Over the period from 1993 to 2013, we had inspected well over 8,000 education establishments from pre-school to colleges, employing over 50 staff over the period and engaging the services of 500 self-employed inspectors. In addition, I was involved with delivering to organisation quality standards such as Investors in People, Business Excellence Model, the Law Society Lexcel quality assurance and other work such as Best Value inspections for the Audit Commission in Wales. Yes, my hands were full, and politics was very low down on the agenda.

A Scotsman takes over

They lost the General Election of that year. Kinnock was expected to triumph, having had a consistent lead over the Tories for a long time before Polling Day. However, the Tories, under John Major, secured their fourth consecutive General Election victory. Kinnock was replaced as Labour leader by John Smith. With his arrival, there was a visible change in emphasis for Labour. With this change came a change of leadership for Labour and with that, a shift back to championing devolution once more. This is what David Melding says in his book, *Will Britain Survive Beyond 2020?*;

> *Between 1976 and 1992, the Labour Party was led successively by three MPs who represented Welsh constituencies. During that time, the Party's commitment to Welsh devolution alternated between insipid indifference and active hostility. It took a Scotsman to transform the Welsh Labour*

Party's attitude to devolution. John Smith's short tenure as leader had a profound effect on Welsh politics and encouraged the Welsh Labour Party to embrace devolution with enthusiasm'.[184]

Labour was back on the devolution issue in 1992. John Smith's arrival influenced, amongst others, the man who would announce the formation of the Welsh Assembly when it eventually happened. Ron Davies had voted No in 1979. John Smith appointed him Shadow Secretary of State for Wales and he then went on to be known as the architect of Welsh devolution. Melding recalls a talk Ron Davies gave in 2003 in Aberystwyth, to the Welsh Political Archive:

He recalls an interview he had on his appointment as Shadow Welsh Secretary by Smith.

'We'll need a proper Parliament in Wales,' John Smith said. 'Just like we'll legislate for Scotland.' He railed passionately against those he described as "silly buggers"—Welsh and to a lesser degree Scottish, Labour Party members opposed to devolution'.

There had been signs before Smith took over from Kinnock that there were some among Labour in Wales who were resurrecting their arguments from the Seventies. It was still a case of legislative devolution for Scotland, but only executive devolution in Wales. But the debating had begun again.

---

184. David Melding: *Will Britain survive beyond 2020?* Cardiff: Institute of Welsh Affairs, 2009, p. 129.

26.

The Nineties Renewal

Just after the 1992 General Election, the Wales TUC passed a resolution at its annual conference calling for the setting up of a 'Welsh Constitutional Convention' along the lines of the one already operating in Scotland. The Welsh Labour Party was alarmed at this and they established their own Constitutional Policy Commission in June 1992

to re-examine policy in relation to the creation of a directly elected Welsh Assembly.

It submitted an interim report to the 1993 Labour conference. It was called The Welsh Assembly: The Way Forward. But the party didn't go very far forward after that report.

As devolution was emerging again, it caused divisions as in previous debates, but any general opposition was far more muted. The same cannot be said about the recurring infighting within Labour. This flared up again, as attempts were made to keep MPs, local government leaders and valley members happy.

The account of this period in *The Road to the National Assembly for Wales*, Barry Jones and Denis Balsom say,

A convention would have meant Labour, in the words of one source, 'having to bring in Plaid and this would have caused mayhem in the valleys....' would only have pushed the Party in Wales close to civil war.[185]

---

185. James Barry Jones; Denis Balsom (eds.): *The Road to the National Assembly for Wales.* Cardiff: University of Wales Press, 2000, p. 36.

Ron Davies, the champion of the Yes campaign.

A Parliament for Wales campaign re-emerged. Another referendum was on the cards, following years of no devolution activity of any note. Within Labour, it was soon a case of MPs Ron Davies, Rhodri Morgan, MEPs Eluned Morgan and David Morris, the TUC's George Wright and Derek Gregory versus MPs Llew Smith and Kim Howells, MEP Wayne David MEP and Trades Unionists, Ken Hopkins and Terry Thomas.

In 1995, Welsh Labour proposed an executive assembly with powers over secondary legislation. This really was the 1970s revisited. But in the previous year, the pro-devolution argument had potentially lost a major influence. John Smith died in 1994. His place as Labour leader was taken by Tony Blair. The cause would not suffer, however, as Blair proved an active advocate for devolution, although he was an inheritor of the momentum already gathered from his Scottish colleagues, Gordon Brown, Donald Dewar and Robin Cook. The battle continued.

But before he stepped centre-stage, it's worth noting a major contribution to this surge in the devolution debate again at the start of the Nineties. The debate was given new momentum by the Scottish Constitutional Convention. It was established in 1989 after prominent Scottish individuals signed a Claim of Right.

They held the first meeting in the Assembly Hall in Edinburgh on 30 March 1989. Canon Kenyon Wright, the convener of the executive committee, opened the meeting. They adopted David Steel and Harry Ewing as co-chairs. They held a second meeting on 7 July in Inverness. Various organisations took part in the Convention, such as the Labour Party, the Liberal Democrats, the Scottish Green Party, the Communist Party, the Scottish Trades Union Congress, the Scottish Council for Development and Industry, the Small Business Federation and various bodies representing other strands of political opinion as well as civic society. Representatives of the two largest churches—the Church of Scotland and the Roman Catholic Church—were involved, as well as smaller church groups, and some non-Christian communities which decided to participate.

Initially, the Scottish National Party (SNP) took part, but the then party leader Gordon Wilson, along with Jim Sillars, withdrew the SNP from participation owing to the convention's unwillingness to discuss Scottish independence as a constitutional option.

The Conservative government of the day was very hostile to the convention and challenged the local authorities' right to finance the convention, although the courts found that they were in fact entitled to do so.

Under its executive chair, Canon Kenyon Wright, the convention published its blueprint for devolution, *Scotland's Parliament, Scotland's Right*, on 30 November 1995, St Andrew's Day. This provided the basis for the structure of the existent Scottish Parliament, established in 1999.

The Blair Factor

At the 1995 Welsh Labour Party conference, the Party recommended the first past the post electoral system. Tony Blair's intervened to insist that there must be an element of proportionality in any Assembly elections. Voting reform proved to be an area of bitter infighting from then on.

Blair was very supportive of another referendum on devolution for Scotland and Wales. Following his sweeping victory in the 1997 General Election, he made plans for such a referendum to happen. Devolution for Wales and Scotland was a commitment in the Labour Party manifesto for

Time to take over the remote control.

YES TO AN ASSEMBLY

National Library of Wales

the 1997 General Election. This Referendum would not have the 40% threshold that the '79 one did.

The referendum happened in September 1997. The words on the ballot paper were as follows:

Parliament has decided to consult people in Wales on the Government's proposals for a Welsh Assembly:
Mae'r Senedd wedi penderfynu ymgynghori pobl yng Nghymru ar gynigion y Llywodraeth ar gyfer Cynulliad i Gymru:

I agree there should be a Welsh Assembly
Yr wyf yn cytuno y dylid cael Cynulliad i Gymru

or

I do not agree there should be a Welsh Assembly
Nid wyf yn cytuno y dylid cael Cynulliad i Gymru

(To be marked by a single (X))

The Yes campaign, Yes for Wales, consisted of Labour, the Liberal Democrats and Plaid Cymru and each party ran its own campaign as well as uniting under the Yes umbrella. This unity between the parties stood in direct contrast to 1979. The campaign chose the strategy of enabling many grassroots organisations to form their own campaigns. Consequently, groups such as Pensioners say Yes were formed.

Nick Bourne, the man called the Conservative spokesperson for Wales, led the No Campaign. He would be the leader of the Conservative group in the Assembly when it was formed. But the No Campaign in the run-up to the 1997 referendum wasn't as organised as the previous one in the Seventies. It didn't have as much money and, of course, the main driving force of the push for No, the Conservative Party, had just suffered a major landslide defeat in the 1997 General Election.

In the final count, the difference between the Yes and the No votes was less than seven thousand. In the end, the result was down to the last announcement of the day—the one from my home county, Carmarthenshire, which included the constituency I had represented as MP. It was with bated breath that Wales waited for the Carmarthen result. Until that point, the overall result was in the balance. When it came, it was 49,115 in favour of devolution and 26,119 against. Devolution for Wales was secured. Once again, Carmarthen was involved in another election result that could be called historic.

David Melding is clear as to the reason Yes carried the day:

In the remarkably close referendum (18 Sept 1997) result that followed, the intervention of Tony Blair has the best claim to be the single most critical factor in securing a 'Yes' vote. The decision to hold a referendum was, of course, forced on the Welsh Labour Party by Blair in the first place.[186]

Martin Johnes adds to that, in *Wales since 1939*:

186. David Melding: *Will Britain survive beyond 2020?* Cardiff: Institute of Welsh Affairs, 2009, p. 131.

Wyn Roberts, left, discusses a second Severn crossing with
Secretary of State for Wales, Nicholas Edwards, centre.

*In September 1997, Tony Blair visited Wrexham to campaign for Welsh
devolution. The Guardian noted—'Ton-ee! Ton-ee! They shouted, not
just the girls waving from Mark and Spencer's, but the young lads as
well…. This is a new phenomenon in British politics; The Prime Minister as a rock star'.*[187]

In the 1997 General Election, the Conservatives had lost all its Welsh
seats. They had campaigned for a No vote during the referendum and
after the result with the legislation to go through the Commons, the
party leader William Hague declared in *Western Mail* on Oct 11 1997,

*'The Conservative Party has no intention of standing idly by and allow-
ing the Union of the United Kingdom to be torn apart and its historic
constitution discarded without the fight of our lives.'*

187.Martin Johnes: *Wales since 1939*. Manchester: Manchester University Press, 2013,
    p. 412.

But there were a few Conservatives who supported Sir Wyn Roberts's more conciliatory and constructive tone. He'd been a minister in the Welsh Office for 16 years and he said he wanted to 'upgrade' the powers of the Assembly. He said in the *Western Mail* October 3, 1997,

'Tories must face up to the reality of an Assembly'

David Melding saw it in this way:

'It was the turn of Tory Unionists to face their midnight hour. Two of the three nations of Britain had declared that they wanted direct control over their domestic affairs... Never again would the Conservative Party win in Wales and Scotland by winning in England. Opposition to what the Victorians called Home Rule could no longer define Unionism'.[188]

1979 and 1997

What then was the difference between '79 and '97? We have dealt with the most relevant points as we've outlined the narrative in this book. But, to summarise, there are many obvious differences.

In the Seventies, Labour was bitterly divided on devolution. Callaghan's heart was not in the battle. The Tories, on the other hand, were riding high on their way to their historic victory in the 1979 General Election. By 1997, the Tories had been in power for 18 years but had just suffered a huge defeat in the 1997 General Election. Blair was swept in and created an immediate impact on the politics of the UK, which included his support for devolution. The backing for an element of proportional representation in any new Assembly also swayed many in '97. The timing of the Welsh vote was also significant, coming as it did one week after the Scottish vote. The Scottish lead bolstered the Welsh support to a degree.

---

188. David Melding: *Will Britain survive beyond 2020?* Cardiff: Institute of Welsh Affairs, 2009, p. 132.

3.50am: Final vote swings the count for an Assembly

Thatcher played her part in one way too. In 1986, she embraced the European Union single market. In doing so, she seemingly undermined the concept of the British state. She also oversaw increased powers for the Welsh Office over several years.

The vote had been won. Wales could form its own Assembly and have its own elected Assembly Members. But the narrowness of the victory showed clearly that such a governing body would be in power over a divided Wales. Eleven of the twenty-two counties in Wales had voted no. It would be no easy task to set up a new governing body under such circumstances. And there were other factors, as J. Barry Jones sums up in the book *The Road to the National Assembly for Wales*:

> *'Wales is a nation of minorities, linguistic, geographic and economic. It has a very high proportion of in-migrants and is more culturally and economically linked to England than either Scotland or Northern Ireland'.*[189]

The new Assembly would have a mountain to climb.

---

189. James Barry Jones; Denis Balsom (eds.): *The Road to the National Assembly for Wales*. Cardiff: University of Wales Press, 2000, p. 135.

27.

Wales 2020

Come 2014 and now retired at 72, it was inevitable that with time on my hands, political matters caught my attention once again. I had attempted to renew my involvement in politics when I re-joined the Labour Party in 1996, with one sole aim in mind—to strengthen the whole case for devolution inside the party. I tried to be accepted as a candidate for the first Assembly elections in 1999. However, that went the same way as my previous three attempts to stand for Labour. I wasn't selected; in fact, I wasn't put on a list of over 200 candidates. Maybe I should have taken more notice of advice given to me by many colleagues—including by Lord Ivor Richard who sent me a letter saying he was glad to see me back in the party, but I shouldn't expect a fatted calf for the prodigal son!

Some fifteen years later, after a long period of hardly any political activity or membership, I re-joined the Liberal Democrats in 2011, but I was very unhappy with the party's later coalition with the Tories. I soon started commenting on political events in the media once again. I was just an armchair critic, as I did not attend a party meeting until the middle of 2015.

When I started attending meetings, the difference between the Welsh Lib Dems of the '80s and 2015 was quite stark. The party had lost its Welsh identity and much of its radicalism. It remains so in 2020. I remain a member, albeit on the very periphery and most certainly not happy with how it has conducted itself in Wales over the last decade.

While I was away from the political scene, the Assembly had been established in Wales, and the devolution I had long been advocating had been implemented. But I am relatively dissatisfied with the way the Welsh Assembly has conducted itself. There is a lack of vigorous and open debate and the debates that actually happen are of poor quality, focusing too much on Cardiff and south-east Wales, with insufficient oversight and monitoring of decisions made and much else. I have never felt that our National Assembly, now a Senedd, has been doing itself any favours with the Welsh public and that remains the case.

Another big change happened for me in 2015—I discovered social media! This has, without doubt, accelerated my political involvement in the last few years. I am an active blogger and I have a YouTube channel which is a vehicle for much political debate. This newfound activity was given a huge boost by the whole Brexit debate and vote in 2016. I was certainly in full throttle by then!

For my part, the Brexit referendum outcome completely transformed the political agenda in Wales. I recall saying at the time that David Cam-

Carwyn Jones, First Minister of Wales 2009-2018

eron will not only go down as the PM who disengaged Britain from Europe but started the process of the eventual dismantling of the UK Union as we knew it.

Membership of the European Union was the glue that kept the UK Union in relative harmony. Once outside, it was only a matter of time until it would come too apparent that Westminster would reassert more and more control and influence. Added to that, Scotland voted to remain within the European Union, as did Northern Ireland, so that would eventually bring further strains and pressures on the Union. Indeed, apart from the aberration of the relatively close Welsh vote, the referendum outcome was essentially an English decision.

It was a time when voices inside the Labour Party, including the then First Minister of Wales Carwyn Jones and the former Prime Minister Gordon Brown, at a conference in Cardiff, came out strongly in favour of a UK Constitutional Convention to examine the future governance of the UK Union. The outcome of the EU referendum was focusing the minds of devolutionists, federalists and many in favour of independence alike.

For my part, together with Lords Elystan Morgan and David Owen, as well as my son Glyndwr Cennydd, we wrote two documents on the issue. One was published in early 2018 and was called 'Towards Federalism and Beyond'.

At the first rally in Carmarthen.

Before that time, I had already joined Yes Cymru when its membership was only a few hundred. I spoke at its first rally in Carmarthen and emphasised the importance of the organisation being non-party. This was both significant and poignant. They held the rally on the occasion of unveiling a plaque in Guildhall Square, Carmarthen to commemorate the 50th anniversary of Gwynfor Evans's by-election victory in July 1966. How time had moved on!

From the outset in 2016, Yes Cymru made an impact and raised the profile of the whole debate on the future of Wales. A year or two ago, I came across a comparative analysis of how often the SNP and Plaid Cymru had highlighted independence in their various party manifestos since 1997. The SNP referred to it almost 50 times between 1997 and 2017, whilst Plaid Cymru did so on 15 occasions. From 2000 to 2011, Plaid Cymru mentioned independence only 5 times in its manifestos.

Whose Wales now?

There's no doubt that the Wales of 2020 has changed out of all recognition to the Wales of my childhood. Over the decades I remember, the way the people of Wales view themselves has adapted and fluctuated. Are we Welsh, British, a mixture of the two? And in the context of recent Brexit arguments, the European dimension has come to the fore once again, with no party being immune from trying to define their stance on Europe.

For my part, I have always viewed myself as being Welsh, European and only marginally British.

The story of devolution and our politics since the 1880s have inextricably been governed by events outside Wales—empire, boundary, industry—coal from Wales to fuel the Empire etc, two World Wars, three if not four major economic, industrial and financial depressions, the Falklands War, the Thatcher years and, in recent times, Brexit. These influencing factors are still there, shaping the way we think of Wales. And what has changed completely is the awareness of a broad Britishness that has disappeared with the demise of heavy industry, particularly coal in Wales. The collier in the Rhondda has no need to stand in solidarity with his comrade in Yorkshire because neither exists anymore. The National Union of Mineworkers has no miners and, subsequently, no need for a 'national' identity.

Community and Communities

In that new, post-heavy-industry world, what has changed significantly over the last few decades in Wales are demographic and communication considerations. These are little looked at factors in the devolution debate, but they play into it, as they do into the Welsh Brexit aberration referred to earlier.

Wales has a 150-mile border with England and by now, well over 48% of its population live within 25 miles of that border. Nearly 140,000 people traverse that border daily for their employment, business, freight or leisure activities. Conversely, the figures for Scotland are vastly different. Only 4% live within 25 miles of the English border and some 30,000 cross the border daily.

Another essential difference with Scotland that undoubtedly must have an impact on Wales' politics and opinions is the fact that, over the decades, the inward migration into Wales has increased at some pace. Some 25% of the population of our country were born in England. I recall making an analysis of the 2011 Census figures when the percentage was only 21%, that there were some 15 Westminster constituencies in Wales where the percentage of people living in them that were born in England ranged between 35 and 50%.

Such a situation has led the Director of the Wales Governance Centre in Cardiff University, Richard Wyn Jones, to look at how homogenous Wales really is. Quoting Saunders Lewis' description of Wales as a 'community of communities', he identifies what he calls six tribes that make up the Wales we live in today. His original article was in the Welsh language current affairs magazine, Barn, and then translated for Nation Cymru, with a few additions.

Before defining the tribes he identifies, Richard Wyn Jones sets the Welsh political context, from the Liberals of the Victorian era to the Labour Party of Welsh government days, which is, of course, the narrative of this book:

In very broad and no doubt crude terms, the electoral dominance of Welsh liberalism was founded on the support of a religiously Nonconformist gwerin and working-class who tended to speak Welsh and were Welsh British in their identity. The social foundations of support for their Tory rivals lay among the Anglican and Anglicized middle class for whom Welsh identity meant less or indeed nothing at all. As numerous historians and other observers have pointed out, Labour subsequent dominance was an extension an adaptation of this earlier Liberal forerunner rather than some revolutionary overthrow of it follow stop true, the religious dimensions of this hegemonic block have faded to complete irrelevance and the Welsh language has been under siege for decades. Yet the interweaving of narratives of class and national identity remains an essential underpinning for Labours remarkable record of electoral success.[190]

He then says that this pattern has changed significantly in Wales today. A more fractured Wales has created a fundamental change in Welsh politics. Richard Wyn Jones then defines the six tribes in Wales—Welsh only, Welsh British, British only (not Welsh), English only, English British, British only (not English). A detailed analysis of each category then follows, which is beyond the remit of this book. I'll mention one example where Richard Wyn Jones applies this analysis—Brexit.

Wales voted in favour of Brexit. But Richard Wyn Jones' analysis breaks that vote down. Those who felt strongly Welsh, but felt no allegiance to Britishness, voted to Remain. The substantial minority living in Wales who describe themselves as strongly English or strongly English (British) tended to vote Leave. The Welsh British also voted Leave. He summarises:

This underlines the fact that, on international matters at least, many of the same attitudes that align with Englishness in England and indeed Wales also align with Britishness in Wales and Scotland.[191]

190. Richard Wyn Jones: "Divided Wales", *Cardiff University Politics & Governance Blog / Blog Gwleidyddiaeth & Llywodraethiant Prifysgol Caerdydd,* 23 September 2019, https://blogs.cardiff.ac.uk/brexit/2019/09/23/divided-wales/ (visited 10.04.2021)
191. Ibid.

Unfortunately, not much attention is paid to the analysis that Richard Wyn Jones draws upon. The information is available, but it is not sought after and not used in analysis by pollsters or media analysts alike. This is a major omission.

The medium and the message

With this analysis of Wales in mind, we can add further that the way the people of Wales get their news and information is also significant.

In 1979, the daily circulation of the *Western Mail* and *Daily Post* was 150,000. By 1997, that figure had decreased to 113,000. Then in 1979, the circulation of the London morning papers in Wales was over 700,000. This had also increased by 1997 so that only some 30% of Welsh people read a Wales-based daily newspaper. Only 6% read Welsh-based papers. In Scotland, the same figure for Scottish-based papers is 46%.

Broadcasting fares a little better than print media. BBC Wales today is watched by 35% of the population of Wales daily, ITV News 17%, Radio Wales 13%. However, UK network news predominates across all outlets.

If we look at Scotland, we see that 90% of the daily papers sold in that country are also produced there. In specific terms of the coverage of the 1997 devolution referendum, we see that in the coverage of the referendum campaign in Scotland, the BBC gave three times as much coverage as it did to the Welsh referendum. In addition to this, in 1997, some 35% of the Welsh population lived in overlap areas where they could watch programmes from English transmitters as well, or instead of. In Scotland, this was only 2.5%.

Further comparative figures for the two referenda, in '79 and '97, show that the *Western Mail* and *Daily Post* daily circulation in Wales in '79 was 150,000. The London daily papers' circulation in Wales was 700,000. UK and TV radio coverage in 1997 gave greater prominence to the referendum results in Scotland. For the BBC, it was 39 minutes for Scotland to 12 in Wales and for ITV, it was 36 minutes to Scotland and 25 minutes to Wales. They fared a lot better.

Such figures surely reflect a broader reality; that Wales is more linked to England than Scotland is in terms of economy, employment and media information distribution. This most certainly influences and impacts our politics. One of the wider implications of this is that the Welsh public is not fully aware of basic information relating to Assembly powers. For example, a recent YouGov poll showed that 49% thought that health was administered by Westminster and 50% for education. That same poll showed that 40% believed that Plaid Cymru had been in government from 2011 to 2016. Recently, the First Minister Mark Drakeford commented on the unsatisfactory nature of the media in Wales:

> *I agree that the weakness of the Welsh media has always been a challenge in communicating the significance of devolution here in Wales.*

In addition to the news access statistics mentioned, and their political influence, we need to note the major change that's happened in recent years in print news specifically. The decline in hard copy newspaper sales has been more than compensated for by online news outlets. The *Western Mail's* online site—*WalesOnline*—has over 300,000 visitors per day, the *Daily Post* with over 80,000 per day and the *South Wales Evening Post* with more than 50,000 visitors per day.

Hyperlocal outlets are also increasing in number and spread. *Wales News Online*, for example, has five hyperlocal sites, based on the five regions of the Senedd. It has attracted over 5 million visitors to those sites in its first four years. There are local TV companies, such as those in Cardiff and Swansea, and plans for a television service for Carmarthenshire next year.

And of course, there is the ever-present and all-pervading social media. Facebook and Twitter especially have entered the political world. United States politics has been directed through Twitter for the last four years. In Wales, Yes Cymru's growth has been largely facilitated by a dominant social media presence.

We wait to see what effect this change in news distribution and information gathering has on the devolution debate in Wales in this election year.

Five Assembly terms

There have been five Assembly terms to date, with the current one ending in May 2021. Having said that, there was a mountain to climb following the Yes vote of '97; Labour has proved that to be the case. They were voted into power in the first Assembly and they have been there since. But they were effectively only in a majority in the first Assembly. They have subsequently been in a coalition with the Liberal Democrats and

Rhodri Morgan and Mike German seal the Lab-Lib Assembly coalition

Ieuan Wyn Jones and Rhodri Morgan launch their parties' One Wales coalition.

Plaid Cymru, and they currently govern with Dafydd Elis Thomas (Independent) and Kirsty Williams (Liberal Democrat) in the government.

There have been four Wales Acts since 1998. The first one, in that year, is the one that led to the establishment of the Assembly and ensured the transference of most of the powers of the Secretary of State to the National Assembly. This meant transferring the responsibility of 21 nominated government agencies in Wales. They introduced the next Act in 2006. This created an executive that was drawn from but separate to the Assembly. It had limited law-making powers and provided for a referendum for further legislative competencies.

Before the next Wales Act, there was, in 2011, another referendum in Wales, one that is easily forgotten. This asked whether Wales should have full law-making powers in the areas where it already had jurisdiction. There was a far clearer majority in favour of this than there was in '97. 63.49% backed increasing law-making powers for Wales, with 36.51% opposing the idea.

The backing of this increase of power for the Welsh Assembly was greeted with the First Minister Carwyn Jones' now-famous line, 'Today an old nation came of age'. That was certainly true. In 2013, Carwyn Jones went further and said that the current constitutional arrangements were no longer functioning and that the UK must continue down the road to becoming a federal nation. He has repeated that call for a federal solution several times since.

In 2014, the third Wales Act increased the areas of devolved responsibility. Stamp duty, landfill tax and business rates were put under the Assembly's remit. It allowed for the provision of devolving further taxes as long as the Assembly and the UK Parliament could agree on it. This is when the name of the body in Cardiff Bay was changed from the Welsh Assembly Government to the Welsh Government. This act gave the provision for a referendum on whether it should devolve elements of income tax.

In 2017, they passed the fourth Act. In technical terms, this Act allowed for a shift from what is known as a conferred matters model to a reserved matters model. In effect, this Act now recognises that there is a body of Welsh law, that the Welsh Government is a permanent body in the UK's constitutional arrangements and a referendum is required for its abolition. Wales also now has the power to vary income tax by 10p in the pound and to increase borrowing powers. It can also change the name and size of the Assembly and other electoral changes.

In October 2017, this Act was welcomed by Lord Elystan Morgan, a veteran of devolution debates for over six decades, but with a word of concern:

> *I am rapidly coming to the conclusion that Wales is being short-changed in regards to devolution. This assertion firstly rests on the willingness of Her Majesty's Government to contemplate nearly 200 reservations in the Wales Act 2017, most of which are so trivial as to give the lie to any sincerity concerning a reserved constitution. Secondly, is the willingness to pretend that a long-term settlement on the division of authority between Westminster and Cardiff could even be contemplated, whilst the very substantial proportion of that authority was not in the gift of the UK Government, but was ensconced in Brussels.'*

What Next for Wales?

Undoubtedly the Wales Act of 2017, the implications for the governance of Wales following the EU referendum, the proposals in the Internal Market Bill, the new UK Shared Prosperity Fund, which will replace the EU Structural Funds and an undercurrent of hints and winks from the Boris Johnson government at undermining devolution, all pose a threat to the Senedd's freedom to govern without Westminster interventions. By now the threat is becoming increasingly more than hints and winks if truth be told. Boris Johnson has said recently that devolution was a mistake. And Jacob Rees-Mogg, in the House of Commons, said that Blairite constitutional tinkering has weakened our parliament and has helped to divide the UK, and that he hoped this government finds an effective way of restoring the constitution to its proper form. He later tweeted,

> *Under Labour, our constitution was vandalised, and we must undo this foolish tinkering.*

First Minister Mark Drakeford

Such comments are threats that have significant dangers for the nation-hood of Wales. Mark Drakeford, the First Minister, has called the Internal Market Bill an

> ... *enormous power grab—undermining powers that have belonged to Wales, Scotland and Northern Ireland for over 20 years... and that will do more to hasten the break-up of the Union than anything else since devolution began.*

Then Jeremy Miles, the Welsh Government Brexit minister, said that the Internal Market Bill is '... an attack on democracy' which will 'sacrifice the future of the union by stealing powers from devolved administrations'. He went on to state that imposing a new UK internal market after the end of the Brexit transition period will 'accelerate the break-up of the Union'.

In mid January 2021 the Welsh Government formally started legal action against the Westminster Government to challenge the Internal Market Act as it is now, because they think that it negatively impacts the Senedd's ability to pass legislation.

But there are indications that this threat is also present within Wales as we witness the emergence of the Abolish the Assembly movement as well as the previous success of UKIP and its allies since 2016 in capturing seats in the Senedd. The latest polling January 2021 indicates that they could capture two to four seats in the Senedd.

But there is a more worrying development. Some Conservative candidates already selected for the forthcoming Senedd elections are not only opposing more devolution, but they too are questioning the need for the Welsh Parliament. Their motive for taking such a stance might well have something to do with the Abolish the Assembly party and Nigel Farage's new named party the Reform UK Party, attracting some ten percent of the vote in early 2021 Welsh polling

The Coronavirus pandemic has also highlighted the influence and powers of the Senedd and Welsh Government. Not only the Welsh public but also the Westminster government and the English public have become more aware than ever of the implications of the devolution settlement and that the United Kingdom has four governments with defined powers. It has been, at times, an uncomfortable concept for them to grasp and accept. They are evidently frustrated that Westminster alone cannot decide for the four nations. I suspect that few imagined that the Welsh government could limit travel from England to Wales and that it can establish its own Covid restrictions.

Emerging from all this is the support for Welsh independence, which is rapidly increasing, with around 21% of the Welsh people willing to embrace the concept. Yes Cymru membership is surging; now, in February 2021, it's at 17,000. Interestingly enough, in a recent poll, it was shown that 51% of Labour supporters would consider supporting independence, but 28% of Plaid Cymru supporters would not!

Plaid Cymru have seen the need to respond to this changing climate by setting up a commission, whose findings have been published in a report called *Towards an Independent Wales*. They have performed an invaluable service by doing this. The report has brought to the forefront the central issues we face in Wales today, and it proposes a way ahead. It is a definite, positive step forward. One aspect of this publication is included in the Appendix to this book.

But as valuable as this contribution is from Plaid, they still have one big question to address—why is it that it's support for Yes Cymru that has mushroomed, not support for Plaid Cymru? Or to put the same question in another way, why is the cause Plaid fight for more popular than the party itself? It surely must be because independence is inherently a non-party political issue. The challenge for Yes Cymru is to make sure it stays as such. It is for all parties and no party. There are many, many Labour supporters who back Welsh independence, but they will never vote for Plaid Cymru. Plaid, on their part, must not politicise independence, stating that it can only happen through them. That won't work today, and it flies in the face of history too. Plaid politicised the language in the late Sixties and through the Seventies. It cannot do so with the independence issue as well.

As for Labour, it's up to them now to tackle the governance of Wales and the future of the United Kingdom head-on. Now is the time. Mark Drakeford is calling for 'a radical reform of the UK' in response to what he sees as the UK Government 'centralising power' and 'undermining devolution'. He also has stated that no UK government has the right to stand in the way of an independence referendum in Scotland or Wales and that

'The break-up of the United Kingdom is a real and present danger'

But the essential missing element amongst all the rhetoric is where does the Labour Party in Wales officially stand? Is it for enhanced Senedd powers, devo-max, a federal or a confederal UK? It is not sufficient for individuals within the Welsh Government or the party to respond to events and make assertions. Labour needs to get its act together. We need more than headline politics from Labour and the other parties. During my period in the Labour Party, there were endless policy documents on devolution. Where are such documents now in the Welsh Labour of these years? Comments such as 'welcoming a discussion on the future of Wales' are meaningless without substance.

It would appear that some action is being taken to address this. In January 2021 Wales' First Minister introduced a report called 'We the People', making the case for 'Radical Federalism'. Although it is a step forward, the key fact is that it's only a report published by a group of Labour members and civic activists. I accept that a few senior members of Welsh Labour understand the urgency of the situation but what about the mass of Welsh party members, Welsh Labour MPs and Labour Senedd Members? My worry is that for far too many of them even a federal situation is a step too far and the divisions within the party, as over an Elected Assembly in the 1970s and 80s will emerge at some point in the future.

It does seem that Sir Keir Starmer, with the encouragement of the former Prime Minister Gordon Brown, is seized of the need to be seen to respond to the ever-increasing threats facing the UK Union as present constituted. Brexit and the handling of the Covid pandemic have further hastened the fragile state of the union. Not just in Scotland and Wales, but also in Northern Ireland and within England itself.

So Starmer has established a Labour Party Constitutional Commission headed by Gordon Brown. There is little doubt that his greatest concern currently is the independence movement in Scotland and the popularity of the SNP in the run up to the Holyrood elections. It is why in announcing the Commission late December 2020 he paid a lot of attention to Scotland and hardly mentioned Wales.

Most certainly Wales has reached a constitutional crossroads but there is a vacuum that the Welsh Government and the progressive parties need to fill. It is why some of us have been calling for several years now for our own Wales Constitutional Convention.

Just like Plaid Cymru, and even the Welsh Liberal Democrats who have called for a federal UK, Welsh Labour must state its official position whether it be by a working group of the party, a Wales conference resolution or any other means. It cannot and mustn't stand on the sidelines. All this applies to Sir Keir Starmer in the wider British context also. He must follow the lead once given by Harold Wilson in 1964 and Tony Blair in 1997.

This book has clearly illustrated why. The two major advances for the Welsh nation came with the setting up of the office of the Secretary of State for Wales in 1964 and then, over 30 years later, the Welsh Assembly, both brought into being by Labour governments.

The support is growing

It has always been my view that the future of Wales requires the Labour Party to step up to the plate but buttressed by a strong Plaid Cymru presence. Yes Cymru has an important part to play too and remember that the aim is to win hearts and minds and not defeat those that disagree with the movement.

I have lived through all the turmoil and travails of struggling to achieve Wales' rightful place in the community of nations. For my part, it is of no use re-fighting the battles of decades past. Labour have called Plaid Cymru 'separatists' and Plaid Cymru have perpetually decried Labour's achievements in Wales over decades. Slogans will get us nowhere now.

I return to Richard Wyn Jones, mentioned earlier in this chapter. The title of the article is a fair summary of the situation we face; *'Why the future of Welsh politics is likely to be much more fractured than its past'.* He concludes his article in this way:

> *In many ways, Wales is now home to the most varied and heterogeneous patterns of national identity of any country in these islands. Because of this, we can expect that its internal politics will also be the most fractured and divided. Is that a way, one wonders, of bridging these divides?*[192]

An extensive survey by the *Sunday Times* in January 2021, carried out by YouGov, contributed further figures to the point that Richard Wyn Jones has been outlining. In a UK-wide poll, it showed that 36% thought of themselves as Welsh or more Welsh than British, 29% more British than Welsh and 23% equal.

Cool and focused minds are necessary to engage with the people of Wales and respond to their concerns and apprehensions. After all, there is a significant body of opinion that remains unconvinced. The latest UK wide polling January 2021 revealed that 52% of the Welsh people oppose independence and 11% don't know. Those two cohorts totalling 63%, are against even holding a referendum on the question. Completely different to Scotland where over 50% support a referendum. The same is true in Northern Ireland, where again over 50% are in favour of a referendum in the next five years on the reunification of Ireland.

Faced with all this Johnson's government is not taking a back seat. He, as the self-declared 'Minister for the Union', and Michael Gove are busy working with a Union defence team in a bid to quash the rising support for Welsh and Scottish independence. Gove, in evidence to the Westminster Public Administration and Constitutional Affairs Committee, said recently:

> *'we do need to look at every part of the current constitutional arrangement to make sure it is fit for purpose ... the Government would be saying a wee bit more early the new year'*

---

192. Richard Wyn Jones, ibid.

The current state of opinion in Wales indicates that no party is sure of crossing the 30-member threshold to form a government. The by now traditional Saint David's Day opinion polls on the political climate in Wales show that Labour will be the majority party in the forthcoming elections. In their 2021 polls, both the BBC Wales/ICM and the Wales-Online/YouGov show Labour with between 24-30 members, the Conservatives with 13-16 and Plaid Cymru 14-15. So Labour could very well have to work in coalition come the 2021 Senedd.

Should that be the outcome, Plaid Cymru's proposal in its report for a Welsh Self-Determination Bill with the establishment of a National Commission, to include Citizens' Assemblies to inform the people of Wales about options for their constitutional future, has obvious merit. There is no reason any democrat in Wales should oppose such a proposal. But I seriously doubt whether Welsh Labour see it that way. But time will tell. Even on the matter of holding a referendum the First Minister, in a recent ITV Wales interview said this:

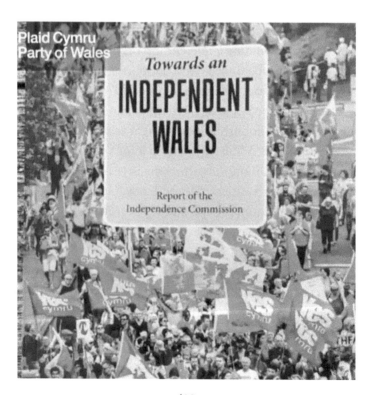

If a party in an election proposes a referendum, secures a majority, of course there should be a referendum because that then has won the democratic approval of the people of Wales. If that isn't the position, there will be no mandate for anybody to go ahead with a referendum because parties not in favour of a referendum will be in the majority.

Too much is at stake now, and there is no room for complacency. The threat to the future governance of Wales is real. Success cannot be guaranteed. After all, it has taken over 50 years of just my lifetime to get this far.

Appendix

A Federal Model for the UK

by David Melding, CBE MS

Federalism could complement the UK's parliamentary tradition

Even when at its most unitary, the British constitution was profoundly heterogeneous, essentially a combination of traditions and practices that coalesced in what we may term the Union *compromise*. We now move on to consider whether this Union can be rejuvenated by a federal *bargain*. But first, a word of warning is needed. As we move from the abstract to the concrete, an imaginative leap is required. The mind must be open to new political configurations. Creating a new Union is more important than defending the old, and a glimpse of this new vision may help to stem the nationalist surge in Scotland. The essence of the British parliamentary tradition could find new life in a federation based on the Home Nations. This would be the best outcome for us, currently British citizens, and for those presently citizens of other liberal multi-national states around the world. For Britain is not Belgium, and the disintegration of the UK would certainly generate a powerful precedent. We have a duty to take an expansive attitude when addressing our constitutional challenges and their potential impact on others.

In an examination of what federal British political institutions might look like, I am not presenting an unanswerable case for a British Federation. Rather, I seek to demonstrate that a British Federation is feasible if there is the political will to create such a Union. Similarly, I hope to be spared the forensic criticism that often follows prescriptions for constitutional reform. I already know that federal institutions would have their own anomalies and imperfections. No constitution can hope to be free of some significant dissonance. What a robust constitution can provide, however, is the necessary harmony for a secure political culture where cooperation, not conflict, reverberates. Whatever its faults, for three hundred years, the Union of 1707 provided such a culture (at least in Britain if not Ireland). Now I want to suggest a federal development of that tradition. Federalism will fall at the first hurdle if it is viewed as a repudiation of British political experience.

Federalism, then, can only hope to work in Britain if it builds on our existing parliamentary tradition. Happily, the precedents are encouraging. Even the USA in the 1780s used the base metal of British political experience to create the first modern federal constitution, and parliamentary federalism was directly forged out of the iron ore of the British constitution during the 1860s. The British North America Act was the final product of this industry and it provided the Canadians with a parliamentary and federal constitution that has endured and even survived its own nationalist challenge in Quebec.

Westminster and its relationships with the other parliaments in a UK Federation

The life of a British Federation would probably begin with a new Act of Union passed by Westminster but with the express consent of the Scottish Parliament and Welsh and Northern Ireland assemblies. Let us put to one side for the moment whether an English parliament would be created at this stage or merely an entrenched English legislative process within Westminster.

Westminster would no longer be, in abstract constitutional theory, an absolutely sovereign body. However, its sovereignty over state-wide matters would be real and entrenched. These matters would include large scale economic policy, welfare, defence and foreign affairs. Although the process of limiting the nature of Westminster's sovereignty in this way may seem a radical departure, it has already occurred in practice.

In accepting that the people of Scotland have a right to secede from the British state, Westminster has acknowledged that here, on the most supreme of constitutional questions, it is the Scottish people who are sovereign. To put it mildly, it is difficult to argue that some of this sovereignty is not now exercised by the Scottish Parliament on behalf of the Scottish people. Westminster could not abolish the Scottish Parliament without sparking a constitutional crisis which would shatter the Union. It is now dysfunctional as well as archaic to maintain absolute parliamentary sovereignty as the essential principle of the British constitution.

Some have sought to argue that Westminster would still have the ability to dominate national institutions via its control of domestic English affairs. And even should an English parliament be established, this would merely change the location of such dominance, not its character. Yet it is difficult to see the federal ideal traduced by such shaky reasoning. The federal arrangement would entrench the existence of the Scottish Parliament and Welsh Assembly—they could not be abolished and would assume sovereign authority over their domestic affairs. Any attempt to encroach on such defined rights would merely make secession more likely, particularly in Scotland. And even before such ultimate remedies were to be considered, attempts at encroachment would face the sizeable barrier of judicial review in the Supreme Court.

The political power of England in a British Federation—whatever form English institutions take—needs to be considered carefully. But the level of government most likely to suffer in any malfunctioning of English institutions is not the national level but that of the state. England could not dominate Scottish and Welsh institutions, but it might dominate British institutions. An English parliament might well overshadow Westminster. There is much to be said for the current approach to developing regional super-municipal entities that could eventually take on legislative and executive powers and resemble perhaps the National Assembly for Wales between 1999-2006. The London Assembly stands as an interesting if often overlooked precedent.

The House of Lords as a Federal Chamber

That House of Lords reform has been imminent since 1911 should cause all contemporary reformers to despair. It has been difficult to design an alternative to an unelected institution that works effectively as a limited revising chamber. However, in a UK Federation, the obvious reform would be for the House of Lords to become the federal chamber. Bicameralism is a feature of many successful federations and the House of Lords could gain a powerful function as the chamber in which the long-term health and vitality of the Union are principally advanced and protected.

In a federation, it would be important for each Home Nation to be represented on a basis that enhances the principle of Union. This could be best achieved by guaranteeing a minimum and disproportionate level of membership for each Home Nation. For instance, in a House of Lords of 250 members, each nation could be allocated a minimum of 30 members. Another possibility would be to guarantee the smaller nations, say, twice their population entitlement of members in the House of Lords. This would build on the pre-devolution precedent in the House of Commons where Scotland and Wales had enhanced membership. Whatever mechanism is used, it should provide a means to check and balance the potentially overwhelming power of England in a federation.

As the chamber expressly entrusted with the health of the Union, the House of Lords would give voice to each Home Nation in influencing and scrutinizing state matters such as defence, foreign affairs, and the operation of the British constitution. This would be a powerful response to nationalist criticism that present arrangements smother the voices of

Scotland and Wales in international affairs, for example. It would not, of course, give the Home Nations their own voice solo—that could only come with full independence—but it would amplify their voice in forming British foreign and defence policy. The House of Lords should gain an absolute veto on constitutional changes that seek to alter the federal bargain. To borrow from Balfour, the House of Lords would really be the watchdog of the constitution.

Intergovernmental relations in a UK Federation

The problem of encroachment between the national governments and Whitehall has been relatively rare though not absent in the devolved era. An obvious and contentious example of encroachment has been the question of which government has the right to call an independence referendum in Scotland. Although settled in favour of the UK government, the principle is still disputed by the SNP. The SNP has also tried to encroach on defence issues, particularly relating to the nuclear submarine base at Faslane. The Welsh government is in a long dispute about the reform of the Barnett formula to fund public services in Wales. Common frameworks to promote shared governance in the UK over such devolved issues as the environment, agricultural policy, and fisheries (amongst many others) are an area to watch carefully in the post-Brexit era. The governance arrangements agreed for such common frameworks will be a good indication of the health of inter-governmental co-operation. Something similar can be said about trade negotiations which, although a non-devolved area, have considerable potential ramifications for the exercise of devolved competencies.

It is fair to say that relations between governments in the UK have broadly been business-like and productive. In a federal bargain, the structures of intergovernmental co-operation would be more formal and focused on meetings of the various premiers—in the UK, the First Ministers and the PM, or their respective ministerial colleagues. The Joint Ministerial Committee in the UK is the prototype that would no doubt be built upon in a UK Federation. Disputes would, of course, occur, and when both persistent and serious, they would be adjudicated by the

Supreme Court if not resolved on a bilateral basis.

The great benefit of the federal bargain is that the general competencies of the different governments would be set out, which would help to reduce troublesome grey areas of ambiguity. Encroachment would be discouraged and, where attempted by one or other level of government, it would be more conspicuous and therefore easier for the Supreme Court to adjudicate should that level of formality be required. The problems of encroachment and jurisdictional ambiguity are ever-present in federations, and when properly resolved by robust constitutional structures, they can be productive.

All constitutions travel through time and have to reconcile fundamental principles with contemporary and mutable demands. Changing circumstances may require a function of government exercised at the federal level to pass to the national, and vice versa. New demands place altogether new functions on government and the appropriate level of executive agency must be agreed if it is absent from the original federal bargain. What always marks federations as essentially healthy is that these currents flow in both directions between the federal and national level. A federation that persistently reduces the powers of the central government is one becoming a confederation. Alternatively, a federation that is persistently drawing power away from the substate level is one becoming a unitary state.

Federal states are often seen as a collection of governments operating in a treaty-style relationship. While the basic rules are fixed—that is the fundamental treaty, which, in a UK Federation, would be the new Act of Union—there is a constant process of amendment, interpretation, and negotiation. Given the success of inter-governmental co-operation in the devolved UK, federal mechanisms should strengthen the culture of co-operation that has operated.

The judiciary in a UK Federation

The most important legal institution in a federal UK would be the Supreme Court. At the moment, the Supreme Court of the UK operates as the final court of appeal for England and Wales, and as the final legal arbitrator of jurisdictional disputes between the executives and legislatures of Scotland, Wales and the UK. The latter function would become more salient in a federal UK and would be an organic development of current practice. As previously remarked, disputes between the devolved institutions and the UK government have been few and far between. And in federal states like the USA, disputes on jurisdiction are surprisingly rare. Nevertheless, when cases occur, they are profound and have extensive ramifications. The US Supreme Court was called upon to determine the constitutionality of President Obama's health reforms which created a federal compulsion for citizens to possess health insurance. In the 1960s, federal civil rights legislation was made possible by the Supreme Court's judgement in Brown v Board of Education (1954) which held that racial segregation in schools violated the 14th amendment of the US Constitution.

The Supreme Court of the UK has already demonstrated its ability to undertake judicial reviews in contentious cases. The court's ruling on the executive's exercise of the prerogative power was ground-breaking in that it held where the prerogative was not limited by convention it could be a subject for judicial review. A Supreme Court has to demonstrate that it can be an impartial arbitrator between national and state interests. A legal culture that always seemed to favour the central state would undermine the Supreme Court's authority in Scotland and Wales. Similarly, a culture that favoured the nations against the state would risk inhibiting the effective operation of UK institutions. Federal states constantly have to deal with this tension and strike a balance that is in the public interest and upholds the rule of law. Judicial review inevitably has, then, a political dimension and it is incumbent on an independent judiciary to act with tact and judgement within the federal bargain. The judiciary would seek to uphold and interpret the federal bargain, although its essentials would remain the reserve of the legislatures in some process of constitutional amendment.

A written constitution would greatly assist the operation of federal institutions in a reformed Union. It is something of a misnomer to describe the current British constitution as unwritten. A more accurate description would be *uncodified* because much of British constitutional practise is found in a constellation of statutes. These are not fundamental, however, because they can be amended by a routine legislative process.

The fundamental law of a UK Federation would be the new Act of Union which would need an extraordinary legislative process for amendment and be subject to a right of veto by the House of Lords. Even a comprehensive written constitution, which may well be required in the longer term, should not seek to anticipate the minutiae of political happenstance.

The monarchy in a UK Federation

The monarchy is Britain's most multi-national institution. In 1707, the dual monarchy of England and Scotland was amalgamated to form the monarchy of Great Britain. Regal recognition of Wales and Northern Ireland did not soar to such heights, but monarchists in Wales take pride in the title 'Prince of Wales' being held by a male heir to the Crown. This is a rich heritage which still reflects the medieval alacrity to cope with overlapping identities and diverse traditions. A federation of the Home Nations would breathe new life into the British monarchy and its central purpose as the symbol of a successful Union.

Regal institutions could accommodate federalism with little difficulty. Should the people of Scotland so wish, the dual monarchy could be restored; and in Wales, the monarch, and not the heir, could hold the title 'Prince of Wales'. The Privy Council could have distinct Scottish and Welsh divisions. Wales, at last, could gain a royal residence (Cardiff Castle would be highly suitable) and the Court could also meet formally in Wales. Another welcome development would be the creation of honours lists for Scotland and Wales, and in Wales, the establishment of a Welsh order of chivalry.

The relationship between the Crown and the Home Nations in a federal UK could be much more direct than that presently between the Crown and the Dominions. Practice is already established in some important respects with the Queen opening the Scottish Parliament and Welsh Assembly after each election. The relationship between the Queen and her Scottish and Welsh First Ministers is a little more distant than that between the monarch and the PM. However, more regular audiences could easily become custom and practice when the Queen visits Scotland and Wales and when the First Ministers visit London.

These are examples of how fully the federal principle could be extended to the monarchy. However, the Britishness of the monarchy would also need to be strengthened because the Crown is the ultimate symbol of the UK. The coronation ceremony could be adapted to reflect and celebrate both the British and multi-national nature of the monarchy. The monarch could have a formal role in the Joint Ministerial Committee, perhaps by hosting an annual meeting of the First Ministers and Prime Minister.

Fiscal federalism in the UK

From the start, devolution in the UK had some of the attributes of fiscal federalism. In 1999, the devolved governments acquired wide-ranging responsibilities for the delivery of public services. Scotland was also given a limited tax-making power to vary the basic rate of income tax by up to 3p. However, the block grant from central government has continued to fund an overwhelming proportion of devolved public spending. This reliance on central government finance is one of the greatest in any western democracy although this is slowly changing.

Block grants tend to be unconditional in federal states and for good reason. The whole concept of fiscal federalism is undermined if central government places heavy restrictions on how block grants can be spent. Unconditional block grants allow a modicum of accountability as citizens hold their devolved governments to account to some extent for local decision-making. Conditional grants can serve a useful purpose for particular programmes that have joint benefits for substate and state governments. Large infrastructure projects and some education and health programmes are suitable for conditional grants when central government wants to encourage a particular approach to public policy.

Finally, it ought to be borne in mind how important equalisation grants are to the concept of a transfer union where economic risks, over the long term, are shared. It is very difficult to see the UK surviving for long if it ceases to be a transfer union. While the long-term objective of a federal UK must be to reduce the level of inequality between the member nations, and this would eventually reduce the need for transfers, the concept of Britain as an economic union is as vital as the social and political union which is more frequently referred to in current debate.

Borrowing: the biggest threat to the Union

It is because the sharing of the income tax base is probably unavoidable in a federal UK that special consideration must be given to borrowing powers. Although income tax is an important and broad-based tax, it is subject to fluctuations in its yield during the economic cycle. Were devolved administrations to use income tax varying powers extensively, then they would need borrowing powers to flatten out the fluctuations in the yield.

As the American political scientist Jonathan Rodden has observed, federalism can lead to substantial debt accumulation and significant failures in macro-economic management. When substate governments are viewed as truly sovereign entities, there is little danger of acute debt accumulation because creditors, voters, and the markets will monitor borrowing carefully. However, despite the theory of divided sovereignty, federal substate governments are rarely seen as financially autonomous. Own source tax revenues rarely generate half of the funding required for the expenditures made by substate governments (indeed often substantially less than half). Instead, substate governments are reliant on grants and shared revenues from central government. In practice, creditors develop bailout expectations and therefore lend more freely to substate governments on the assumption that central government will ultimately prevent any debt default.

Rodden has described what he calls a bailout game where substate governments are reluctant to adjust their fiscal policies and instead hold out for a bailout. One state that has faced difficulties of this kind is the Federal Republic of Germany. While the reputation of the German government for fiscal rectitude is very strong in the international markets, this rigour has not always been present among the Länder. The problem is aggravated, of course, by the German government's horror of debt default and this has inadvertently provided a guarantee to investors lending to impecunious Länder. The problem is clearly not cultural in Germany's case; rather, it stems from a poorly designed form of fiscal federalism where the federal government has no effective control on borrowing by Länder.

The fiscal structure of a UK Federation

As in most federations, fiscal federalism in the UK should retain sizeable grant funding from the Treasury to the national governments. Most of this would be unconditional but it could be complemented by some conditional grant-giving to fund programmes that bring both national and Union-wide benefits. However, conditional grants should be used sparingly and their use would require more tact than in most federations, given the national character of a UK Federation. Treasury grants are likely to account for at least two-thirds of total devolved expenditure, but in principle, this share should be reduced if and when possible. In general, it can be stated that substate governments with a relatively high level of own-source revenue tend to be more autonomous. Such a situation would seem to suit the UK because there is a strong preference for national autonomy in Scotland and Wales. Practically speaking, this ideal situation might take a long time to achieve.

A smaller block grant would not preclude an equalisation process to ensure that there is reasonably equal revenue capacity across the Union. Given the scale of such transfers is likely to remain high for the foreseeable future, coupled with the national dimension in British politics, the grant settlements should be determined by an independent Grants Commission. This would be appointed by the UK government but subject to the approval of the House of Lords as the chamber of Parliament charged with maintaining the wellbeing of the Union. The Commission's criteria would include factors such as need, derivation, and equalisation. Grant levels would be set for several years—subject to adjustment for inflation or major economic shocks—to allow for stability in fiscal planning and to avoid the friction generated by an annual allocation process.

Income tax would be the main source of revenue for the devolved administrations. Powers over income tax should be wide-ranging—including the ability to vary differently the higher and lower rates—and be a tax on base model. Corporation tax should not be devolved, but as an alternative, payroll taxes could be considered for transfer to the nations. Income tax and payroll taxes have the advantage of encouraging governments to promote economic enterprise. However, care is needed to discourage beggar-thy-neighbour tax competition which ends in a race to the bottom and dysfunctionally low taxation rates.

Borrowing powers would be sufficient to allow national governments to manage fluctuations in revenue and to permit a fuller capital programme. However, access to international markets by national governments would be prohibited. Instead, a UK agency—perhaps the Grants Commission—would be the source of lending for large and long-term capital programmes.

The importance of intergovernmental relations in a federal UK needs to be clearly understood. A useful start would be to give the JMC a statutory footing and a permanent secretariat charged with preparing data, studies and reports. At the heart of the strengthened JMC should be an authoritative Finance Minister's Committee to discuss the parameters for resource allocation in the Union and macroeconomic issues of common concern. A reformed House of Lords could periodically receive a 'state of the Union' report from the JMC.

Confederalism—a coherent alternative?

Confederations are not sovereign states. Consequently, they have no central government with the independence that flows from the permanence guaranteed in a constitution or fundamental law. Rather, any confederal authority can be dissolved at will by one of its constituent members. They may do this comprehensively—abruptly depart altogether—or piecemeal by simply not enforcing policies that are deemed disagreeable or financially unrewarding. In the 1830s, South Carolina sparked the Nullification crisis by declaring that it was not obliged to enforce the federal laws its legislature rejected. A similar approach was taken by Eurosceptics (before they became outright Brexiters) when they argued that

UK membership of the EU would only be tolerable if Parliament could overturn EU directives and set aside ECJ judgements.

Alexander Hamilton designed the American federal constitution expressly to create an independent and efficacious central government. Federalism is not about de-fanging central government but an attempt to make it palatable, authoritative and permanent. This fact stands prior to everything else when examining federalism, yet it is repeatedly overlooked.

There is then a categorical distinction between federalism and confederalism of immense depth. Some leading figures, such as the former First Minister Carwyn Jones, have called for a new Union to be constructed from the absolute sovereignty of the Home Nations. Once each Home Nation is recognised as the source of sovereignty, they could then lease some sovereignty to a UK government. The difficulty here for those who are genuinely attempting to create a legitimate central government by such means is that sovereignty leased is sovereignty retained. No central government would operate successfully with the constant threat of dissolution. Quite simply, central government must be independent and constitutionally self-sustaining. That is why Hamilton and the other founding fathers divided sovereignty into spheres that were independent and indissoluble.

Should the Union dissolve and the Home Nations become fully sovereign entities, then confederalism becomes a possibility and perhaps even a very creative one. Confederations can pool sovereignty and enable deep co-operation and even integration. Many Eurosceptics rejected the EU because it was moving in such a direction. But secession is always an active principle in confederalism, and, as we have seen with Brexit, ultimately limits the scope of central authority. That said, a British Confederation could emerge in the future should the Union collapse, and it might become as extensive in its policy reach as the EU.

February 2020

Member of the Senedd for South Wales Central since 1999
Deputy Presiding Officer, National Assembly for Wales 2011-16

A Sovereign Wales in an Isle-Wide Confederation

by Glyndwr Cennydd Jones

This piece, produced in October 2020, is conceived as a reflection on my constitutional writing over recent years and particularly how I came to settle on a model of a League-Union of the Isles which has gratifyingly attracted some attention.

My first essay, **Towards Federalism and Beyond** (June 2016), was a swift response to the outcome of the Brexit referendum, highlighting the challenges facing today's Wales in economic and social terms. It advocated the immediate need for a campaign to redefine the UK as a federation so that those competencies returning from the European Union (EU) could be suitably allocated to the nations, along with other much-needed reforms to the arrangements underpinning devolution.

Devolution

It was Ron Davies, former Secretary of State for Wales, who said, before the dawn of the Welsh Assembly in 1999, that 'devolution is a process, not an event.' Since then, Wales has experienced executive devolution with secondary law-making powers from 1999 to 2007, executive devolution with enhanced secondary powers between 2007 and 2011, legislative devolution under a conferred powers model from 2011 to 2018, and legislative devolution under a reserved powers model from 2018 to the present day. During this period, there have also been three Scotland Acts, each augmenting powers north of the border. Nevertheless, England continues to be omitted from the devolution reforms without its own discrete national parliament.

Today, Wales and Scotland hold legislative competence over all matters not explicitly reserved to Westminster, which implies a form of federalism, but without the usual sharing of sovereignty across parliaments. The statutes founding the devolved institutions are analogous to the constitutions regulating federal systems, both providing for and limiting powers of the legislatures and administrations, and dividing responsibilities between the territories and the centre. Established by approval through referenda, the parliaments in Cardiff, Edinburgh and Belfast hold a measure of political entrenchment which has legal foundation in the Wales Act 2017, Scotland Act 2016 and Northern Ireland Act 1998, confirming devolution as a permanent component of the UK constitution, and detailing that the UK government will not normally introduce bills in Westminster to legislate on devolved spheres of competence. Still, Brexit challenges this.

More broadly, as highlighted by Dr. Andrew Blick in his article '*A United Kingdom Federation: The Prospects*' (*Federal Union* 2018), the Human Rights Act 1998 partly reflects the Bill of Rights existing in most federal systems, while the UK Supreme Court operates several roles associated with a similarly titled body in a federal jurisdiction. The Joint Ministerial Committee, though found wanting in its application, somewhat replicates a federal mechanism for states to participate in important central decision-making. Despite this constitutional scaffold, the Senedd in Wales remains an institution lacking true influence and power. The customary argument that parliamentary sovereignty should rest solely at Westminster is under question.

The 'Towards Federalism' component of the essay's title was a pragmatic acknowledgement of what could actually be achieved in the short to mid-term. However, it was mostly understood that the 'and Beyond' element had more significance than simply echoing the catchphrase of a well-known Hollywood film franchise.

A Constitutional Continuum (December 2016), my second essay, explored the developing momentum for change and reform amongst many academics, politicians and the public at large, specifically investigating potential models of governance based on partnership principles.

Federalism

In a federation, sovereignty is shared between central and constituent national or state governments. Each level has clearly articulated functions, with some powers pooled between them, but none has absolute authority over the others. An individual is a citizen of the central overarching structure and the state within which they reside, participating democratically in electing representatives to the legislative parliaments at both levels of government, usually with a party political system operating across the whole. Central institutions are in place to implement many taxes. Examples of federations include Germany and the USA.

Agreed practices and rules are confirmed through a written constitution, which articulates the division of responsibilities between the federal and state tiers. It identifies those powers assigned to the centre which may typically cover: the armed and security forces; border, diplomatic and international affairs; shared public services; cross-recognition of legal jurisdictions; currency and monetary policies; a single market, and select taxation. The remainder rests with the states. The constitution also apportions powers across two chambers of a central parliament. Representation of the states in the second chamber is desirable, allowing a firm place for them to consider laws on behalf of the whole federation, with decisions such as joining or leaving international bodies, and constitutional changes made subject to its approval. The constitution and charter of rights, by which public institutions must abide, are enforced by a Supreme Court.

A federation sets out to provide constitutional clarity and stability across the states, with shared mechanisms in place for advancing joint interests and resolving disputes. It also capitalises on potential for realising some economies of scale in delivering centrally held functions, allowing for a proportional redistribution of the joint prosperity generated by the federal capital to the states. However, in the UK context, questions remain on how England, with approximately 85% of the total population, could be integrated successfully into a federation without causing disputes between both UK and English levels, and also whether the intended benefits of various functions being exercised closer to the people could be realised in such a large unit. England's regions may well be the only practical option for inclusion in a UK-wide federal system.

Confederalism

A confederation is a union of sovereign member nations that for reasons of efficiency and common security have assigned a limited portfolio of functions and powers to a central body. Confederations are usually established by treaty, in contrast to a federal constitution, addressing crucially shared interests such as internal trade, currencies, defence, and foreign relations. Returned representatives take part in central decision-making processes more in the nature of trustees acting on behalf of their member nation's affairs. National parliaments, not individuals, are formally represented in central institutions, with people first relating to their member nation and next to the confederation. Collective budgetary funds are raised annually through each member nation's contributions of a defined proportion of their Gross Domestic Product (GDP). The nations operate distinct tax regimes and are free to act unilaterally in all areas unless centrally assigned. The Benelux Union has developed along these kinds of lines.

In the UK context, a confederal treaty typically enables Westminster to continue as the parliament of England, with a Confederal

Assembly established to deliver a limited range of central powers. Each member nation adopts its own institutions within a broad constitutional framework—protecting the integrity of political processes and ensuring fundamental rights—whilst encountering the advantages and challenges of running a sovereign state within what is best summed up as a loose alliance or partnership. A treaty on issues of shared concern aims to mitigate any risks and costs associated with fragmenting previously held joint functions, noting that competitive considerations between member nations inevitably complicate relationships in the context of a confederation.

Two of the more pressing challenges of adopting a pure confederal model concern the matters of large-scale economic management and currency controls. Since the central body is relatively weak, decisions made by a Confederal Assembly require subsequent implementation by individual member nations to take effect. These pronouncements are therefore not laws acting directly upon members, but instead have more the character of agreements between nations, which are always open to challenge and review, creating uncertainty in collective, strategic aims. However, the attraction of a confederation, comprising member nations of radically different sizes, is driven by a view that the UK already has more diversity than is often found in federations.

It was around this time that I stumbled on 'Confederal Federalism and Citizen Representation in the European Union' (Western European Politics, Volume 22: 1999, Issue 2) by Professor John Kincaid, which took my developing continuum considerations to more nuanced ground. In a nutshell, the article explains 'what seems to have developed in the EU is... a confederal order of government that operates in a significantly federal mode within its spheres of competence.' This find was, without doubt, a timely piece of good fortune. The realisation had dawned on me that the constitutional choice between federalism and confederalism need not be binary.

My third essay, **A Federation or League of the Isles?** (July 2017) was, as it says on the tin, an in-depth exploration of federalism, confederalism, and more significantly—that possible middle ground—confederal-federalism. Not wishing to alienate the generally moderate elements of both unionism and nationalism to the substance of the proposition, I labelled the model a League-Union of the Isles and embarked on setting out a detailed description of what such a framework might look like, a summary of which follows.

Confederal-federalism: A League-Union of the Isles
Devolution involves a sovereign Westminster, in effect, delegating a measure of sovereign authority to the devolved institutions. A League-Union of the Isles turns this constitutional approach on its head, advocating four sovereign nations of radically different population sizes (Wales c. 3.2m, Scotland c. 5.5m, Northern Ireland c. 1.9m and England c. 56m), delegating some sovereign authority to central bodies in agreed areas of common interest.

The model proposes a confederation of Wales, Scotland, Northern Ireland, and England, with aspects of federal-type control built into key policy portfolios to reflect the principles of equality and solidarity among member nations. Each nation holds all powers and rights which are not by treaty delegated to joint institutions, operating distinct legal jurisdictions. The British monarch continues in role as Head of the League-Union of the Isles.

A Council of the Isles acts with mechanisms in place to address the asymmetry between population sizes of member nations, specifically through the composition and distribution of seats. Members of the Council are typically elected for a four-year period by the electors of each nation, convening annually for a fixed time unless urgent business is demanded. The Council assumes its own standing orders, confirming a Presiding Officer and Executive whose Prime Minister and Ministers are responsible for enacting power on specific matters involving defence, foreign policy, internal trade, currency, large-scale economic considerations, and isle-wide affairs.

Each Bill considered by the Council is circulated to the National Parliaments of Wales, Scotland, Northern Ireland, and England, in advance of final reading, with member nations empowered to make objections or suggest amendments before voting. This provides a counterweight to any aspirations of the centre to aggregate power within its core, and to act unilaterally on issues such as defence and foreign affairs. On passing, the Head of the confederation confirms the Bill as an Act of the Council of the Isles. The ultimate authority on the legitimacy of any law and treaty remains with the Supreme Court.

A Committee of Member Nations (comprising the Council's Prime Minister and Minister for Isle-wide Affairs, and the First Minister of each member nation), convenes regularly to discuss more general considerations which demand a degree of cooperation and harmonisation of laws across borders, over and above the key functions enacted in Council. These include: postal, telephonic and internet communications; railways, roads and associated licensing; airports, ports and traffic controls; coastguard and navigational services; energy, water and related infrastructure; income and corporation taxes; rates of sales, weights and measures; copyrights, patents and trademarks; scientific and technological research; broadcasting; meteorological forecasting; environmental protection; civil defence; emergencies, and the prevention of terrorism and serious crime.

The Committee, with the support of the Council, also holds controls for confirming contractual-type arrangements for supplying any requested public services to member nations. To cover the common functions and agreements in place, the Council levies charges upon each member nation according to a defined proportion of their GDP annually relative to that of the League-Union of the Isles as a whole. These monies are paid into a consolidated fund from which the interest on the UK public debt continues as a standing charge. The centre aims to promote equality across all territories by sharing a measure of baseline investment for infrastructure projects, operating formal instruments for resolving disagreements. National Parliaments are discouraged from misusing any advantages they possess in areas of potential contention including, for example, the economy of England, the oil of Scotland, and the water of Wales. Some central responsibility is also assigned for pensions and what is currently termed National Insurance Contributions (appropriately renamed), mitigating elements of financial risk and promoting ongoing solidarity. Further, federal-type mechanisms may be introduced to support fiscal decentralisation from the UK position.

The National Parliament of each member nation sits as the sovereign, legislative and representative body of its people, enacting powers and laws on every issue not identified as the Council's competence. A Government with executive powers, comprising a First Minster and other ministerial positions as required to oversee the various offices, is appointed from the nation's parliamentary members. The superior judges are nominated on the advice of an independent authority. Nations further sub-divide their lands through Acts of National Parliament, defining the composition and responsibilities of local or regional authorities.

A Federation or League of the Isles? appeared in a joint booklet with Lord Elystan Morgan, Lord David Owen, Gwynoro Jones and Martin Shipton. The publication was called *Towards Federalism and Beyond* (perhaps an unwise reuse, on my part, of the title given earlier to essay number one), which was launched in September 2017 to celebrate the 20th anniversary of the vote to establish the National Assembly of Wales. A second joint booklet, topically named for the time *Brexit, Devolution and the Changing Union,* followed in February 2018. Both documents remain available electronically and are lodged in the libraries at Cardiff Bay and Westminster, where I hope they will stimulate further discussion amongst parliamentarians.

Moving onwards, I had always imagined constructing an argument that would encompass the main drivers and influences of geography, history, industry, peoples and politics on our island story, whilst corralling, researching and synthesising the evidence in a manner clearly to present the case for a constitutional compromise of strategic significance. The resulting essay, my fourth, **These Isles** (April 2019), is a work with which I remain pleased, viewing it as a useful contribution to the developing debate not only in Wales, but in the context of the UK as a whole. The Institute for Welsh Affairs undertook to release the text in four parts during Spring of that year, and the complete piece is accessible at: https://www.iwa.wales/wp-content/media/These-Isles-by-Glyndwr-Cennydd-Jones-June-2019.pdf

In summary, it affirms that most states are synthetic constructs and are subject to change. That said, unitary states face ongoing challenges in acknowledging the partial autonomy and diversity of their constituent nations, especially in cultivating and sustaining a sense of allegiance and belonging to the larger political body. The exposition frames the UK constitutional question as follows.

> With many today asserting a multicultural Welsh, Scottish, Northern Irish, or English character along with a form of dual nationality which embraces a British personality, it is reasonable to reconsider the nature of Westminster's parliamentary sovereignty. The pressing issue of our time relates to whether sovereignty, as currently understood, should be shared across these five territorially defined identities (including that of Britain) in a traditional federal arrangement, or instead assigned individually to the four nations—Wales, Scotland, Northern Ireland, and England—which, in turn, could delegate parts of their sovereign authority to common central institutions of a fundamentally British composition, and/or European.

These Isles was followed by the briefing paper **Constitutional Relationships and Sovereignty in these Isles** (September 2019) and its infographic supplement **Illustrated Constitutional Models and Exemplar Principles** (September 2019). They upheld the line of reasoning that Britishness as a concept is much older than the UK and it is unrealistic to argue that the Welsh or Scottish people, in notional independent territories, would start considering the English as fellow Europeans instead of fellow British.

Broadly speaking, British ideals and values are forged by cultural, historic and topographic influences, which usefully bridge the demands of world interdependence and the desire for increased autonomy in the nations. The challenge is to capture these principles in a new constitutional framework which improves arrangements for self-government—through emphasising common respect for human dignity, freedom, democracy, equality, and rule of law—within an isle-wide civic societal structure typified by pluralism, non-discrimination, tolerance, justice, and solidarity.

The papers, in essence, summed up the constitutional options as below, and included the more challenging scenario of an independent Wales acting exclusively within the EU, for the purposes of encouraging wider comparative conversation.

- Devolution. A sovereign Westminster delegating some sovereign authority to the devolved institutions.
- Federalism: A partially sovereign Wales sharing sovereignty within a UK Federation.
- Confederalism: A sovereign Wales pooling a few key functions within a British Confederation.
- Confederal-federalism: A sovereign Wales delegating some sovereign authority to a League-Union of the Isles.
- Independence: A sovereign Wales delegating some sovereign authority to the EU.

An independent Wales within the EU

Wales acting as a sovereign nation within the EU is, in principle, a workable model. However, a practical difficulty rests with Wales' largest trading partner England and its uncertain relationship with Europe. A form of isle-wide constitutional framework is essential to facilitate the necessary economic, political and social understandings, or at least an Atlantic Union, of EU nations, comprising treaties between Wales, Scotland, Northern Ireland, and the Republic of Ireland. In June 2016, the Welsh public effectively voted against EU membership, creating some doubt about the likely political traction of a future sovereign Wales joining the EU, but there are indications the mood may be changing, if only steadily.

Hypothetically, an autonomous Wales could be underpinned internally by five regional authorities partially mirroring the geographical composition of present regional seats for Senedd elections and constituted by the amalgamation of enclosed principal areas or unitary authorities for local government, and restructuring of other relevant bodies. These may cover the health boards, police, fire and rescue authorities, and consortia for education, social services, transport, and trunk roads. Enacting Welsh government policy, such authorities would promote economies of scale; clarity in directing long-term planning and delivery; accountability for achieving shared outcomes across geographical areas; improved governance, and increased capacity.

The potential for Wales to act unilaterally outside any European or isles-wide agreements is impossible in the era of enhanced cross-border cooperation, which demands some pooling of sovereignty within supra-national frameworks. It has been suggested that Wales' operational interactions with England could be addressed through a bilateral treaty of sorts, but this approach is likely to prove unsustainable, with uncertainty over collective aims resulting in a drift of capital and employment prospects towards the larger neighbour to the east. The challenge is highlighted in the report *A Constitutional Crossroads: Ways Forward for the UK* (Bingham Centre for the Rule of Law 2015) which highlights that the 'border between England and Wales is crossed about 130,000 times each day' and that '48% of the Welsh population lives within 25 miles of the border with England.' The picture as we move into the third decade of the 21st century is more complex still.

By December 2019, having recently participated in the joint discussion article '*Unionism, Federalism and Nationalism*' with David Melding MS and Helen Mary Jones MS for *Welsh Agenda* magazine, I somewhat accidentally but interestingly found myself acting as a commissioner on Plaid Cymru's constitutional Independence Commission. Its report *Towards an Independent Wales* (yes, 'towards' had become a buzz word) was published by Y Lolfa in September 2020. The model of a League-Union of the Isles informed much of the Commission's explorations of confederalism and was publicly presented as an option alongside the Benelux model, proposed by Adam Price MS. During summer 2020, I also had the pleasure of liaising with Professor Jim Gallagher on his developing thoughts for *Could there be a Confederal UK?* which is an important paper by a past Director-General of Devolution for the UK's Ministry of Justice.

So, reflections aside, I am now actively considering the fundamental 'nuts and bolts' of a founding treaty that might hypothetically underpin the introduction of a League-Union of the Isles—for the purposes of promoting deeper debate in 2021. It is now timely for me to clearly state on the record why an isle-wide constitutional model of confederal-federalism is a more suitable proposition than that of federalism, a loose confederation, or an independent Wales acting solely within the EU.

So, why a League-Union of the Isles?

This preferred option presents the opportunity to empower the peoples and countries of these isles within an overarching collaborative framework that aims to promote national sovereignty, or 'independence', on the one hand, and effective working relationships for key shared interests on the other. To this end, it defines a realistic and sustainable proposition of sovereign nations successfully coexisting in close geographical proximity, whilst firmly recognising longstanding interactions between our peoples and their common journeys through history.

The model is underpinned by the principles of social, economic, defence, cultural, and indeed political, equality and solidarity amid member nations, efficiently tackling our mutual interests, whether regional or global, and empowering each territory to address their own distinct combinations of challenges and needs. In constitutional terms, the new relationship is introduced through a codified confirmation that all powers and rights rest with the individual nations, which in turn delegate or pool a balanced portfolio of strategic functions and objectives to the centre by means of an agreed confederal treaty, with aspects of federal-type controls built into specific mechanisms.

- To sustain our economic union, the proposition assumes a common currency, bank and market, as well as an isle-wide responsibility for macro-economic decision making. This particularly aims to support fiscal decentralisation away from the current UK arrangements with borrowing monitored.
- The social union is maintained through the guarantee of individuals' rights of movement, residence and employment across

all member nations, along with the continuation of the British monarch in a role as the Head of the League-Union of the Isles.

- In upholding our joint security, the forces of defence and organisation of foreign policy are both held centrally. This is the protective rock on which our shared principles and values, as projected through common, practical functions, can develop, be maintained and prosper.

- The cultural union is supported through official recognition of the extant isle-wide language, English, and those tongues indigenous to each territory. These languages' longstanding contributions to the story of Britain and its new future are formally acknowledged.

In application and execution, the balance of social, economic and defence interests are effectively and efficiently enacted through a limited but mature political union comprising a central Council of the Isles to which individuals elect representatives, in addition to their respective National Parliaments. With usual consideration of legal structures, each territory, operates their own jurisdiction, with a Supreme Court of the Isles acting as the ultimate authority on the legitimacy of any laws and rights which are assigned to the Council by treaty.

This measured equilibrium of selective unions allows empathy for the principle of convergence to be understood and actually realised, to a degree, across the League-Union of the Isles, with individuals relating to their member nation, initially, and to the centre next. A Committee of Member Nations which comprises the First Ministers of the individual territories and the Prime Minister of the Council promotes cooperation, where necessary, on matters that, whilst requiring cross border coordination, are the direct responsibility of the National Parliaments. Further, the sovereign member nations independently hold four seats at the UN General Assembly but aspire to retain, subject to negotiation, the single collective permanent seat on the UN Security Council so as strongly to represent our shared geopolitical and geographical interests at the top diplomatic table, balancing change with continuity.

Therefore, confederal-federalism embeds the values of equality and solidarity within its strategic objectives and practical structures, providing opportunities for these ideals to be reinforced in action through promoting partner members' financial robustness and security going forwards. As a counterweight to any encroachment or misuse of powers in enacting the shared, central functions, and since sovereignty rests with each nation, the right of secession is implicit in the model, subject to appropriate referenda and other treaty-bound checks and balances.

Why not a loose confederation?

The proposition of a League-Union of the Isles clearly contrasts with a looser confederal order focused mainly on the successful operation of a common market treaty, where Wales would in effect opt to use the British pound, along with maintaining elements of a social union. In such a scenario, likely facilitated by an Assembly of Member Nations, the driver for meaningful economic union is reduced as the influencing motives for adopting common long-term stances are not complemented by joint political and defence structures. England will likely see no reason to reform the Bank of England and share monetary controls to any consequential extent within this option. The values of solidarity would be weakened, with the principle of convergence having little incentive and traction across the nations.

It could be possible for Wales to introduce its own currency, but this situation would present significant challenges and risks, demanding additional gears and mechanisms to articulate with neighbouring positions. Such a development would 'water down' any firm confederal arrangements in place and potentially prove the relationship unsustainable, due to the uncertainties around collective aims. It is doubtful that England would agree to a form of unstable confederation, seemingly motivated, at least from Wales' perspective, by the overwhelming desire to ensure some access to its neighbour's greater market wealth.

The peril is that this approach could result, by default, in a sovereign Wales standing separately and suddenly outside any isle-wide and European treaties. Equally, it could lead to a trail of events where the Welsh public sought greater assimilation with England as a counter to the dis-

integration of an increasingly fragmented relationship—and the consequential economic hardships experienced. The Benelux treaty, which has
been suggested by some for confederal consideration, appears appealingly
light touch on the surface because it is now established alongside the
more substantial EU, of which all Benelux countries are members. In the
context of Brexit, it is not possible for obvious reasons to replicate such
a framework for Wales, Scotland, Northern Ireland and England today.

Therefore, the option of a loose confederation underpinned by an
Assembly of Member Nations, which convenes to agree stances only on
matters affecting economic and social unions, does not provide the constitutional traction, public confidence and structural stability required
for the values of equality and solidarity to be applied in good faith across
the various territories. It is only when elements of the weighty matters of
defence and foreign policy are included in the portfolio of shared functions, facilitated by a limited, but meaningful, political union enacted
through a Council of the Isles that the proposition coalesces into an effective confederation of depth and longevity.

But, a federalist may ask, what is the difference between a League-Union of the Isles and a UK Federation?

It is the case that many of the central functions map across and, in both
models, individuals participate democratically in electing representatives
to established legislative parliaments at two levels of government. However, a fundamental difference rests in the nature of decision-making processes underpinning the application of shared functions.

In a UK Federation, a top-down model of representational authority
remains within an overarching framework of clearly delineated responsibilities assigned to the territories and that of the core, which remains
the centre of gravity. This is especially true in party political terms. Like
a spider sitting in the middle of a web, there is no mistaking which body
both spins and holds the threads. The territories must remain within their
bounds, discouraged from taking on a greater role in governing their

peoples in time. The umbrella political identity is a powerful construct, likely constraining genuine national development, progress and reform.

In a League-Union of the Isles, on the other hand, the weight of influence and purpose rests with the nations. The centre exists to serve in facilitating the delivery of the common social, political, economic, defence and cultural aims, as already outlined. Individuals elect representatives to take part in central policy decision-making processes mostly on behalf of their member nations' interests.

A federal solution, such as the one proposed by the Constitutional Reform Group (CRG), acts only to entrench many of the structural difficulties extant in the present devolution arrangements, which largely mirror a federal order but without the formal sharing of sovereignty across national parliaments. The UK constitutional debate has moved substantively beyond the context in which the CRG admirably started to advocate a federal solution in 2015. Views in Wales about the nature and quality of Cardiff's interactions with Westminster have changed a good deal, especially due to Brexit and, more recently, Covid-19—and the mood in Scotland is increasingly shifting towards independence. However, the Scottish National Party's present platform of pursuing an independent Scotland within the EU is problematic in today's circumstances. By definition, it necessarily confines and restricts the nation's ability to facilitate a single market with its largest trading partner, England, fundamentally because of contrasting positions on Brexit.

Accepting that the federal horse has already bolted, particularly before the relentless wave of SNP electoral successes in recent times, never has there been so much at stake for the future of our nations' relations. We are approaching an uncertain moment in this island journey, if not too, in our collective affairs internationally, with the UK's standing much reduced across the globe. Separatist tendencies are increasingly prevalent, whether nationally in Scotland and Wales, or at a UK level driven by Brexit. There is a crucial need for us to explore some form of broad, strategic compromise, which embraces the concerns of both unionists and nationalists, in moving away from a narrow 'winner takes all' answer to the constitutional question posed. If successful, the long-lasting rewards could be enormous, with fresh political narratives promoting a new kind of partnership across these isles—one which draws on past and present experiences in forming an underlying bedrock of successful collaboration for the century ahead. Interestingly, David Melding MS in his essay *Unionism and Nationalism in Welsh Political Life* (May 2019) emphasises that unionists and nationalists 'will always have to strike some bargain to manage and utilise the forces created by the geography, culture, and economic needs of the British Isles.'

So, are we any nearer to modernising and reforming those political structures that define today's Britain?

After the failed referendum vote on devolution in 1979, it was not until 1997 that a measure of acceptance that change was required emerged. The establishment in 1999 of a National Assembly for Wales was a step in the right direction, with four Wales Acts since bringing in two broad phases of executive and legislative devolution respectively, leading to the current status quo. During this time, a greater body of understanding has been fostered in Wales with regards to its specific needs, distinct from those of the UK as a whole. However, the Senedd's limited managerial, rather than strategically empowered, approach to governance still fails to deliver effective democratic representation of the aspirations, needs and values of the people of Wales within an increasingly complicated, developing isle-wide context.

At the time of writing, in autumn 2020, the world is embroiled in the Covid-19 pandemic. The four constituent nations of the UK have taken different tacks in their responses to the social distancing challenges presented, including the application of lockdown conditions. This has reaffirmed the national borders extant within these isles. The trend for significant divergence in policy stances across the various parliaments has compounded other clear political disagreements centred on constitutional change, with different parties holding power in each institution for over ten years. These influences will become a substantial source of crisis as we move on from the EU. Furthermore, Wales' economy is likely to be disproportionally affected in the aftermath of Brexit and Covid-19, with the nation carrying many underlying structural dependencies and unre-solved issues of industry and enterprise. These considerable challenges require responses devised by those who better understand their impact on our cities, towns and rural communities—and are well-positioned to build the required connections and relationships, at home and over-seas, effectively to bring together both public and private expertise and resources in delivering change.

If we were offered a hypothetical opportunity to constitute Britain from 'scratch' once more today, would we consciously choose the model of a centralised unitary state that we have inherited? I suspect England would not have any real intent or interest in pursuing such a proposition as the nation has its own marked difficulties of internal inequality and tensions to overcome (as highlighted by the recent Covid-19 stand-offs between the Prime Minister and the metro-mayors of Northern England.)

The UK is the legacy of a different era in world history, one which was embroiled by conflict, empires and two World Wars. Indeed, the main political groupings of our age remain those which rallied and formed around the issues of those times. The constituent nations of Britain have long since travelled at differing economic rates. More recently, the EU has been part of the fabric that holds the UK together. The pre-eminence of EU law, and its interpretation by the EU Court of Justice, has safeguarded legal and regulatory norms across copious fields, including the devolved areas. The UK internal market has been sustained by the conventions of the EU internal market. Brexit risks these interrelated competencies becoming increasingly unsound. The need for a renewed isles-wide frame-work made fit for purpose for the 21st century is now paramount.

I am truly an admirer of the concept of Britain, if not of the UK unitary state, an oxymoron in all but name now. In its defence, there has been no sustained, successful attempt to pretend that the 'whole' or the 'sum of all parts' does not in fact comprise a number of separate nations respected in their own right within European history. Even before the age of devolution, the various identities of the UK's constituent territories were deeply rooted despite occasional, sporadic attempts to standardise across the piece. The fact that such efforts were unproductive places a spotlight on the synthetic nature of our unity, which is possibly at the heart of our current condition of constitutional soul-searching.

If we had a second chance, would we not simply recognise the sovereignty of the different nations and peoples in these Isles and seek to work within a robust social, economic and security partnership directed by a limited, but mature, political legislature? I am sure that England would no more want to take on the challenges of Wales than Scotland would seek to control the future of England. All nations together cannot solve the issue of Northern Ireland, but we can empower the territory to have the useful conversations required to seek resolution of a conflict that now thankfully belongs to a different time.

Globally, these isles are known, amongst many other things, as home to the mother of all parliaments. Would it not speak powerfully of our stature, confidence and foresight, if we acted together, but as individual nations, to enact the mother of all reforms too? What an example our *Prydain*, and our nations' peoples would be showing the world. Our collective shoulders would have to be broad in setting aside any differences, whether substantial or petty, real or imagined, firmly to embrace shared interests and responsibilities in continuing this remarkable island journey, hand in hand as sovereign nations, but within a League-Union of the Isles of Britain…

Glyndwr Cennydd Jones is an advocate for greater cross-party consensus in Wales and for a UK-wide constitutional convention, and has been published on these themes by the Institute of Welsh Affairs, Cardiff University, Centre on Constitutional Change, *Welsh Agenda* magazine, *Western Mail*, *Golwg* and *Y Cymro*. A catalogue of his articles and essays can be found on: https://constitutionalcontinuum.blogspot.com/

Index

People

Wilson, Harold, 82, 156, 158,
169-171, 178-179, 186-187,
189-190, 203, 205-206, 226,
247, 252, 265, 277, 281-283,
287, 290, 295, 304-305, 397

Wright, George, 325, 339, 376
Wright, Canon Kenyon, 377
Wynne, Richard, 137, 196

Main Political Parties

Conservative Party (Tories),
14, 17-18, 27, 32, 34, 37-38,
40, 50-52, 57, 83, 95-97, 99,
108-113, 116-119, 122, 130,
132, 146, 149-151, 159-160,
166-167, 191-192, 207, 217,
228, 238, 242, 246-248,
256-259, 269, 275-277, 281,
295, 298, 308, 312, 319, 323,
325-328, 332, 335, 338, 342,
352, 355, 357, 369, 371-372,
377, 379-381, 383, 388, 395,
400, 455

Labour Party, 8, 12-14, 17-18,
25-27, 32-39, 47, 53-56, 61-62,
69, 72-73, 77-85, 88-90,
93-119, 122, 124, 132-133,
139, 145-173, 177, 179-185,
187-192, 195, 199-203, 206,
210-212, 218-223, 226-229,
232-239, 242, 246-249,
251-259, 262, 267-268,
272-277, 281-296, 304,
307-311, 315-322, 325-331,
333, 335, 337-346, 350-352,
355, 357-373, 375-401, 455-457

Liberal Party, 17, 21, 26-27,
32, 35-58, 73, 76-77, 83-84,
89, 93-95, 97, 102, 132, 134,
152, 177, 187, 199, 207, 228,
232, 238, 242, 258-259, 277,
279, 281, 295, 298, 325-326,
331-335, 337, 361, 363-364,
371-379, 383, 387-388,
391-392, 397

Plaid Cymru (National party
of Wales), 8, 11-13, 17-18,
26, 31- 33, 35-39, 61-69, 73,
75-77, 79-82, 84-85, 87-90,
93, 96-100, 104-108, 114,
117, 121, 123-124, 128-148,
151, 161, 164-175, 180-188,
191-204, 207, 209, 211-218,
221-223, 226-228, 231-232,
236-239, 241-242, 246, 249,
252, 254, 256-258, 264-265,
267-275, 279, 281, 285,
287-291, 295-297, 309-311,
325-335, 340-342, 350, 355,
359-361, 364, 369-371, 375,
379, 386, 390, 392, 395-400,
429, 455-457

Scottish National Party (SNP), 13, 132, 156, 292, 310, 350, 377, 386, 397, 409, 434

SDP, 18, 27, 96, 274, 361-366, 371
SDP-Liberal Alliance, 364-365, 371

Press and Broadcast

Y Ddraig Goch, 65, 274, 311
Y Faner (Baner ac Amseau Cymru), 143, 341
Y Lolfa, 429
Young Wales, 43, 53
YouTube, 384
Yr Wythnos (HTV), 267

Movements, Associations, Organisations

Places

Acts, Bills, Commissions

Bibliography

Callaghan, James: *Time and Chance*. London: Politico's Publishing, 2006.

Davies, John: *A History of Wales*. London: Penguin Books, 2007.

Davies, Pennar: *Gwynfor Evans: golwg ar ei waith a'i feddwl*. Abertawe/ Swansea: Tŷ John Penry, 1976.

Edwards, Andrew: *Labour's Crisis: Plaid Cymru, the Conservatives and the Decline of the Labour Party in North West Wales 1960-1974*. Cardiff: University of Wales Press, 2011.

Evans, Gwynfor: *A National Future for Wales*. Cardiff: Plaid Cymru, 1975.

Evans, Gwynfor: *Land of my Fathers: 2000 Years of Welsh History* (transl. from Welsh). Swansea: John Penry Pr., 1974.

Evans, Gwynfor: *Fighting for Wales*. Tal-y-bont, Ceredigion: Y Lolfa, 1991.

Evans, Gwynfor: *The Fight for Welsh Freedom*, Tal-y-bont, Ceredigion: Y Lolfa, 2006

Evans, Gwynfor: *Wales Can Win*. Llandybie, C. Davies, 1973.

Evans, Gwynfor; Stephens, Meic; Dubè, Steve: *For the Sake of Wales: The Memoirs of Gwynfor Evans*. Cardiff: Welsh Academic Press, 2001.

Evans, John Gilbert: *Labour and Devolution in Wales*. Tal-y-bont, Ceredigion: Y Lolfa, 2019.

Evans, Rhys: *Gwynfor Evans: Portrait of a Patriot*. Tal-y-bont, Ceredigion: Y Lolfa, 2008.

Foulkes, David; Jones, J. Barry; Wilford, R. A. (eds.): *The Welsh Veto: The Wales Act 1978 and the Referendum*. Cardiff: University of Wales Press, 1983.

Gibbard, Alun: *Into the Wind: The Life of Carwyn James*. Tal-y-bont, Ceredigion: Y Lolfa, 2017.

Gieschen, Hubert: *The Labour Party in Wales and the 1979 Referendum*. Frankfurt: Haag and Herschen, 1999.

Gooberman, Leon: *From Depression to Devolution: Economy and Government in Wales, 1934-2006*. Cardiff: University of Wales Press, 2017.

Griffiths, James: *Pages from Memory*. London: J. M. Dent and Sons, 1969.

Hopkin, Deian; Tanner, Duncan; Williams, Chris (eds.): *The Labour Party in Wales 1900-2000*. Cardiff: University of Wales Press, 2000.

House of Commons, *Wales and Devolution* (19 May 1997), https://commonslibrary.parliament.uk/research-briefings/rp97-60/

Jenkins, Geraint H.: *Cof Cenedl VI: Ysgrifau ar Hanes Cymru*. Llandysul: Gomer, 1991.

Jenkins, Geraint H.: *Cof Cenedl VII: Ysgrifau ar Hanes Cymru*. Llandysul: Gomer, 1992.

Jobbins, Siôn T.: *The Phenomenon of Welshness 2, Or 'Is Wales too poor to be independent?'*. Llanrwst: Gwasg Carreg Gwalch, 2013.

Johnes, Martin: *Wales since 1939*. Manchester: Manchester University Press, 2013.

Jones, Carwyn (with Gibbard, Alun): *Not Just Politics*. London: Headline Accent, 2021.

Jones, Gwynoro; Gibbard, Alun: *Gwynoro a Gwynfor*. Tal-y-bont, Ceredigion: Y Lolfa, 2019.

Jones, James Barry; Balsom, Denis (eds.): *The Road to the National Assembly for Wales*. Cardiff: University of Wales Press, 2000.

Jones, Richard Wyn: *The Fascist Party in Wales? Plaid Cymru, Welsh nationalism and the accusation of Fascism*. Cardiff: University of Wales Press, 2014.

Jones, John Robert: *Gwaedd yng Nghymru*. Lerpwl, Pontypridd: Cyhoeddiadau Modern Cymreig, 1970.

Lewis, Saunders: "Deg Pwynt Polisi", in: *Canlyn Arthur*. Aberystwyth: Gwasg Aberystwyth, 1938.

Melding, David: *Will Britain survive beyond 2020?* Cardiff: Institute of Welsh Affairs, 2009.

Morgan, Derec Llwyd (ed.): *Emlyn Hooson: Essays and Reminiscences*. Llandysul: Gomer, 2014.

Morgan, Elystan; Williams, Huw L.: *Elystan: Atgofion Oes*. Tal-y-bont, Ceredigion: Y Lolfa, 2012.

Morgan, Kenneth Owen: *Rebirth of a Nation: Wales 1880-1980*. Oxford: Clarendon Press, 1981.

Morgan, Kenneth Owen: *Wales and British Politics, 1868-1922*. Cardiff: University of Wales Press, 1963.

Morris, John: *Fifty Years in Politics and the Law*. Cardiff: University of Wales Press, 2013.

Osmond, John (ed.): *A Parliament for Wales*. Llandysul: Gomer 1995.

Phillips, Dylan: *Trwy ddulliau chwyldro...?: Hanes Cymdeithas yr Iaith Gymraeg, 1962-1992*. Llandysul: Gomer, 1998.

Price, Emyr: *Megan Lloyd George*. Caernarfon: Gwasanaeth Archifau Gwynedd, 1983

Price, Emyr: *Yr Arglwydd Cledwyn o Benrhos*. Caernarfon: Cyhoeddiadau Mei, 1990.

Prys Davies, Gwilym: *Llafur y Blynyddoeedd*. Dinbych: Gwasg Gee, 1991.

Prys Davies, Gwilym: *Cynhaeaf Hanner Canrif: gwleidyddiaeth Gymreig 1945-2005*, Llandysul: Gomer, 2008.

Rees, D. Ben: *Cofiant Cledwyn Hughes*. Tal-y-bont, Ceredigion: Y Lolfa 2017.

Rees, D. Ben: *Cofiant Jim Griffiths: Arwr Glew y Werin*. Tal-y-bont, Ceredigion: Y Lolfa, 2014.

Roberts, Wyn: *Right from the Start: The Memoirs of Sir Wyn Roberts*. Cardiff: University of Wales Press, 2006.

Smith, J. Beverley; Griffiths, James: *James Griffiths and his Times*. Labour Party Wales, Llanelli Constituency Party, 1977.

Steel, David: *A House Divided*. London: Weidenfield and Nicholson, 1980.

Stradling, Robert A.; Hearder, Harry: *Conflict and Coexistence: Nationalism and Democracy in Modern Europe: Essays in Honour of Harry Hearder*. Cardiff: University of Wales Press, 1997.

Thomas, George: *Mr Speaker: The Memoirs of Viscount Tonypandy*. London: Century Publishing Co. Ltd., 1985.

Thomas, Wyn: *Hands Off Wales: Nationhood and Militancy*. Llandysul: Gomer, 2013.

Wade-Evans, Arthur W.; Jones Pierce, T., et. al.: *Seiliau Hanesyddol Cenedlaetholdeb Cymru*. Caerdydd/Cardiff: Plaid Cymru, 1950.

Williams, Phil: *Voice from the Valleys*. Aberystwyth: Plaid Cymru, 1981.

WJEC, *Austerity, Affluence and Discontent 1951-1979*, https://resources.wjec.co.uk/Pages/ResourceSingle.aspx?rIid=555

Lightning Source UK Ltd.
Milton Keynes UK
UKHW020951100821
388609UK00005B/139

9 781802 270396